Age, Accent and Experience
in Second Language Acquisition

SECOND LANGUAGE ACQUISITION

Series Editor: Professor David Singleton, *Trinity College, Dublin, Ireland*

This new series will bring together titles dealing with a variety of aspects of language acquisition and processing in situations where a language or languages other than the native language is involved. Second language will thus be interpreted in its broadest possible sense. The volumes included in the series will all in their different ways offer, on the one hand, exposition and discussion of empirical findings and, on the other, some degree of theoretical reflection. In this latter connection, no particular theoretical stance will be privileged in the series; nor will any relevant perspective – sociolinguistic, psycholinguistic, neurolinguistic, etc. – be deemed out of place. The intended readership of the series will be final-year undergraduates working on second language acquisition projects, postgraduate students involved in second language acquisition research, and researchers and teachers in general whose interests include a second language acquisition component.

Other Books in the Series
Age and the Acquisition of English as a Foreign Language
   María del Pilar García Mayo and Maria Luisa García Lecumberri (eds)
Effects of Second Language on the First
   Vivian Cook (ed.)
Fossilization in Adult Second Language Acquisition
   ZhaoHong Han
Learning to Request in a Second Language: A Study of Child Interlanguage Pragmatics
   Machiko Achiba
Portraits of the L2 User
   Vivian Cook (ed.)
Silence in Second Language Learning: A Psychoanalytic Reading
   Colette A. Granger
Studying Speaking to Inform Second Language Learning
   Diana Boxer and Andrew D. Cohen (eds)

Other Books of Interest
Audible Difference: ESL and Social Identity in Schools
   Jennifer Miller
Context and Culture in Language Teaching and Learning
   Michael Byram and Peter Grundy (eds)
Cross-linguistic Influence in Third Language Acquisition
   J. Cenoz, B. Hufeisen and U. Jessner (eds)
Developing Intercultural Competence in Practice
   Michael Byram, Adam Nichols and David Stevens (eds)
English in Europe: The Acquisition of a Third Language
   Jasone Cenoz and Ulrike Jessner (eds)
How Different Are We? Spoken Discourse in Intercultural Communication
   Helen Fitzgerald

Please contact us for the latest book information:
Multilingual Matters, Frankfurt Lodge, Clevedon Hall,
Victoria Road, Clevedon, BS21 7HH, England
http://www.multilingual-matters.com

SECOND LANGUAGE ACQUISITION 7
Series Editor: David Singleton, *Trinity College, Dublin, Ireland*

Age, Accent and Experience in Second Language Acquisition
An Integrated Approach to Critical Period Inquiry

Alene Moyer

MULTILINGUAL MATTERS LTD
Clevedon • Buffalo • Toronto • Sydney

Dedicated to my loving family, my sons Martin and Joseph
and my husband Aviel, whose encouragement and support
have made all the difference

Library of Congress Cataloging in Publication Data
Moyer, Alene
Age, Accent, and Experience in Second Language Acquisition: An Integrated
Approach to Critical Period Inquiry/Alene Moyer. 1st ed.
Second Language Acquisition: 7.
Includes bibliographical references and index.
1. Second language acquisition. 2. Child development. I. Title. II. Second language
acquisition (Buffalo, NY); 7.
P118.2.M68 2004
418–dc22   2003017737

British Library Cataloguing in Publication Data
A catalogue entry for this book is available from the British Library.

ISBN 1-85359-718-X (hbk)
ISBN 1-85359-717-1 (pbk)

Multilingual Matters Ltd
UK: Frankfurt Lodge, Clevedon Hall, Victoria Road, Clevedon BS21 7HH.
USA: UTP, 2250 Military Road, Tonawanda, NY 14150, USA.
Canada: UTP, 5201 Dufferin Street, North York, Ontario M3H 5T8, Canada.
Australia: Footprint Books, PO Box 418, Church Point, NSW 2103, Australia.

Typeset by Wordworks Ltd.
Printed and bound in Great Britain by the Cromwell Press Ltd.

Contents

Acknowledgments

I would like to gratefully acknowledge several people who were kind enough to comment on various aspects of this manuscript: David Birdsong, Richard P. Meier, and Teresa Pica. Their insightful suggestions have undoubtedly improved this work, though all errors and omissions are strictly my own.

I am also grateful for the generous support for this project from the University of Maryland College of Arts and Humanities and the School of Languages, Literatures and Cultures.

Chapter 1
Contextualizing Critical Period Inquiry

> Coming into contact with a foreign language means hardship which
> usually brings euphoria quickly to an end, making it a short episode for
> the individual – and also for groups and nations.
> Konrad Ehlich, 1994

> [A second] language emerges through necessity ... because I want it,
> urgently want it, and because I urgently attend to it.
> Peter Bichsel, 1995 [translation mine]

The Problems of Scope and Classification

The field of second language acquisition (SLA) has long sought relevant factors to explain differential attainment for early and late learners. Since the appearance of Lenneberg's *Biological Foundations of Language* (1967), the idea of a critical period for language learning has guided a great deal of the research on second language acquisition.[1] Though Lenneberg made little specific mention of SLA, his critical period hypothesis has evolved into a full-blown theory for the field, often assumed to be a 'unitary account of non-native like outcomes' (Birdsong, 1999: 9). Still, the question remains why late language learners typically perform in notably 'non-native' ways. In the search for answers, we too rarely recognize the highly individual and complex nature of the endeavor. This is an especially salient issue given that SLA is most often an uninstructed, i.e. non-classroom, process among immigrants to foreign lands who face harsh social and economic conditions, possibly remaining culturally isolated for years.

Given this context of great challenge, many fall far short of a native speaker ideal, while others succeed beyond all expectations. By all accounts, we cannot yet explain either extreme of the success scale: entrenched fossilization and exceptional learning. The empirical evidence points to no specific faculty or mechanism in either the neurological or cognitive realm to explain exceptional performance in L2 (Obler, 1989; Schneidermann, 1991 as cited in Birdsong & Molis, 2001). Why, then, do more learners *not* attain to this level? In a recent review of cognitive research on bilingualism, Gonzalez and Schallert (1999) confirm that language processing is a multi-level task, incorporating knowledge from structural, semantic, discursive and cultural levels of language. This suggests that barriers to new knowledge reside not only in linguistic transfer, but in negative transfer of cultural knowledge as well. If so, transcending barriers to native-like acquisition requires adaptation on a number of complex levels beyond the neuro-cognitive realm. Narrowly focused explanations for SLA outcomes do little to advance an appreciation for such complexity.

By and large, critical period research has emphasized differences in phonological and morpho-syntactic performance between native and non-native speakers with little reference to the individual learner (Flege *et al.*, 1995; Johnson & Newport, 1989; Olson & Samuels, 1982; Oyama, 1976; Patkowski, 1980; Snow & Hoefnagel-Hoehle, 1982). Production tasks and grammaticality judgments are typically isolated, and language attainment is described in structural terms, i.e. emphasizing explicit errors or grammaticality judgments. Age of onset is then offered as the explanation for non-native attainment, with few notable exceptions (Birdsong, 1992; Bongaerts *et al.*, 1997; Ioup *et al.*, 1994; White & Genesee, 1996). What is striking about this research is what it lacks: an account of individual factors *in context*.

With a legacy of early work on bilingualism in Canada, socio-cultural perspectives in SLA, by contrast, emphasize the importance of contextual factors in understanding second language (L2) development (Clément *et al.*, 1993, Clément *et al.*, 1994; ; Clément & Noels, 1992; Clément & Kruidenier, 1983; Gardner, 1983, 1985b; Gardner & Lambert, 1972; Gardner, *et al.*, 1997; Hamers, 1994; Lambert, 1977; Norton Pierce, 2000; Taylor, 1977). These factors include: identity, assimilation, psychological distance, and even instruction for second language attainment (Clément & Kruidenier, 1983; Gardner, 1983, 1985b; Giles & Johnson, 1981; Labrie & Clément, 1986; Lambert, 1977; Schumann, 1978). A fundamental contribution of this collective work is the understanding of SLA, not as an abstract phenomenon, but as a process that essentially connects the individual to a community, where language is closely tied to one's sense of self – an important consideration for long-term integration both in linguistic and in cultural spheres (Lantolf, 2000; Lantolf & Pavlenko, 1995; Norton Pierce, 2000; see Pavlenko, 2002 for review).

Early work on German as a second language (*Zweitspracherwerb Italienischer und Spanischer Arbeiter, Heidelberger Forschungsprojekt*) also highlights the importance of personal contact with native speakers (Dittmar & Rieck 1977, as cited in Loeffler, 1985; Meisel *et al.*, 1981). While much of this research sets out in search of universal, internally-driven, mechanisms in uninstructed SLA, the range of background factors tested points to the primacy of interaction as key to developing morpho-syntactic fluency. Similar results come from grammatical-functional research, where pragmatic and semantic processing mode preferences are seen to result from interactive experience (Broeder, 1991; Dietrich, 1995; Dittmar, 1992; Pfaff, 1987, 1992 – see Moyer, in press, for summary). If interactive experience is critical to long-term attainment, then opportunities for such engagement in the target language community must be accounted for.

Equally problematic is the fact that adult language performance is frequently described as substandard, in spite of an early emphasis on creative construction in interlanguage (Ellis, 1985; Selinker, 1972 and 1992). In essence, the focus on documented patterns such as simplification and free variation has perpetuated stereotypes of foreigner talk through an emphasis on reduced interlanguage features. Fennell summarizes the unfortunate result for German as a second language:

> ... All such [classificatory] behavior, whether exhibited by linguists, pedagogues, officials, or everyday people, serves to ethnicize both the minorities, and concomitantly, the Germans themselves ... Here we return to Bourdieu's contention that the act of naming and classifying is a very strong exercise in power ... Comparing *Gastarbeiter* German with standard German has stacked the cards against foreign workers, begging the labels 'inadequate,' and ultimately 'inferior.' (Fennell, 1997: 92f)

Indeed, it is all too rare to focus on what learners are doing well. Marinova-Todd *et al.* suggest that 'rather than focusing on the low probability that adults will acquire fluency in L2s ... it is more productive to examine the factors that typically lead to native-like proficiency ...' (Marinova-Todd *et al.*, 2000: 10). To this end, the influence of age should be examined in terms of how it may relate to availability of authentic input, instruction, interaction, etc., as well as to the learner's intention to attain to a certain level. These aspects of late language learning can be ascertained only through careful measure of L2 experience.

Second language experience effectively constitutes a 'black box' for SLA; many of the relevant mechanisms may be unobservable. Yet, in spite of these empirical challenges, the nature of late language acquisition suggests the need to move beyond simplistic analyses and interpretations. To understand how new knowledge is acquired, *we must discover how learners actively participate in the learning process itself.* This requires an appreciation of the socio-psychological aspects of learning approach, including an examination of motives, beliefs, and sense of linguistic and cultural identity (Liebkind, 1999; Norton Pierce, 1995). Even the target language commu-

nity's expectations for non-native speaker assimilation may play a significant role in how the learner engages with available resources and
negotiates learning and feedback opportunities against the backdrop of
perceived expectations for 'success' (see Genesee *et al.*, 1983; Pavlenko,
2002). These issues deserve deeper investigation in applied linguistics
research in general.

The problems of scope and classification may thus be due in part to
fundamental incomparability between research on what could be termed
'privileged' learning, typical of classroom foreign language instruction,
and that of naturalistic language acquisition. Social, instructional, and
psychological conditions cannot be compared for such disparate experiences. The social and political status of immigrants affords them few
opportunities to receive supportive feedback on their developing
interlanguage (see Norton Pierce, 1998). Moreover, their experience with
the target language may accumulate in a somewhat haphazard, or reactive,
manner. This is quite another matter for the classroom learner, who is
essentially guaranteed a comfort zone for linguistic revision and gradual
L2 identity development. These internal and external differences are not
addressed by structural descriptions of interlanguage development, much
less by isolated statistical analyses. It is therefore necessary to empirically
integrate critical period perspectives with data on individual access to
input and instruction (see Moyer, 1999).

In this book, I will integrate and critically review current literature on
age effects, and add new data to the discussion as I test the biological basis
of the critical period hypothesis *relative to the impact of socio-psychological and
experiential variables*. This integrated methodology relies on descriptive and
statistical analyses of relationships between multiple biological, psychological, and experiential factors. The interpretation of these relationships is
then strengthened through ethnographic data on the *individual's perspective*
on the process. Accordingly, the significance of these factors becomes
clearer as we understand how the learner responds and adapts to the target
language and its community *over time*. Given the context for most SLA
today, a more holistic understanding of personal and communal opportunities to build L2 experience is appropriate. To this end, the data in this
study focus on immigrants to Berlin.

Contextualizing SLA: Germany as an Empirical Framework

For immigrants who must learn a second language, the complex conflation of maturation, socio-psychological orientation, and cultural identity is
very real. Present-day Germany provides an excellent empirical basis for

exploring issues of identity and milieu in the SLA process. Currently, Germany claims about 9% (7.3 million) of its population as 'foreign' (not including *Aussiedler*, or ethnic Germans seeking asylum from neighboring Eastern European countries). Fluency in German is critical to the potential of these people for long-term assimilation and acceptance. Skutnabb-Kangas points out that, while the mother tongue may be necessary for psychological, cognitive, and spiritual survival, the official language of the state is needed for 'social, economic, political, and civil rights ...' and may determine further education, job prospects, and participation in wider society (Skutnabb-Kangas, 1999: 58). Acknowledging the juxtaposition of forces toward social integration as well as isolation, the adult immigrant's difficulties with acquiring German go beyond possible cognitive and neurological constraints. By exploring the experience of the learner, we may better understand how language acquisition proceeds, or fossilizes, according to predictable influences.

With this context in mind, the current study (see next section) presents linguistic and non-linguistic data gathered from immigrants to Germany from the US, Britain, France, Russia, Poland, Slovakia, and Turkey. The analysis of language attainment is thus contextualized here through a broad accounting of experiential and socio-psychological influences on language attainment. Furthermore, these immigrants provide an inter-esting contrast to the uninstructed data presented in earlier studies depicting L2 learners/acquirers, with little or no access to formal, or instructional, experience in the target language. Because of their combina-tion of both formal and informal exposure, these immigrants have had what might be considered an optimal acquisitional experience. They are also well-educated, and as such, social separation is perhaps less dramatic for them than for many *Gastarbeiter* and *Asylbewerber*.[2] They also tend to see themselves as actively engaged with the language and its culture for both personal and professional reasons. Given these potential advantages, these learners may 'defy' the critical period, in the sense that age effects may be weaker when external opportunities (i.e. access to L2) are greater, and internal orientations are relatively positive.

The numerous studies on immigrant language acquisition have revealed surprisingly little regarding such personal and communal issues. The history of *Gastarbeiterlinguistik* goes back to the mid-1970s with the ZISA (*Zweitspracherwerb Italienischer und Spanischer Arbeiter*) and HFP (*Heidelberger Forschungsprojekt*) projects (for discussion, see Fennell, 1997; Larsen-Freeman & Long, 1991).

Objectives of the many published studies from these, and subsequent, databases include seeking evidence for: (1) universal developmental pathways to syntactic and morphological acquisition; (2) the temporary (or permanent) nature of reduced varieties, i.e. so-called Pidgindeutsch or Foreign Worker German; and (3) potential access to Universal Grammar in the acquisitional process. Overwhelmingly, the emphasis has been on structural descriptions of morphosyntactic simplification. A number of studies have led to hypotheses concerning universal routes of development, and the role of instructional intervention (see Jordens, 1996 for discussion). Recent research has focused on areas of transfer from L1 features (Felix, 1980; Kaltenbacher, 1994; Meisel, 1983; Pfaff, 1984), processing strategies, stages in syntactic development and verbal movement patterns (Beck, 1998; Eubank, 1992; Vainikka & Young-Scholten, 1996), and potential access to Universal Grammar for specific features (Clahsen & Muysken, 1986; Felix 1991). More recently, analyses of developmental strategies have focused on possible 'dual mechanisms' for language learning, combining memory and analysis in the acquisition of regular and irregular morphological markers (Clahsen, 1997; Elsen, 1997).

To be sure, this ongoing descriptive and theoretical work has provided rich data and thought-provoking hypotheses concerning the nature of early versus late language learning. However, it acknowledges social and cultural concerns of immigrant learners in minimal ways. Moreover, the resulting theoretical interpretations have been criticized, given the small number of participants in many studies, the relative paucity of methods reporting, and the vastly different access among participants to interactive learning opportunities (see Hudson, 1993; Jansen, 2000; Mellow, 1996; Rogers, 1995).

Alternative studies from sociolinguistic and functionalist perspectives have expanded our understanding of immigrant language acquisition and the social circumstances of guest workers, especially in terms of the purpose and function of their interactions in German (Broeder, 1991; Frischherz, 1997; Jordens et al., 1989; Perdue, 1990; Pfaff, 1985, 1987, 1992; Röhr-Sendlmeier, 1990). Summarizing results from a number of studies, robust patterns emerge across a range of methods. Factors correlating to higher levels of linguistic attainment include: motivation to integrate into German culture; consistent interaction in German beyond survival situations, sustained peer relationships with native Germans, institutionalized integration assistance; and participation in German education programs (Barkowski et al., 1976; Buss, 1995; Esser, 1982; Götze & Pommerin, 1988; Horn, 1996; Lalleman, 1987; Pfaff, 1985; Worbs, 1995). For early German language acquisition (GLA), parental expectations and support for education are correlated to success in language attainment and overall educational achievement (Götze & Pommerin, 1988; Röhr-Sendlmeier, 1990).

These findings confirm that consistency and support in the learner's interactive community are key to ultimate attainment. Such close examinations of opportunities for L2 contact over time are rare in the empirical research.

In this charged socio-political context, explanations for attainment in German arguably go beyond cognitive or neurological explanations (see Moyer, in press). Linguistic development, and its role in social acceptance, must be seen as a highly individualized phenomenon. It is not easily reduced to predictable patterns and outcomes, but depends on myriad social and psychological factors, played out in both public and private spheres.

The Current Empirical Study

Because of its focus, this work fills an important gap in the critical period research, which has been recently criticized for weak and/or narrow methods and explanations, particularly with regard to non-biological factors (see Bialystok & Hakuta, 1999; Birdsong, 1999; Scovel, 2000). If ultimate attainment is influenced by one's ongoing *opportunities* and *intentions* to build L2 knowledge and abilities, then maturation may have an impact on these levels of engagement in several (unexplored) ways. This assumption is the guiding principle for an exploration of how language acquisition may proceed, plateau, or stagnate on the path to native-like competence.

Empirical evidence in SLA has confirmed a pervasive neuro-cognitive influence, evident in the apparent loss of flexibility for the native-like acquisition of new patterns, especially in the phonological realm. Cognitive and psycholinguistic research have confirmed transfer effects from L1 to L2, similar patterns of development for certain features regardless of L1, and the likelihood of fossilization short of native-like production. At the same time, SLA is characterized by great individual variation. Each learner brings to bear his or her own talents, needs, style, and limits. At this point, the significance of attitude, motivation, and other affective and social-psychological factors is unquestioned in the research. This juxtaposition of individual and universal aspects of acquisition often confounds empirical investigation. Perhaps no other level of language ability demonstrates this juxtaposition more clearly (and consistently) than phonology. Because of its combination of higher- and lower-order functions, i.e. its reliance on both motor and higher analytical skills, it has unique potential to reveal both neurological constraints and individual ability. The oft-cited disparity between production and perception skill underscores how difficult it is to fully account for all operative mechanisms in SLA – a process that is marked by individual approach as well as possibly universal constraints after a certain age. In short, phonological attainment, more so than any other aspect of SLA, may offer the greatest opportunity for more integrative explanations of (non)native-ness among late learners.

A primary objective of this investigation is to discover which factors (and combinations thereof) predict the persistence of foreign accent, as judged both by outsiders and by the individual him or herself. Linguistic and ethnographic data are gathered through several instruments, focusing on spoken tasks, both controlled and free. Native speakers judged authenticity and perceptions of native-ness according to various criteria. Following a statistical analysis of the connections between such factors and performance ratings, the book turns to a close analysis of social-psychological constructs including identity, perceptions of acceptance, and connections to heritage and target language community. The one-on-one interviews allow for an exploration of how statistically significant factors may be understood from the perspective of the learner, with special focus on his or her overall desire for cultural and linguistic assimilation. Above all, the learner's active engagement with these various support systems is shown to be a powerful basis for linguistic and cultural assimilation (see Hamers, 1994).

Acknowledging the importance of the learner's perceptions of belonging, along with formal and informal support systems for linguistic development, reflects the fundamental aim of this work: to advance a predictive model for SLA that substantiates the relevance and balance of age, identity, and L2 experience in ultimate attainment.

The Structure of the Book

A brief review of empirical research in SLA reveals a rather dichotomous approach to understanding differences in early and late language acquisition: the tendency to claim universality of patterns, versus an accounting of individual aspects of the process. These perspectives have hardly been reconciled for any particular aspect of L2 acquisition, and the phonological realm is no exception. Based on the patterns revealed across approaches, however, some reconciliation may be warranted.

Chapter 2 therefore explores these dichotomous approaches in the context of the Critical Period Hypothesis and theories of ultimate, or end-state, attainment. Entitled 'Accounting for Universal and Individual Factors in Ultimate Attainment: Focus on Phonology,' it highlights the quest to understand both *process* and *product* in late SLA, characterized by mutually exclusive methods and approaches. By and large, the idea of 'fundamental difference' between early and late language acquisition

(Bley-Vroman, 1989) is found in cognitive, modular, Universal Grammar, instructional, and social-psychological approaches to SLA. This chapter reviews the usefulness of these approaches for explaining phonological attainment – a uniquely complex phenomenon given that the gap between perception and production ability appears to be a persistent, vexing aspect of late SLA.

Even if phonology is uniquely constrained by neuro-motor changes, these influences probably operate across levels of language, since age effects are also apparent in morpho-syntactic acquisition (Scovel, 2000). Nonetheless, phonology's (exclusive) power to predict outcomes has been overstated. Maturational constraints may reasonably be a function both of neurological changes and of socio-psychological and cognitive conditions as well. Therefore Chapter 2 also reviews the research on individual factors in phonological acquisition, including identity, motivation, empathy, and concern for native-ness.

The chapter concludes by emphasizing that the linearity of the age–outcome relationship appears to fade at maturation (around age 12 or so), suggesting that declines in language learning after that point are due to factors other than age. An argument is therefore made for a merger of psycholinguistic and sociolinguistic perspectives, based on contextual and experiential realities of the late learner. Finally, I point to the centrality of accent for judgments of native-ness and belonging in the target language community.

Chapter 3, 'Verifying the Relative Strength of Maturation, L2 Experience and Psychological Orientation: The Quantitative Findings,' outlines the empirical basis for this book: an integrated study of immigrant learners/ acquirers of German in Berlin ($n = 25$) from various L1 backgrounds. These participants have experienced a range of exposure domains for German through personal friendships, academic or work-related acquaintances, and formal instruction, beginning at different ages. Research questions outlined in this chapter include:

- How does age of onset with L2 relate to formal and informal opportunities to build L2 experience?
- How does consistency in these opportunities affect long-term attainment?
- How is age of onset related to social-psychological factors that may shift over time, for example, motivation and self-perceptions of native-ness in L2?

In order to both test and expand the critical period research paradigm, this study examines four primary clusters of factors as they relate to phonological attainment:

(1) *biological-experiential* factors such as age of onset, gender, native language, level of education, length of residence, etc.;
(2) *instructional-cognitive* factors such as duration and types of L2 instruction, indirect instructional exposure to German through other coursework (in Germany), phonological instruction and feedback, learning strategies for improving pronunciation, etc.;
(3) *experiential-social* factors such as the acquisitional context for initial onset with German, consistency of contact with (and feedback from) native speakers, frequency of written versus spoken use of German, contexts for using German, etc.; and
(4) *social-psychological* factors such as motivation (intensity and consistency over time), behaviors undertaken in response to that motivational drive, self-perceptions of fluency, satisfaction with attainment, necessity of fluency in German for future plans, and so forth.

All these data were collected through background surveys, coded as either continuous or categorical variables for the quantitative analysis, and verified through the interviews for qualitative analysis.

For the quantitative analysis, the significance of age of onset is compared to the significance of other contextual and experiential variables for linguistic performance, which were rated by native speakers for both controlled and free-response items (nine native speakers served as controls for these tasks). The impact of maturation is therefore discussed in relation to both opportunity (contexts for access) and intention to pursue native-like fluency. According to the statistical analyses (including ANOVA, t-tests, correlation, and multiple regression), instructional and psychological factors significantly relate to native-like attainment *as well as to age of onset*, and their influence can be substantiated across tasks. This demonstrates that maturation is indicative of certain social and psychological constraints on the process, i.e. beyond neurological and neuro-cognitive developmental changes in the individual. Further insights from the regression analyses point to the independent impact of several variables, i.e. their strength is not simply due to a conflation with other factors. Special attention is given to the variables *length of residence* and *age of onset*, as well as to *age* versus *maturation* as possibly exerting distinct effects.

Chapter 4, 'Understanding Identity, Intention, and Opportunities for L2 Contact: The Qualitative Findings,' strengthens and expands upon the descriptive and statistical analysis in Chapter 3 through qualitative data. Interviews provided an opportunity to ask individuals about their attitudes toward the target language country, their sense of belonging, cultural and linguistic identity, etc. A secondary aim of this instrument is to understand the *dynamic* nature of L2 experience and motivation, i.e. how those notions may have shifted over the course of time. I consider the following specific questions, based on the observed data:

- How do psychological orientations and experiences in the target language country influence specific behaviors and goals, such as the pursuit of greater contact to native speakers, formal language instruction, etc?
- Which aspects of L2 experience should be considered fundamental to ultimate attainment? For example, can consistent, personal contact with native speakers mitigate predicted age effects?
- Are cultural and linguistic identity pivotal to attainment, particularly as they may influence intention to reside and/or affiliate with the target language culture?

Accounting for such influences reflects the fundamental objective of this work: to understand age of onset in relation to one's opportunities for building L2 experience, essential connections to the language itself, and intentions to develop native-like fluency. In addition to addressing common themes that emerge in the interviews, I also contrast ideas of 'belonging' for some individuals of non-European descent. The ways this particular construct may impact perceptions of oneself as a user of the target language and participant in the target language community are underscored here as important considerations for future work.

Chapter 5,' Conclusions and Proposals for Future Research,' emphasizes that critical-period research in SLA should not only acknowledge non-biological factors in maturational effects, it should revise its empirical approach accordingly. As these data demonstrate, decontextualizing age of onset leads to a potential misinterpretation of its influence on ultimate attainment. While it may be a formidable influence, constraining L2 development in multiple ways, maturation does not, in itself, provide a full explanation for processes and outcomes in SLA.

As a final note, the construct of experience, particularly as a reflection of active engagement on the part of the learner, is characterized in terms of *duration, quality, consistency* and *intensity* – four considerations deserving greater attention in the future.

Conclusion

Language acquisition beyond early childhood is essentially a personal and social process; one that is hardly appreciated in the confines of structuralist, product-oriented interlanguage data. If a comprehensive theory of SLA is possible, then the learning environment, L2 experience, orientation to the learning task, and the learner's perceived reception as a speaker of L2 are all elements to be explored, not underestimated. Given that acquisition is neither a predictable continuum nor a mere accumulation of rule-based behaviors (Long, 1990, as cited in Brown, 2000), ultimate attainment inquiry should more consciously focus on the dynamic nature of SLA in its sociocultural context. Today's shifting migration trends underscore the validity and urgency of such issues.

The linguistic analyses in this study rely on native-speaker interpretations of 'native-ness' for acquirers who are very advanced in the second language (German). While I acknowledge that 'native-ness' is a murky construct, one whose usefulness has been recently debated (Davies, 2000 and 2003; Graddol, 1999), the notion nonetheless remains a psychologically real aspect of the foreigner's experience of him or herself in the target language country. In practice, non-native-ness is perhaps most often associated with foreign accent. Yet, up to now, very little research has explored the relevant factors that determine long-term phonological attainment in L2 (cf. Bongaerts *et.al.*, 1997; Flege *et.al.*, 1995; Moyer, 1999; Purcell & Suter, 1980; Young-Scholten, 1994). Phonological attainment may be tied to neuro-cognitive, psychological, and even psycho-motor constraints, e.g. as articulatory habits from L1 become entrenched. It is therefore an especially relevant area of investigation for critical period studies. At the same time, phonological performance is perhaps the most salient factor in determining comprehensibility, native-ness, fluency, and belonging. As this investigation attests, accentedness, and the inclination to push beyond it, are significantly tied to contact with native speakers, motivation, duration of formal instruction, and length of residence, in addition to age of exposure.

Notes

1. Lenneberg (1967) assumed that at some point near puberty, beginning at approximately 9–10 years old, language recovery (and, by extension, foreign language learning) would be less complete. This point was made in reference to phonology especially.
2. *Gastarbeiter* refers to the many foreign workers who came to Germany after World War II to power the *Wirtschaftswunder* from Italy, Yugoslavia, etc.; it also refers to their families, well-established now in the second and third generations. The children of these workers are referred to as *Migrantkinder* (a somewhat outdated term considering that most grow up attending German schools and acquire the German language to a native level). Socially and culturally, however,

there may still be separation based on the fact that their 'non-German' status is often emphasized in public and political discourse. *Asylbewerber* is a term referring to the many political refugees who have entered Germany over the past 15–20 years in particular, often from non-European countries, but also from Bosnia, and the provinces of the former Yugoslavia, the former Soviet Union, etc. *Asylbewerber* have a much harsher existence in Germany since the *Asylkompromiss* of 1993 which placed restrictions on those seeking asylum from neighboring countries that are seen as politically secure. (For more discussion, see Moyer, in press.)

Chapter 2

Accounting for Universal and Individual Factors in Ultimate Attainment: Focus on Phonology

Introduction: Differences in Child and Adult Language Learning

If children universally master their mother tongues (assuming no serious impairments or deprivation), late language learners arrive at highly variable end states. Understanding both the *universal* and the *individual* aspects of their developmental process, and its outcome, is one essential task of SLA research. Up to this point, neither theory nor empirical research has clearly bridged these two essential forces in one unified model. Instead, an entrenched division of interests is pervasive in the field. Facing this divide, 'ultimate attainment' studies have been overwhelmingly concerned with universal patterns of influence in late language acquisition. This focus has arguably led to a dead end of sorts; evidence and counterevidence have mounted, with no clear direction for moving the investigation forward. Getting beyond this impasse requires a new approach, or perhaps an *integration* of approaches.

As early as 1978, Schumann described the complexity of language learning among immigrants, calling attention to neurological, affective, cognitive, instructional, and social factors important to the process. Table 2.1 is adapted from that early list.

Schumann's thorough catalogue is a reminder both of how far SLA research has come, and how far it must still go. Many of the influences shown in Table 2.1 have been verified as significant, sparking no small measure of debate along the way. With greater understanding of interlanguage development, researchers have been able to point to several possible explanations for the differences between L1 and L2 acquisition. This second chapter critically reviews these current theories and approaches to empirical study. Throughout, I stress their applications for phonological acquisition – possibly the area most often associated with critical-period effects, as well as judgments of 'non-native-ness.' For these reasons, phonological abilities are also emphasized in the empirical study presented in the following chapters.

Table 2.1 Taxonomy of factors influencing second language acquisition

Neurological factors:
• Lateralization
Affective and personality factors:
• Motivation • Ego permeability • Tolerance for ambiguity • Sensitivity to rejection and self-esteem • Introversion/extroversion • Culture shock
Cognitive and aptitude factors:
• Cognitive maturity and processes (imitation, generalization, memorization) • Strategies and styles • Intelligence/IQ • Interference from L1 • Field dependence/independence
Instruction and input factors:
• Teacher and class dynamics and reaction to feedback • Curriculum: Method, texts, approach • Intensity and duration of instruction • Saliency
Social factors:
Group/community level: • Dominant versus subordinate status • Assimilation and acculturation • Preservation of ethnic and cultural identity • Degree of enclosure, size, cohesiveness of community • Attitudes toward TL (dominant) group • Intended length of residence
Personal level: • Transition anxiety • Social strategies • Linguistic shock

Adapted from Schumann (1978)

In comparing acquisitional outcomes among children and adults, several studies have revealed notable patterns. For instance, in a longitudinal study by Snow and Hoefnagel-Höhle (1982), older children (aged

8–10 and 12–15) and adults scored higher on pronunciation tests, for both imitation and spontaneous tasks. These results held for subsequent measurements, though the differences between age groups decreased over time. For all tasks and age groups tested, 3–5 year olds scored the lowest, and 12–15 year olds showed the most rapid acquisition in all skills tested: pronunciation, morphology, syntactic judgments, and listening comprehension. These results are significant, in that these repeat measures demonstrated that older learners can achieve as well as younger learners. In another study, Fathman (1975) found that 6–10 year olds were more accurate in producing elicited phonological structures, while 11–15 year olds performed better in morphological and syntactic tasks. Specifically, older learners were able to learn morphosyntactic structures more quickly than younger learners when the amount of exposure was held constant. And in a two-year study, Ekstrand (1976) found that older learners outperformed younger ones on a range of tasks, including reading, writing, listening comprehension and speaking (cited in Larsen-Freeman & Long, 1991).

Summarizing these early studies, Krashen *et al.* (1982) make the following generalizations: (1) adults and older children show advantages over young children in rate of learning, especially in the areas of syntax and morphology; and (2) earlier exposure generally indicates higher proficiency. There have been very few studies, however, that have tested actual long-term *retention* of learned features, not to mention comparing phonological development with morphosyntactic development. Examining the 'end-state' of the learning continuum is one way to investigate differences between early and late learning potential across levels of language. This approach and its empirical shortcomings are outlined below.

Ultimate attainment

A few studies have focused on true end-state abilities, or *ultimate attainment*. In their well-known 1989 study, Johnson and Newport examined adult learners' performance in relation to their age of arrival in the target language country. On a test of grammaticality judgments, those who arrived in the US after the age of 7 showed a significant and continuous decline in ability to judge grammatical vs. ungrammatical items at a level considered 'native.' This steady decline continues until the age of 17, at which point performance levels off, showing no further relationship to age. This study has been widely cited as proof of the influence of age of onset (AO) on the second language (for critique, see Bialystok, 1997). In a second study, Johnson and Newport (1991) provide similar evidence for universal features (the subjacency principle) among learners with AO ranging from 4 to 38. Results indicate age effects similar to the earlier study (see Schachter, 1996, for discussion).

By contrast, Birdsong (1992) found that adult learners of French did exhibit native-like grammaticality judgments. In fact, native speakers (NS) and non-native speakers (NNS) diverged significantly for only 22% of the items, and overall, 15 of the 20 NNS performed at a native level. The NNS subjects were all post-pubertal learners (defined in this study as 11 years or older). None had been immersed in the target language country before the age of 19, and the earliest age of instruction was 11. Thus, in spite of a late onset, native-level attainment in grammaticality judgments was possible for an impressive number of subjects. Recent studies provide similar evidence (Birdsong, 1992; Ioup *et al.*, 1994; Juffs & Harrington, 1995 – cited in Bialystok, 1997; White & Genesee, 1996). However, non-native attainment is still widespread, especially for phonology, and grammaticality judgments themselves have come under attack as poor measures of real language ability (see Nunan, 1996; Sorace, 1996).

In light of these ongoing controversies and debates, in order to situate the current study theoretically and empirically, I review here several major approaches to understanding age effects. Particular attention is paid to phonological acquisition as unique and intriguing, given the common consensus that foreign accent is widely cited as an intractable feature of late SLA. Whether phonology inherently requires certain skills, i.e. that it may be less 'attainable' than morphology and syntax, is an important question in the debate on age effects.

The critical period and SLA

Age of onset is typically cited as the critical factor in the debate on child and adult differences in attainment. In his book, *Biological Foundations of Language* (1967),[1] Eric Lenneberg outlined the likely impact of late exposure on language learning, emphasizing phonology as particularly subject to neuro-biological constraints. However brief, Lenneberg's comments reflect the common wisdom that foreign languages are learned through extensive conscious effort, and that accent 'is not easily overcome' (Lenneberg, 1967: 176). His work has influenced SLA research in profound ways; the idea of a critical period quickly became the fallback explanation for non-native outcomes, particularly in the phonological realm.

The neurological basis for a critical period for language learning may lie in electro-chemical changes in the brain, many of which reach a steady state around the age of 10–12 years (Lenneberg, 1967). It could further be due to lateralization, or the assignment of specific (language) functions to either the right or the left hemisphere. After lateralization is complete (by early puberty, according to Lenneberg), language acquisition is predictably much less complete or successful because the brain is less flexible or 'plastic.'

To take a specific example, new phonetic categories may be incompletely formed owing to the consolidation of pyramidal axon connections by the age of six or eight years (Walsh & Diller, 1981: 12), i.e. occurring even earlier than Lenneberg proposed. These connections, responsible for 'lower order cortical functions' such as sensory-motor skills, are 'minimally neuroplastic,' meaning they do not continue to develop and adapt to linguistic input or demand (Walsh & Diller, 1981: 17). Walsh and Diller speculate that this is why early learning of phonology is most effective, while morphological and syntactic development likely remain somewhat open through later ages. The 'higher order processes' required for morpho-syntax may fall under the domain of cognitive development, originating in cortical regions in which neural functions continue to develop into adulthood.

In similar fashion, Abuhamdia (1987) outlines specific changes in plasticity and myelination (formation of sheathing surrounding brain cells) according to their differing paths of development. Neurons associated with 'higher order processes' (such as syntax, morphology, semantics, and creative language use) continue to develop over several decades, while those associated with articulatory movement do not:

> ... The existence of the foreign accent seems to be related to the early maturation and myelination of the Golgi type 1 neuronal cells which are preponderant in the language motor area. These cells lose their plasticity early in life, and it is only during this period that one or more languages may be acquired natively, i.e. without a foreign accent. (Abuhamdia, 1987: 209)

In short, the differential development and maturation of cell types may exert influence on the various levels of language (syntax and morphology versus phonology), and thus explain the differential achievement in these areas. If phonology resides in a part of the brain that ceases development early in life, this would further substantiate the Critical Period Hypothesis (CPH), thereby explaining the difficulties in mastering a new phonological system.

The potential fallacy in assuming a biological link to accent is that such a factor should operate more or less equally across learners, and it should demonstrate an obvious drop-off or decline at maturation – the presumed close of the critical period. Pallier *et al.* (1997) found that even those exposed to the target language in early childhood may not be able to produce phonemic distinctions that they can perceive with accuracy. And as Flynn and Manuel (1991) point out, there are instances of adult learners with accent-free speech, as well as child learners with slight accents. They further argue that the decline in plasticity has not been linked causally to poor language learning ability: '... It is hard to reconcile the fact that older children and adults are initially more successful producers of L2 speech [in spite of] an age-related loss in plasticity' (Flynn & Manuel, 1991: 121). If this is true, then language acquisition relies on more than just neurological processes, and the idiosyncratic balance of relevant mechanisms may explain the range of outcomes observed.

The neurological emphasis of the Critical Period Hypothesis has resulted in a great deal of research on brain activity, especially on bilingual language processing (Obler, 1993; Obler & Gjerlow, 1999; Obler & Hannigan, 1996; Weber-Fox & Neville, 1999). Positron emission tomography (PET) now allows for online observation of brain activity during language reception and production tasks. Similarly, functional magnetic resonance imaging (fMRI) localizes differences in brain activity for L1 and L2 in bilinguals, permitting a comparison of these zones of activity for late and early learners of L2. Results show that syntactic and semantic processing, as well as certain aspects of morphological processing, may be differentially affected by age of exposure to the language (see Weber-Fox & Neville, 1999). Yet Marinova-Todd *et al.* (2000) criticize claims of hemispheric activity patterns as proof of critical period effects on actual language *ability*, as opposed to neurological activity. According to their argument, the implications of this work have been too broadly interpreted. Bialystok and Hakuta also downplay the significance of neural organization as a reflection of actual ability:

> It is not surprising that the experience and knowledge we accumulate as we grow changes the way in which new information, including new languages, will be represented, and that these differences can be detected as different patterns of neural organization in the brain. (Bialystok & Hakuta 1999: 178)

As the authors also point out, some individuals show right hemisphere dominance for language processing, thus, language processing does not work in the same ways for all. It is only through behavioral evidence, i.e. performance, that real arguments may be made for ability, and thus far that evidence is contradictory across cases (Bialystok & Hakuta, 1999).

Given that some learners do appear to attain to native levels, other factors must be at play, and age effects are probably more complex than we have assumed. Long (1990) is one researcher who has supported the idea of a 'sensitive period' (separate ones, in fact, for phonology, morphology, etc.), allowing for some individual variation, while downplaying the significance of affective and cognitive factors. In a different interpretation altogether of these competing influences, Schumann (1994) suggests that affect and cognition are interdependent and equal processes – inseparable even – and that the brain's emotional system modulates cognitive processes of perception, attention and memory (Schumann, 1994: 240). He differentiates between two kinds of learning: (1) that which is highly influenced by 'stimulus appraisal,' indicating an important role for affective evaluation, and (2) learning that is less affected by emotional response and thus shows less individual variation. According to Schumann (1994: 238), long-term, 'sustained, deep' learning, such as language learning, is 'extensively modulated by affect,' meaning that affect can prevent development at any point, leading to fossilization.

The bottom line is that we must account somehow for individual variation as well as for any possible universal constraints. Viewing certain influences *in isolation from one another* has thus far led us to some premature and possibly erroneous conclusions.

The age factor

In a recent review, Birdsong (1999) delineates several factors relevant to a possible critical period for SLA: loss of neural plasticity, loss of access to something like a language acquisition device, an overwhelming tendency toward cognitive processing and analysis for adult learners, and the possibility that factors of input, experience, and psychological orientation may determine both process and outcomes in SLA. The question is: can these influences be adequately observed (much less measured)? Perhaps one major appeal of the CPH is this: It has been 'operationalized' in SLA research as a simple measure of age of onset (AO). This approach raises obvious questions of internal validity, some of which are briefly mentioned here.

To begin with, age is an especially unsatisfying explanation, scientifically speaking, since it is a continuous variable, it coincides with the increasing significance of so many other variables, and it is impossible to observe separately from these co-occurring factors (Hatch, 1983; Wode, 1994). In short, age is neither isolatable, nor falsifiable. Thus, its influence cannot be determined until it is conclusively tested in relation to other factors. For example, Bialystok and Hakuta (1999) maintain that cognitive processes constitute a primary, qualitative difference in child–adult learning; for adults, previous knowledge domains prevail (e.g. transfer).

Such influences have yet to be sufficiently tested, especially *against* maturation. Bialystok and Hakuta offer this critique:

> ... Observationally, there is a co-occurrence between two events: the age at which a person starts learning a second language corresponds in some way to the ultimate success that the person will attain after years of having used that language ... there may well be a correlation ... but it does not necessarily follow that age is a causal factor in that relation. It may turn out that it is, but the data would need to show convincing evidence for causality. (Bialystok & Hakuta, 1999: 162)

Birdsong (2002) articulates a further problem: the need to differentiate general age effects from maturation itself. Where *age effects*, per se, are manifest in steady, linear relationships between AO and attainment outcomes (i.e. over a person's lifetime), *maturation* is a stage in the aging process, generally realized by the age of 15. Its impact on attainment would present itself as a clear drop off, or obvious decline in linearity, *at that point in an individual's life*. Birdsong therefore urges caution in assuming that *either age or maturation* account for end-state abilities; he emphasizes that the impact of age is not well understood:

> ... If there is a linear decrement in performance over all ages of immersion, this suggests a general age effect, with the possibility that experiential factors co-varying with age may be implicated. If, on the other hand, the age effect ceases at a maturationally-defined developmental point, and is not predictive thereafter, this suggests a qualitative change in learning.' (Birdsong, in press)

In sum, several arguments may be made *against* age as a strict account of non-native outcomes. For one thing, our inability to directly observe underlying skills and mechanisms in language processing makes this a tenuous position to take. Therefore, 'an independent neurophysiological account is probably somewhat artificial, or at best, partial' (Long, 1990: 279). In addition, we know that developmental phenomena are marked by patterns of universality as well as idiosyncracy. As Müller (1996: 611) puts it, 'human brains are characterized by multifactorial, inter-individual variability, and strict universality of functional organization is biologically unrealistic.' Finally, Wode (1994) argues that no 'absolute biological baseline' has yet been established *beyond which language learning becomes qualitatively different*. 'What needs to be shown is that there are differences not in what children and adults actually do, but in what they *can* do' (Wode, 1994: 341). According to the studies cited, it appears that adults (beyond the age of 15 or so) are capable of high levels of mastery, and are particularly advantaged in terms of rate of initial learning. Still, it is not clear whether native-level production is impossible, or just improbable owing to physiological or psychological hindrance. These questions are particularly relevant for the realm of phonology, taken up in the following sections.

Ultimate Attainment in L2 Phonology

Lenneberg's CPH sets up a critical window of opportunity, beyond which the development of native pronunciation is unlikely, if not impossible. He made special note of the intractability of foreign accent after the age of 9 or 10, and this is largely upheld by subsequent evidence, even among advanced learners (Moyer, 1999). Scovel (1981: 37) noted early on the 'inability of non-primary language learners to acquire perfect, accentless speech in the target language, even though they may become completely fluent in the target language vocabulary and syntax.' Many researchers believe that phonological attainment is limited by a much earlier age than Lenneberg proposed. Yet results from various studies do not lend themselves to simple conclusions about maturation's influence, particularly as it is conflated with multiple experiential factors, and 'for all natural populations, exceptions abound' (Scovel, 2000: 217).

Within L2 phonological research, both long-term and short-term attainment have been measured across a wide age span, for various languages. Oyama (1976) tested 60 Italian male learners of ESL (English as a Second Language) to compare the effects on phonological attainment of age of arrival in the US and length of exposure. Using a read-aloud task, as well as narration, subjects were rated for degree of foreign accent. The results indicated a very strong effect for age of arrival, but not for number of years of exposure. Olson and Samuels (1982) discovered that older subjects performed better than younger subjects on an imitation task of phoneme drills, although these results demonstrate only immediate imitative ability. As mentioned, Snow and Hoefnagel-Hoehle (1982) surveyed reading-aloud abilities of native English speakers learning Dutch. They found that older subjects and adults outperformed children in the early learning phase. However, within 10 months younger learners caught up to and exceeded the older subjects' phonological accuracy. The authors interpret their results as unsupportive of a critical period for pronunciation, since adults and older learners demonstrated superior accuracy for short-term performance.

Correlating pronunciation accuracy with multiple background factors, Purcell and Suter (1980) found four variables that accounted for 67% of the variance in a regression analysis: (1) the first language (L1); (2) aptitude for oral mimicry (based on self-report); (3) length of residence in the target language country and/or living with a native speaker of the target language; and (4) degree of concern for pronunciation accuracy. This study is noteworthy for two reasons. First, age at initial exposure did not correlate significantly to degree of accent. Second, the authors surveyed many linguistic and psychological factors, including motivation, assessment of cultural identity, and concern for pronunciation accuracy.

In a test of experiential factors among very advanced learners, Moyer (1999) found that non-native performance did not overlap with that of native controls; however, motivation and instruction were significant to ultimate attainment. The presence of suprasegmental instruction and feedback was specifically correlated to performance ratings closer to native, a variable that has not been specifically isolated before.[2] Learner factors that did not exhibit significant correlations include: self-evaluation of nativeness and satisfaction with pronunciation abilities in L2 (German), concern for sounding native (concern for accuracy), and extent of cultural and linguistic assimilation while in the country. Task differences indicated some effects for formality of task – more isolated tasks were rated closer to native than spontaneous, conversational ones – but these differences were not statistically significant.[3] It is worth noting that Moyer's study included an outlier, or exceptional learner, whose overall rating reflected a 'more native' accent than some of the native-speaker controls. This participant had a German spouse, recalling Purcell and Suter's (1980) finding that living with a native speaker is significant for degree of accent. Exceptional learning could therefore be a result of optimal input, feedback, and motivation (see Chapters 3 and 4.)

In similar studies, Bongaerts *et al.* (1995) and Bongaerts *et al.* (1997) found overlap between native and highly-motivated non-native speakers for pronunciation across various task types. As a cautionary note, these participants were specifically targeted for their exceptional abilities, as identified by 'experts,' and some had received intensive training in the perception and production of target speech sounds. Thus, generalizing these findings to wider populations is not possible. Importantly, however, Bongaerts *et al.* (1997) cite access to instruction and authentic interaction with native speakers as highly relevant to the participants' experience in L2. Further evidence for the strength of learner background variables is found in Flege *et al.* (1995) and in Bongaerts *et al.* (2000), particularly for instruction, motivation, concern for pronunciation, and even gender[4] (Flege *et al.*, 1995), though the tasks relied on non-spontaneous performance.

In a detailed summary of phonological studies over the past 30 years, Piske *et al.* (2001: 197) conclude that age may be central to ultimate attainment, but that 'no study has as yet provided convincing evidence for the claim that L2 speech will automatically be accent-free if it is learned before the age of about 6 years and that it will definitely be foreign-accented if learned after puberty.' Too little data is available across an age-of-onset (AO) spectrum (cf. Flege *et al.*, 1999; Leather, 1999), and even some early exposure has shown accented speech (Flege *et al.*, 1997). On the whole, then, overwhelming support is not found for critical period effects, depending on task type and learner background factors. Flege (1987a) argues against an actual critical period, and bases his argument on the fact that age is confounded with: (1) developmental and anatomical differences between children and adults, (2) differential access to L2 input, (3) the prominence of motivation and anxiety for adults, and (4) the differential phonetic processing due to pre-existing categories in the adult's knowledge base. Furthermore, there are widespread discrepancies in methodological approaches across studies, in terms of elicitation measures, presence or absence of native speaker controls, and performance rating types (Piske *et al.*, 2001), leaving possible generalizations tenuous at best.

Overall, attainment in L2 phonology is highly variable, probably because of multiple factors of experience[5] that exert differential influence across learners and learning situations. At the same time, some aspects of phonological acquisition are predicted to be a function of universal influences, such as: modularity in phonological knowledge, universal patterns of development, and possible access to a Universal Grammar (UG) in phonology. These points are raised in the following section.

Modular and Universal Perspectives on Phonological Abilities

One prominent view in universalist approaches assumes the existence of a language learning module, i.e. a specialized, separate faculty that is not necessarily integrated with other types of skills (see Müller, 1996; Munsell *et al.*, 1988). According to this view, language acquisition relies on its own specialized mechanism, which may or not function at peak levels in adulthood – possibly accounting for differences in child and adult achievement (see Bickerton, 1984; Fodor *et al.*, 1974).

Ideas on the modularity of language and its neural subsystems and processes inform a lively debate, particularly relevant to phonological processing. From research on the acquisition of L1, it is apparent that infants are capable at birth of differentiating phonetic categories based on voice onset time (VOT) in spite of a continuous acoustic signal (see Barsalou, 1992).[6] Kuhl (1991) notes that infants organize speech sounds according to prototypes, read lips (demonstrating connections between auditory and visual perception), and practice vocal imitation. In these ways, they connect auditory and articulatory abilities. Within the first year of life, infants develop 'perceptual biases' to reflect the phonetic categories in their input, possibly losing the ability to develop new categories later, or relying on other acoustic processing strategies to do so (Gierut, 1996; Kuhl & Iverson, 1995; Polka & Werker, 1994; Werker, 1995; Werker & Pegg, 1992; Wode, 1992, 1994). Sparks and Ganschow (1993) further theorize that deficits in phonological processing do not impact on general language or metacognitive processing abilities, thereby demonstrating the independent, modular nature of phonological abilities. Moreover, research in second language phonological acquisition has yielded some evidence supporting the view that categorical knowledge is not necessarily open to restructuring beyond early childhood (treated below).

Asymmetries in perception and production

Several investigations have examined asymmetrical abilities in perceptual and production abilities for late learners. Flege (1987b) describes differences between adult and child phonological acquisition as stemming from differential processing of new phonetic categories. According to Flege's Speech Learning Model, adult learners may rely on preexistent phonetic categories from L1, preventing the development of phonetically accurate targets for L2 sounds (Flege, 1991). At issue is the adult's reduced sensitivity to specific phones that are not members of his L1 inventory. Evidence shows that, with or without training, an adult can *perceive* these contrasts with accuracy, but may not be able to *produce* them accurately. This raises the question of an age-related decline in motor control over articulatory organs. Countering Flege's version of asymmetrical abilities, Dupoux (2003) argues that perception is no longer plastic, but that production can be, i.e. that late learners can sound native-like even without forming accurate perceptual distinctions between L1 and L2 phonemic categories. Exactly what is the nature of the relationship between perception and production, and does each proceed independently? Clarifying this relationship could go a long way toward clarifying age effects in phonological acquisition.

As a part of his Universal Theory of Acquisition, Wode (1992) maintains that adults actually *modify* perceptions of L2 categorical boundaries based on their existing L1 phonetic inventory. These findings are verified by Flege's (1991, 1992) studies on the difficulties experienced by late learners acquiring phones very similar to those in the L1 repertoire. In cases of close similarity, the learner is likely to perceive the two counterpart sounds as equivalent, and establish a close, but inaccurate, target for the new sound.

Foreign accent may therefore persist because of this tendency (see also Bohn & Flege, 1992; Flege & Hillenbrand, 1987). To verify such effects, Wode (1992) stresses the importance of measuring abilities *over time*, arguing that some mechanisms do naturally decline, and categorical perception clearly evolves owing to external stimuli.

Other studies that deserve mention come from Schneidermann *et al.* (1988) and Neufeld (1987, 1988), as they specifically test the impact of prior knowledge and training on perceptual and production abilities. The results for these studies are actually contradictory and methodological problems mar their generalizability (particularly for the Neufeld studies). Therefore, it is unclear whether prior discrimination training is helpful for accurate production (this is looked at later in the chapter).

One thing should be noted regarding tests of production accuracy: the task itself may impact on performance. Read-aloud elicitation tasks may indicate greater attention to phonetic accuracy than free response items that inherently provide meaningful context (and a presumed greater focus on meaning). Tarone (1982) and Dickerson (1975) both conclude that target-like production of phones is more likely on isolated tasks. On the other hand, Sato (1987) and Oyama (1976) found greater accuracy on casual speech tasks (or non-elicited speech) than for reading aloud. As Larsen-Freeman and Long (1991) point out, differing task demands and discourse considerations (length, authenticity, context) can all affect learner performance.

Developmental processes and universals

Beyond specific L1/L2 contrasts, research on phonological acquisition has focused a great deal of attention on universal patterns of development, particularly markedness constraints, commonly manifest in syllable structure preferences. This essential question informs the research: How does the adult learner construct a new phonological system from the available input? According to James (1987, 1989), words themselves allow the learner to tie form to meaning, and phonemes to phonetic reality. Later, prosody and rhythm become important cues in phonological processing. Once learners become aware of segments in their actual phonotactic realizations, a multi-level 'phonological grammar' can be constructed. James (1987: 247) maintains that the nature and course of this construction is determined by universal structural characteristics. These processes are generally termed 'developmental,' since they proceed regardless of linguistic background, target language, or learning situation.

Support for universal processes comes from evidence on markedness constraints and simplification strategies. One of the first studies to look at the effects of position in the syllable on the pronunciation of specific segments was Brière (1966). Since then, Tarone (1982, 1987, 1988) and Sato (1985, 1987) have presented studies on syllable structure constraints from a contrastive analysis point of view. Their results, however, lead them to different conclusions. Tarone (1987) maintains that closed syllables (consonant-vowel, or CV) are the preferred pattern for all learners, such that learners revert to this simple structure in the early stages of development by deleting consonants and inserting vowels into complex clusters. She also found this tendency for syllable types that were present in the subjects' native language (Korean, Cantonese, Portuguese), i.e. where no difficulty was predicted. Sato (1987), on the other hand, found a preference for closed syllables (CVC), along with a tendency to restructure and simplify in syllable-final position – indicating a possible markedness constraint on complex syllable codas.

In studies specifically looking for markedness effects, developmental difficulties are presented as predicted by markedness concerns. For example, Eckman's (1977) early research looks at terminal devoicing (the deletion of voice from syllable-final and word-final obstruents) in terms of a markedness differential hierarchy.[7] Taking his example, a German speaker learning English will assume voiced obstruents are possible only in initial and medial position (since voiced final obstruents are marked), and thus experience difficulty acquiring voiced final obstruents in English (see Eckman 1987a, 1987b). Weinberger (1987) similarly explores simplification strategies and finds that both epenthesis (vowel insertion) and deletion occur, but not in ways predicted by either contrastive analysis or Eckman's Markedness Differential Hypothesis. First, the degree of simplification increases as the numbers of consonants in the final cluster increase. Second, the degree of simplification increases as task formality *decreases*. Thus, error frequency, as well as epenthesis and deletion ratios, may differ according to whether the task is contextualized, or authentic. More recently, Kløve and Young-Scholten (2001) look at metathesis – the repositioning of segments within a word (as opposed to deletion and epenthesis) – as a strategy to simplify clusters. This allows learners to cope with L2 structures that violate L1 constraints or universal principles of syllable structure, such as numbers of consonants allowable in syllable onset or coda.

The fine line between universal and cognitive interpretations of influence is certainly blurred in much of this research. It is often difficult to separate developmental effects from transfer effects, and errors produced could be traceable to either source. As an example, Wode (1983) finds evidence for overlap in vowel and consonant substitution, devoicing and overgeneralization across learners of German with various L1s (including Hindi, French, Arabic, and Spanish). This leads him to support universal developmental feature influence, but based on cognitive processes such as transfer (i.e. prior knowledge). Similarly, Kaltenbacher (1994) finds transfer effects for syllable stress among Egyptian Arabic speakers learning German, and argues that markedness concerns constrain the specific rules transferred from Arabic as follows: the least marked are most likely to be transferred, as are rules that are similar across L1 and L2. Finally, Hammarberg (1993) finds that both creative strategies and natural constraints operate simultaneously in a balance tipped most often by L1 transfer (cf. Eliasson & Mattsson, 1993). In essence, it is likely that there is some interaction of universal, cognitive, and even stylistic concerns at play (Major, 2001), but that interlanguage forms adhere to the same constraints and principles of any natural language (i.e. according to Eckman's 1991 Structural Conformity Hypothesis).

It is unclear what underlying mechanisms are responsible for these patterns: an independent language module, or general processing skills (Kuhl, 1991). The complexity of these issues may lend support to the idea of an innate phonological grammar that guides the acquirer to parse the input in specialized ways. An innate faculty could explain, for example, which parameters occur across languages for syllable structure and stress patterns (see Kaye, 1989; Pater, 1997; Young-Scholten, 1994, 1995, 1996). It could also explain to what extent the same mechanisms are responsible for early and late acquisition of phonetic categories (see Archibald, 1998; Brown, 1993; Young-Scholten, 1994, and whether acquisitional orders occur based on universal properties, or according to language-specific parameters (see Archibald, 1998; Flynn & O'Neil, 1988).

Again, these questions point to essential cognitive processes such as transfer, utilization of positive and negative evidence (if available), and learnability constructs (such as the Subset Principle – see Archibald, 1993, 1997; Rutherford, 1995; Young-Scholten, 1994). Ultimately, differentiating universal from cognitive processes is most difficult. Furthermore, the UG question constitutes a conundrum of sorts, since a learner's recognition or intuition regarding 'universal properties' of language may be attributable to general neuro-cognitive processes and capabilities. Finally, if, as James (1989) argues, a modular approach can best accommodate the complexity of phonological rules systems and constraints, these arguments tend to dismiss *interaction* and *context* as key to acquisition. These weaknesses must be borne in mind. Searle (2002) is one who has recently criticized the fundamental inattention in innatist approaches to such matters as meaning and context.

Searle's critique reminds us that, over time, language acquisition inquiry has divided into many strands, some of which hardly acknowledge the relevance of others. At issue is not only the nature of language development, but how this changes fundamentally over the learner's lifetime. Therefore, any model of acquisition must take into account learning circumstances, access to both positive and negative evidence, previous knowledge (L1, etc.), and socio-psychological factors, such as attitude, motivation, and identity. The following sections will highlight some of the relevant findings for these areas of influence in L2 phonology.

Cognitive Considerations in L2 Phonological Development

Cognitive and psycholinguistic research on SLA focuses on the development of knowledge and know-how built from meaningful, continuous practice (McLaughlin, 1987). According to cognitive accounts, early stages of L2 comprehension and production rely strongly on simplification, transfer from L1, and overgeneralization as knowledge accumulates and is restructured through hypothesis formation and testing. Backsliding and sudden bursts of rapid progress are also part of the process (see McLaughlin, 1987; McLaughlin & Heredia, 1996). According to Bialystok, such processes define both L1 and L2 acquisition:

... First and second language acquisition differ in the extent to which they are under the control of biological or cognitive processes of development. This is because they begin with different initial representations and frequently occur at different points in cognitive development. To some extent, first language acquisition unfolds as a function of a biologically, or innately, prescribed set of constraints. Second language acquisition, in contrast, has more room for cognitive factors to influence and direct the course of its development. In both cases, however, it is the cognitive processes of analysis and control that are responsible for propelling the system toward greater mastery. (Bialystok, 1994: 162)

Some of the more interesting research in this tradition has investigated individual learning styles, awareness and attention, and the differential impact of new versus familiar forms, while questioning such assumptions as the efficacy of instruction and self-monitoring, and whether transfer is necessarily detrimental (something to be avoided) or a natural by-product of learning (Bialystok, 1994; Ellis, 1994; Ellis & Sinclair, 1996; Faerch & Kasper, 1987; Felix, 1981, 1985; Hulstijn, 1987; Kellerman, 1983; O'Malley & Chamot, 1990; Oxford, 1990 – for discussions, see Gass & Selinker, 2001).

These questions are relevant to phonological acquisition as well, as outlined in the following sections.

Transfer and interference

It is no surprise that the influence of L1 may hinder the complete acquisition of phonological, morphological, syntactic, or semantic features in L2. Transfer appears to contribute to the faulty or incomplete acquisition of any number of linguistic features.

For phonological acquisition, phenomena such as phonemic substitutions are generally thought to occur owing to transfer, while devoicing, consonant cluster simplification, and epenthesis are developmental (see Altenberg & Vago, 1987; Major, 1987a). To complicate matters, Hecht and Mulford (1987) maintain that transfer controls the acquisition of vowels, while developmental processes influence affricates and stops. Other researchers point to autonomous factors not easily traced to either transfer, developmental, or markedness concerns (Altenberg & Vago, 1987; Piper, 1987). As noted in the previous section, various processes may interact, probably depending on AO, learning environment, experience, and even interlocutor relationships (see Odlin, 1989; Major, 1987b, 1987c; Stotzer, 1989).

In order to circumvent transfer, a contrastive presentation of L2 features has traditionally been included in the early stages of L2 instruction. This instructional approach highlights differences between L1 and L2, assuming that habit (i.e. previous knowledge) must be overcome so that new learning may proceed (Lado, 1957). Minimal pair practice is the traditional method for overtly practicing both similar and divergent sounds, but there are many problems with this method. Lehtonen and Sajavaara (1984) point out that phonetic descriptions of 'equivalence' are often erroneous, since the same consonants and vowels may have slight acoustical differences from one language to the next. Orthographic representations and even distinctive feature descriptions are also not sufficiently precise, as they often recall predetermined (L1) categories (Lehtonen & Sajavaara, 1984). Furthermore, real speech includes suprasegmental features such as stress, pitch, intonation, and loudness – not just isolated segments. Contrastive analysis approaches – the primary 'contribution' to language instruction from the phonological realm – do not sufficiently represent natural context or extended discourse. Their inadequate predictions of what will be easily acquired are particularly questionable given that *similar* sounds may be more difficult to acquire than dissimilar ones (Major & Kim, 1999).

Since the mid-1970s, behaviorist approaches such as contrastive analysis have lost favor to investigations of learner intuitions, strategies, and perceptions, i.e. creative, rule-based processes driving language development. According to both socio- and psycholinguistic perspectives, a systematic progression is observed in phonological development, in which a feature enters the system somewhat 'weakly' but gradually becomes a categorical rule, replacing a previous version of the same rule or feature (Preston, 1989; see also Ellis, 1985 and Selinker & Lamendella, 1981). Long-term acquisition is thus marked by periods of stability and change, including both systematic and unsystematic use of functionally similar forms. The first language may actually assist the learner in the early stages of forming categories. An overly negative view of its influence assumes that transfer can only hinder, not facilitate, the learning process (Corder, 1983). It is also important to recall that the learner has adaptive, creative strategies for dealing with approximation problems (including underproduction and avoidance).

Approximation and self-monitoring

Further support for a creative, process-oriented view of SLA may be found in studies of approximation and matching behaviors. In an article discussing popular beliefs about interlanguage phonology, Beebe (1984) discounts phonemic transfer as the primary process in L2 phonological acquisition. With data from read-aloud word list and paragraph tasks for 25 Asian ESL learners, Beebe's data show that phonetic errors are common, but that phonemic substitution is minimal, leading her to conclude that most errors are approximation attempts or overgeneralizations of the target sounds; they are not due to phonemic confusion. Beebe (1984: 56) interprets some of the approximations as 'mergers' of L1 and L2 sounds, particularly in consonant clusters. On the way to mastery, intermediate learners may have a large inventory of such approximations, which are eliminated gradually. Beebe acknowledges that some unexplained variation exists, but in her view, learners systematically develop ever-closer approximations to target sounds.

A somewhat broader term for this phenomenon is 'the matching problem,' or the learner's continual comparison of his own L1 output with the target language norm (Klein, 1986). At the early stages of acquisition, matching may be a constant endeavor, yet it becomes increasingly difficult as the learner advances toward more native levels because the discrepancy between output and the target becomes smaller. In Klein's estimation, the learner can focus on only a limited number of aspects of his 'defective language performance' at a time (Klein, 1986: 138.) Monitoring the effect his output has on his interlocutor, the learner may self-correct, negotiate, or avoid problematic structures. Without such a conscious evaluation, he will not be able to overcome it:

... The learner must constantly operate with the rules he has developed at a given point in time, but at the same time, he must consider these rules to be preliminary hypotheses which are subject to revision. If he prematurely takes them to be confirmed, then his acquisition process freezes at that level with respect to these rules. (Klein, 1986: 147)

So how are periods of stagnation or fossilization overcome? According to Klein, if communicative needs are already met, feedback may be ignored. Does this mean that late learners who push predicted plateaus possess some special abilities, or do they simply make better use of the feedback they receive? Derwing *et al.* (1997) tested fossilized learners (defined as learners immersed for more than 10 years in L2) who had undergone a pronunciation training program. Of 13 participants, only three improved significantly on measures of comprehensibility and accent, with four actually showing 'weaker performance' on one measure following 12 weeks of instruction. Apparently instruction alone is not enough to make a considerable difference for more than a few. By contrast, Moyer (1999) found that long-term learners did appear to benefit from phonological instruction according to native-speaker ratings of accentedness, with the greatest benefit from overt training on stress, pitch, and intonation, not just on segmental contrasts. These studies point to the need for more research on the roles of conscious engagement in self-monitoring and formal feedback.

Exploring such a construct presents a difficult empirical problem: how can the presence and extent of self-monitoring be ascertained? In practice, constructs of awareness and monitoring are either reported by the learner, or are assumed by the researcher to be due to the task or previous knowledge (e.g. training). In an attempt to determine when formal rule knowledge assists with inferring implicit rules, Dickerson (1987) set up a study to track learner awareness of phonological rules. In keeping with Krashen's assertion that reference to explicit rules requires time and overt attention to accuracy, Dickerson's experiment presented two types of read-aloud tasks with different amounts of time to focus on accuracy (the second task allowed no time to analyze or repeat items). Participants were pre-tested, then instructed explicitly on phonological rules, and finally post-tested. When recorded samples were evaluated for word-level vowel and consonant quality and stress, samples from the un-timed first task showed more improvement from pre-test to post-test. Dickerson concludes that formal pronunciation rules can facilitate improvement when used for *monitoring* speech, but they can also interfere with production when *initiating* speech (similar to Krashen's 1981 Monitor Theory).

There is relatively little research on phonological accuracy according to amount of time and attention devoted to task, and results have been contradictory, as mentioned (see Dickerson, 1975; Sato, 1987; Tarone, 1982). Moreover, the roles of implicit versus explicit knowledge and processes has not been determined for phonological development, but there are indications that explicit study is advantageous, particularly when it crosses modes, i.e. combines auditory with visual input (Michas & Berry, 1994).

Support for the effectiveness of self-monitoring is similarly tentative at this point, as it may or may lead to gains in fluency (see Berry, 1994; Ellis, 1994; Krashen, 1978; Paradis, 1994). Other relevant concerns include the reception of one's language output by native speaker interlocutors, based on social and contextual considerations (see Gass & Selinker, 2001: chapter 8), and whether overt monitor use impacts on phonology, morphology, or syntax differentially (Van der Linden, 1995).[8]

Aptitude, style, and the ideal learner

To what extent can accurate perception and production be taught, and to what extent do these abilities appear only among very advanced or exceptional learners? The search for the ideal language learner has motivated research on style and skill, pertaining to the following: language learning aptitude, short- and long-term memory capacity, deductive reasoning skills (analysis and hypothesis formation based on available input), and degree of conscious attention or focus. At the same time, some take the position that SLA utilizes essentially the same processes and mechanisms as first language acquisition, e.g. in terms of abstract concept learning and decoding and encoding strategies (see Brown, 2000; Felix, 1981), and that aptitudes present no significant influence. Research on aptitude has been scarce for the past 20 years or more, and new ideas on its critical relevance for SLA are rare (cf. Skehan, 1989).

There are plenty of reasons to tread lightly in this area. For example, Cook (1991) cites several problems with defining and analyzing aptitude based on actual performance. First, any given learning situation may not address a learner's particular aptitudes. Second, there are many types of aptitude, making collective labels of 'language learning aptitude' for definitive clusters of abilities erroneous. In the end, it is difficult to identify skills that are advantageous for all learning situations since abilities will be affected differently according to the particular context.

Support for the role of talent and exceptional abilities is also rare (and controversial) in the general SLA literature (Obler, 1989; Schneiderman & Desmarais, 1988a, 1988b – cited in Markham, 1997). Considering the lack of empirical data, it is impossible to say whether talents and abilities are affected by maturation, and whether a *lack* of certain talents may be over-ridden by other factors, such as motivation.

More recent research advocates a reframing of these issues in terms of 'expert versus novice' systems, a notion that refers to essential differences in processing strategies between experienced language learners (bilinguals, multilinguals) and novices (monolinguals) (see Nation & McLaughlin, 1986). McLaughlin (1990), citing his own empirical work, supports the original categories set up by Carroll (phonetic coding, grammatical sensitivity, etc.)[9] based on numerous explorations of these abilities in SLA. McLaughlin (1990: 170f) concludes that expert language learners 'use more systematic and useful problem-solving and comprehension strategies' and 'show greater plasticity in restructuring their internal representations of the rules governing linguistic input'. This indicates a faster jump to what McLaughlin terms the 'meta-procedural level,' allowing measured reflection on the strategies they employ.

Markham (1997: 30) emphasizes the point that ability, aptitude and talent are rarely researched for phonological acquisition: 'The good learners go largely ignored, at the sake of pondering the failure of the majority ... .' As an exception to this rule, Elliott (1995a) has verified significant relationships between pronunciation accuracy and cognitive style, in terms of both field independence (associated with highly analytical individuals) and degree of right hemisphere specialization (associated with accuracy in discriminating meaning through cues from intonation). This is particularly interesting because other factors tested (including instructional duration, other languages known, gender, and informal exposure to L2) do not stand out impressively in regression analyses. In a follow-up study, Elliott (1995b) shows that instruction plays a significant role in pronunciation accuracy. Attitude (here: concern for pronunciation accuracy) is also highly significant. These results suggest that certain cognitive styles, along with instructional input, hold some advantage for phonological acquisition.

Elliott's findings indicate the need to further investigate cognitive style – one's collective, preferred strategies – as a factor in attainment. This would highlight the link between personality and cognition (see DeWaele, 2002; Leventhal & Scherer, 1987; Schumann, 1994, 1997). Obviously, strategies must be identified through self-report, which can be problematic. Furthermore, their teachability is questionable, meaning that strategies may not be transferable to individual learners; even one's own learning strategies may not be transferable to new tasks (O'Malley & Chamot, 1990). Still, these preliminary indications of the importance of cognitive style point to the need for more research in this area, particularly regarding long-term impact.

The efficacy of instruction and feedback

Up to this point, I have reviewed universal and individual factors in cognitive approaches to SLA, noting some of the difficulties in researching these issues. Despite numerous studies on classroom techniques, certain kinds of instruction or training, etc., we still understand little about how targeted input and feedback may facilitate acquisition, especially in the long-term. Still, positive effects from instruction have been verified through regression analyses that isolate the differential strength of several variables in predicting phonological performance (Elliott, 1997; Moyer, 1999). Since phonological instruction has seen little emphasis, not to mention pedagogical innovation, in the past several decades, the efficacy of specific instructional approaches is yet to be determined.[10] Some recent proposals are mentioned here for their decidedly holistic focus on phonology as a significant aspect of overall linguistic competence.

Traditional phonological training is phoneme-based, restricted to segment and word-level accuracy. The prevailing (and outdated) pedagogy has assumed that pronunciation is a 'set of habits for producing sounds,' thus repetition and correction lead to accurate production and the elimination of errors from L1 transfer (Cook, 1991). There is no evidence that repetition of phonemic and phonetic drills is necessary or effective, nor that consistent feedback is typically available in any given classroom. As Nystrom (1983: 170) describes it, 'some errors are ignored, while others of a similar type receive significant amounts of attention in the teacher's response ... [and] teachers are often ambiguous in their delivery of error responses'.

The inconsistency of feedback is but one problem among many. The treatment of phonology across language programs (and even among teachers within the same program) is typically sporadic, at best. In Moyer's 1995 study, advanced learners report exposure to all types of phonological feedback in their classroom and non-classroom language experience, ranging from informal feedback from native speakers, to formal drills, to entire courses devoted to L2 phonology. Most participants find these sources of feedback to be useful, and would appreciate more attention to phonological accuracy in the classroom. However, they also report a strong desire for more individualized feedback, especially emphasizing extended discourse contexts (such as dialogues and paragraph-length utterances) to get beyond isolated segmental features. Such activities can be incorporated naturally when integrated throughout the instructional sequence (beginning through advanced) (Chela-Flores, 2001).

Pennington and Richards (1986: 212) describe SLA as requiring a 'wide range of complex and subtle distinctions' involving articulatory, interactional, and cognitive processes. In order to ease the transition from controlled to automatic production of phonological features, Pennington and Richards (1986) and Leather (1983) suggest highlighting the inter-dependence of phonology and other language skills. In such a 'top-down' approach, voice quality and prosodic features would be emphasized (including stress, rhythm, and pitch); pronunciation would be presented as inherently 'non-segmental, non-discrete, and non-autonomous' (Pennington, 1989: 21), i.e. its contribution to semantic, syntactic and pragmatic processing would be overtly treated.[11]

Many specific techniques have been suggested for such an integrative approach, including: self-observation in mirrors, peer correction, overt training on gestures and body language to accompany stress and rhythm instruction, visualization aids for pitch and stress, self-evaluation via recording, and greater emphasis on discourse negotiation (Anderson-Hsieh, 1989; DeBot & Mailfert, 1982; Dieling, 1989; Leather, 1983; Pennington 1989; Thornbury, 1993; Yule, 1989). A more recent proposal by Iandoli (1990) draws attention to the importance of identity in the target language as key to developing authentic intonation and stress. Her proposal incorporates the common philosophy of the approaches cited above – a more holistic appreciation of the importance of authentic pronunciation:

> There is a distinct pleasure in being able to interact with native speakers without paying undue attention to one's 'foreignness,' and an even greater pleasure in being thought to come from ... [the country] where the language is spoken. This achievement requires an integration of skills that unfortunately are too often taught separately. Phonemic system, stress, intonation, gesture, appropriate vocabulary, cultural mores, morphology, syntax... discourse and pragmatics – all need to fit together as a harmonious whole ... Dividing the elements of language acquisition by postponing attention to one facet, for instance, until the advanced level or until there is immersion in the target culture, hinders the learner. (Iandoli, 1990: 27)

Many newer approaches to phonological training advocate the utiliza-tion of specialized computer software programs for their provision of immediate visual and auditory feedback. These programs may be superior for tracking suprasegmental output, allowing the student to approximate native-like intonation curves 'online' and to store records of their own performance, thereby tracking progress (Lindner, 1988). DeBot (1980, 1983) and DeBot and Mailfert (1982) cite improvements in production abilities following an instructional phase using glottographs, spectrographs, and computer recordings of intonation. The authors report that audio-visual feedback was found to be more effective than audio feedback alone (DeBot, 1983), confirming the efficacy of cross-modal presentation in focus-on-form activities.[12]

Recently, an interest in improving phonological training is evident in the teacher training literature (Burgess & Spencer, 2000; Macdonald *et al.*, 1994; Seidlhofer & Dalton-Puffer, 1995 – for reviews of specific techniques, see Anderson-Hsieh, 1989; Chun, 1991; Pica, 1994a). In Germany in particular, there is a healthy debate about how to gauge phonological accuracy. This debate underscores two prevalent problems:

(1) one standard of accuracy can hardly be assumed, given great regional language variation, as well as social and stylistic variation in pronunciation (Bohn, 1989; Konig, 1991; Petrenko, 1989; Wolff, 1991);

(2) the presence of immigrants with so many different mother tongues requires effective tools (and possibly specialized teacher training) to address student difficulties in perception and production.

Looking forward, a unified approach for effective phonological training is not likely until we know which techniques are most helpful, and where in the instructional sequence they will be most efficacious.

Summary of cognitive and instructional issues

Several issues remain controversial in the literature on cognitive processes and universal influences in SLA. First, it is clear that learning relies on previous knowledge and that overt instruction may guide the learner to attend to the salient properties and distinctions in the input (Tomlin & Villa, 1994). Likewise, repeated exposure to the same structure increases the likelihood of its recognition, and cross-modal presentation (e.g. visual plus auditory stimuli) increases memory and comprehension. However, O'Malley and Chamot (1990) stress that not all learning takes place in the classroom, i.e. not all rules are learned consciously, and some may 'emerge ad hoc,' belonging neither to L1 nor to L2. Most importantly, it is not known whether effects of feedback and training continue long-term. A closer specification of contextual and situational aspects of learner experience are needed regardless, given that cognitive processes are affected by differential sources of input, instruction, and one's particular attitudes and levels of awareness (see Oxford, 1990).

It is a common truism that students learn what they do, i.e. what they experience formally or informally. Yet it seems equally true that the amount of practice and repetition necessary varies for every learner. These concerns of access and opportunity are surely critical to the long-term attainment potential of any learner. Seliger (1983) reports that those learners who seek input and the opportunity to interact in the second language are more effective and proficient in the output they generate. Obviously, some learners seek more opportunities to interact than others, possibly owing to risk-taking tolerance, motivation, etc. Which input sources learners attend to most (peers, teacher, parents, and so forth) are probably influenced by individual judgments of status or willingness to go outside of one's group or individual identity boundaries (Beebe, 1985).

These associations between practice opportunities and personal engagement reflect the importance of context in SLA, so often lacking in cognitive approaches to the research. Klein (1996) argues that context is key to understanding such phenomena as fossilization, since SLA depends upon (at least) three factors: (1) the learner's 'propensity' or motivation to learn language after childhood; (2) processing abilities, defined as 'the appropriate use of acquired knowledge for communicative purposes;' and (3) access to the target language, meaning quality linguistic input which is both authentic and appropriate (e.g. not Foreigner Talk). Indeed, these three components, according to Klein, vary with the learner's 'particular communicative needs and life plans' – a consideration that may differ widely for instructed as compared to uninstructed learners (Klein, 1986: 248f).

Social and Psychological Issues in L2 Phonology

As this discussion suggests, SLA is largely incomparable to first language acquisition, given the prominence of differing goals, cognitive style, learning strategies, and potential access to instruction and feedback. Furthermore, adults are exposed to much more complex language from the onset, and are expected to parse (and produce) accordingly (see Newport, 1991). As Lightbown and Spada (1993) point out, children are praised for their efforts, regardless of accuracy, and have ample time and opportunity to listen and learn before producing. By contrast, adults are often 'embarrassed by their lack of mastery of the language and they may develop a sense of inadequacy after experiences of frustration in trying to say exactly what they mean' (Lightbown & Spada, 1993: 42). Such frustration affects self-evaluation, possibly increasing anxiety, and negatively impacting on motivation and perseverance. This circular relationship between internal orientation and external feedback is likely to affect all language acquisition situations (MacIntyre, 1995). Noels *et al.* (1996: 249) suggest that linguistic competence may actually 'mediate' such stresses, especially in acculturation-type situations (in-country). If so, L2 fluency may not only stem from, but also enhance, contact with the target language community and its speakers.[13]

In the current literature, the central influence of affective variables is rarely disputed. Early work clearly establishes the interconnectedness of attitudes, motivation, and self-perceptions of fluency, even as they affect *future* attitudes and experiences (Gardner *et al.*, 1999).[14] As MacIntyre (1995) describes it, without a 'positive contribution from the constellation of affective factors,' a learner is unlikely to persist, and if anxiety is great, his learning will surely be hindered (see Ramage, 1990; Skehan, 1989).

This section provides a brief introduction to several affective influences relevant to phonological acquisition, with two caveats noted:

(1) Any discussion on social-psychological factors often separates constructs arbitrarily, as if their influence were independently exerted (e.g. anxiety as separate from motivation). In reality these factors may be more appropriately understood as *clusters*, leading to some predictable behaviors. For example, constructs such as identity, empathy, and ego permeability may be considered to be closely related, but often they are isolated for the sake of the empirical investigation.

(2) There has been relatively little *comprehensive* survey of these variables for late phonological attainment (cf. Moyer, 1999; Purcell & Suter, 1980). The few studies that measure multiple factors find significant correlations to outcome for only a few, e.g. concern for pronunciation accuracy (Elliott, 1995a and 1995b; Purcell & Suter, 1980), attitudes toward the target language and culture (Major, 1993; Stokes, 2001) and motivation (Bongaerts *et al.*, 1997; Moyer, 1999). The current study therefore surveys a number of these factors as potentially relevant to ultimate attainment, testing their impact relative to one another.

Motivation

I begin here with motivation, as a construct that uniquely represents many orientations simultaneously: conscious effort, intentionality, and planning toward a specific goal. Motivation is generally thought to rely on interest or curiosity to know more, along with perceived likelihood of success and reward (Crookes & Schmidt, 1991), and therefore touches upon self-concept as well (Crookes & Schmidt, 1991; Dörnyei, 1994a; Gardner & Tremblay, 1994; Harré *et al.*, 1985). The traditional distinction between integrative and instrumental motivation has been recently reconsidered to allow for greater complexity of motivational types. For example, integrative motivation may imply a sociocultural interest in the target language, as well as a desire for new challenges (Dörnyei, 1994b). In essence, many manifestations of motivation are possible, and will depend on the individual's experience (Dörnyei, 1994b).[15]

Gardner and Tremblay (1994: 366) admit that it is difficult to 'capture the essence' of motivation because it is complex, dynamic, and affected by 'several intervening variables.' Not surprisingly, measuring motivation has proven difficult. Originally, Gardner's (1985a) Attitude/Motivation Test Battery (AMTB) was developed to correlate integrative motivation with proficiency.[16] Over time, survey-based research has strengthened its methods through interviews (often with parents, teachers, and others in the learner's community) in order to better assess the strength of these layers, and to account for the impact of different contact domains (Spolsky, 2000). Accordingly, newer approaches have turned to deeper explorations of the interplay between motivation, attitude, and learning situation as they contribute to long-term attainment (Clément *et al.*, 1994; Crookes & Schmidt, 1991; Dörnyei, 1990, 1994a, 1994b; Gardner & Tremblay, 1994; Spolsky, 2000).

The strength of motivation has been shown to correlate to phonological attainment, measured as the perceived need for achievement (Coates, 1986 – cited in Major, 2001), but particularly for professional orientations for L2 learning (Bongaerts *et al.*, 1997; Moyer, 1999). These factors cannot be easily separated from concern for pronunciation accuracy, noted earlier as a predictor of attainment to varying degrees across learners and studies (Flege *et al.*, 1995, 1999).) As Piske *et al.* put it:

... Most studies examining the effect of motivation on degree of L2 foreign accent have reported at least some influence of motivation on the outcome measures. On the whole, however, the results obtained so far clearly suggest that factors like professional motivation, integrative motivation or strength of concern for L2 pronunciation accuracy do not automatically lead to accent-free speech. Apparently, they are rarely so strong that late learners will still be able to attain a native-like pronunciation of the L2. (Piske *et al.*, 2001: 202)

Much more research is needed to determine whether motivation plays a primary role in accent across learner groups. It may prove to be imprudent to conceive of motivation as *separate* from related concerns, such as desire to sound native, desire to acculturate, and access to contact with native speakers. Anecdotally and empirically, we know that some late learners have no interest in sounding native (see Moyer, 1999), while others may pursue such a goal in spite of their own limits (e.g. limits in perceptual abilities and limited access to authentic input, etc.). Motivation, especially as it is linked to specific behaviors or learning strategies, likely contributes in fundamental ways to ultimate attainment, but its influence may be accurately appreciated only in connection with other social and cognitive considerations.

Empathy, acculturation and identity

For some time, cultural empathy has been identified as an indicator of acculturation potential. Discussed initially by Schumann in his Acculturation Model (1978), and more recently in studies of speech accommodation, cultural empathy is defined as approval or understanding of the cultural orientation of another group (Berkowitz, 1989). Brown (1987) describes it as the ability to understand the experience and feelings of another, which implies self-awareness as well as identification with another person. As interlocutors, we 'permeate our ego boundaries so that we can send and receive messages clearly' (Brown, 1987: 108). In second language learning, the learner must attempt this even when linguistically and culturally insecure. Over the long run, the extent of one's ethnic and cultural identification, along with the desire to acculturate, can have a marked impact on linguistic attainment (see Young & Gardner, 1990).

Even before contact with the target language community, or the target language itself, the individual learner may have preconceived attitudes that can impact on developing experience – as Baker puts it, this is circular: favorable attitudes and expectations may precipitate positive outcomes, and vice versa (Baker, 1992; see also Kniffka, 1992). In addition, identity and attitudes may be constructed collectively, not just individually, and these two levels may conflict (Gardner *et al.*, 1999 – for research implications, see Baker, 1992). Considering the complexity of these issues, it is not surprising that very few researchers have investigated their influence. Here, I mention the few studies relevant to phonological acquisition.

Famous for their research on empathy, Guiora *et al.* (1972) explored the notion of language ego as a barrier to authentic pronunciation. While the methods employed have been questioned by many, the underlying assumption of these studies may be sound: the ability and desire to transcend one's own ego boundaries, which are linguistically and culturally bound, can have profound impact on phonological production. Early on, Guiora described the uniqueness of pronunciation compared to other levels of language ability as follows:

... To learn a second language is to take on a new identity. Since pronunciation appears to be the aspect of language behavior most resistant to change, we submit that it is therefore the most critical to self-representation. Hence we propose that the most sensitive index of the ability to take on a new identity ... is found in the ability to achieve native-like pronunciation in a second language. (Guiora *et al.*, 1972: 422)

As Guiora noted, children learning their first language presumably have a malleable ego. It is later in life, when identity is well-established, that fluctuations in the ego become uncomfortable. More recently, Guiora (1992) has distinguished cognitive from affective conceptions of language ego, arguing that the affective ego protects the sense of self (critical to pronunciation performance) while mastery of lexicon and morpho-syntax (involving the cognitive ego) do not challenge or engage the affect in the same ways. Pronunciation, according to Guiora's view, subjects the individual to a domain of insecurity, thereby interfering with his or her established sense of identity (cf. List, 1989). I would argue further that pronunciation is an aspect of linguistic ability that allows the speaker to be identified immediately as either native or non-native, and as such, is psychologically 'loaded;' it is inherently associated with identity for these reasons. Getting beyond a non-native accent as a late learner requires great effort, a desire to sound native, as well as optimal experience in the language. (These arguments are reiterated in the following chapters.)

The question of ego permeability has also been studied from the point of view of interactional behavior. Zuengler (1985, 1988) has found that certain sounds in the L2 are considered 'social markers' of non-native speech, revealing L1 identity and cultural affiliation. Non-native speakers, according to Zuengler, are aware of these markers, and may deliberately employ them in order to preserve their non-native status. These same phonological variables are also susceptible to style-shifting, in order to accommodate to the interlocutor when empathy is felt. Coupland (1984) offers an extensive discussion on the limits and difficulties in supporting such assumptions based on the evidence available. Those concerns notwithstanding, discussions of empathy, accommodation, identity, etc., are highly relevant for research on phonological acquisition – they remind us that accent is both socially and psychologically real and meaningful *in context*. The learner is at all times a *user* of L2, and this status has far-reaching implications in the context of the target language community.

Conclusion

This chapter has outlined a number of factors believed to affect late language acquisition. As discussed, the following phenomena are commonly cited as universal in SLA:

- neurological developments that may mean a loss of flexibility in establishing new phonetic patterns;
- the transfer of knowledge from a pre-existing system (L1);
- the existence of similar developmental orders and preferences for unmarked feature or syllable structure types;

- the reliance on hypothesis testing and creative analysis to approximate L2 target forms; and
- the probability of fossilization as a result of poor approximation abilities, faulty hypotheses, or lack of motivation to advance.

At the same time, SLA is essentially an individual process, experienced uniquely by each person within his or her own learning context. There is compelling evidence that affect, attitude, and experience (including instruction) also influence ultimate attainment, given that an individual brings pre-existing orientations and abilities to the task, and responds to L2 learning in idiosyncratic ways, depending on motivation, risk-taking, identity and acculturation desires, etc. As noted, all such factors are dynamic; subject to shifts according to new experience and judgment. Similarly, the input available is not a stable element in the process, but undoubtedly shifts over time in terms of quality and quantity.

The search for 'the good language learner'

Throughout its relatively short history, SLA research has been preoccupied with two essential charges: (1) describing the structural qualities of non-native interlanguage, from both *process* and *product* points of view, (2) exploring potential causal factors for variation in attainment. For some researchers, the quest for what constitutes 'good language learning' emphasizes cognitive strategies, personality or 'talent' factors (neuro-cognitive abilities), and even proficiency in L1 (Bialystok, 1994; Genesee, 1976; Hulstijn & Bossers, 1992; Ioup, 1989; Naiman *et al.*, 1978; Obler, 1989; O'Malley & Chamot, 1990; Oxford, 1990; Rubin, 1975; Schmidt, 1992). The hope is to discover particular traits or strategies that might predictably lead to high levels of L2 attainment. More recently, that discussion has benefited from a socio-cultural perspective. Notions such as context, community, and the individual learner's communicative and social *intentions* are key to understanding how second language competence develops (Lantolf, 2000; Norton Pierce & Toohey, 2001; Pavlenko & Lantolf, 2000). Ultimate attainment studies, however, consistently focus on the age factor, rather than on specific talents, contextual factors, or orientations to the task. The idea of *constraint* pervades the literature, reinforcing the notion that 'successful' SLA is *exceptional*.

In exploring optimal language learning, advanced language learners may be our best source of information. They can provide invaluable introspective data throughout the process, but we may never discover all the underlying mechanisms involved. As Seliger points out, the more that SLA inquiry evolves, the more complicated the picture becomes:

... Surely, if it is found that good language learners breathe deeply before producing a hypothesis, the implication is that this must be related to SLA. From here it is but a short step to identifying all kinds of things that learners do while in a language learning context.... The point is that learners do an infinite variety of things while in the process of learning a language. (Seliger, 1984: 37)

The trick is to identify which behaviors, orientations, and experiential factors are crucial to long-term success.

Is phonological acquisition fundamentally different?

By all accounts, late language acquisition is characterized by sporadic development, fossilization of some features, and predictably incomplete acquisition. Bley-Vroman (1989) offers an insightful discussion of this 'logical problem of foreign language learning,' in which he states that the task of the adult foreign language learner is vastly different from the child learning his or her first language; this led Bley-Vroman to conclude that SLA is a 'fundamentally different' process. In the interest of accounting more thoroughly for these differences, Spolsky makes a compelling argument for the integration of neuro-biological and socio-psychological approaches in to the study of SLA:

... Essentially, then, what these studies start to demonstrate is a two-way process, one the embodiment of language acquisition in its neurophysiological location (the brain), and the other, the contextualization of the language acquirer in his or her social situation. The recognition and exploration of these two contexts ... explain why we cannot be satisfied with a narrow view of applying linguistics, but must continue to find ways of incorporating psycholinguistics and sociolinguistics in our work. (Spolsky, 2000: 166)

Precisely such a convergence of sociolinguistic and psycholinguistic perspectives is needed to understand constraints on late phonological acquisition. Phonology, as this chapter has emphasized, involves both lower and higher order analytical skills and motor abilities. It is also an essential marker of 'foreign-ness.' At the beginning of this chapter, I articulated two basic questions: (1) are late learners even less likely to reach native levels in phonology than in morpho-syntax, and (2) if so, can these differences be predicted across learner groups and L1–L2 pairings?

It appears that phonological attainment can be native-like for some, yet it may also be prone to special constraints, shown by asymmetries in production and perception. As for consistency across learners and language pairs, there is simply not enough replication at this point to definitively, or even comfortably, answer that question. Even purported universal features of markedness do not exert consistent impact across language pairs, which leads to the conclusion that other factors are at play.

Some years ago, Tarone (1987) succinctly summarized several popular explanations for the intractability of a foreign accent:

(1) the articulatory organs are no longer physically able to adjust to new sounds;
(2) the onset of formal operations implies an overuse of analysis, interfering with 'natural' processes of acquisition;
(3) L1 phonological habits are psychologically and/or neurologically difficult to transcend; and
(4) the interest in preserving one's cultural identity precludes complete acquisition.

It is possible that there is some truth in each explanation, highlighting the need to expand our perspectives in order to fully appreciate these constraints. Tarone offers this prediction:

> ... In viewing interlanguage as a variable system, can we account for those relative influences? What are the physiological and social constraints on interlanguage phonology? Is it possible for adults to acquire an L2 without an accent? If not, why not? In our attempts to answer questions such as these, undoubtedly we will learn much about the complex interrelationships of language, mind, body, and society in the process of second language acquisition. (Tarone, 1987: 84)

Phonology and 'native-ness"

As a final consideration, the issue of foreign accent should be placed in its wider social context. While many adult learners attain fluency, many more retain a noticeable accent, thereby evoking certain reactions and judgments from others. This inescapable fact reminds us that pronunciation is somehow a central reflection of how we judge native-ness and, by extension, identity. Parrino states:

> We define ourselves by what we say, but more notably by how we say it. The accents that color the languages we speak impact significantly on our identity. Our pronunciation allies or isolates us from a community of speakers ... It precedes our intentions and completes our utterances. (Parrino, 1998: 171)

The fact is that phonological ability implies much more than phonetic accuracy. It includes knowing how to use intonation, loudness, and even silence appropriately in context (Nihalani, 1993). Parrino's hope is that we will re-examine our expectations for adult phonological acquisition, bringing them more in line with reality. If, as Munro and Derwing (1999) maintain, foreign accent, *per se*, is no absolute deterrent to comprehensibility, then pronunciation instruction should focus on aspects of learner speech that can truly interfere with comprehension.

If native-level pronunciation is neither a reasonable nor a desirable objective, what standard should be invoked for assessing language ability? Although the ideal of the native speaker is no more than that – an ideal – it probably cannot be given up easily (Davies, 2000), as it remains a useful notion in the study of language acquisition, especially ultimate attainment. We need a yardstick by which to measure attainment, and the native speaker ideal serves that function. Defining who is a native speaker is much more complex.

What is 'native-ness,' then, and in what ways is it different from fluency? Under the broad umbrella of SLA research, several diverse perspectives address this issue. In general terms, Schmidt (1992) describes fluency as a reflection of speed, appropriacy, creativity, idiomatic language use, etc., which implies more than accuracy, speed, and knowledge combined. A psycholinguist may define fluency in terms of automaticity in processing, or the application of native-like intuitions of grammaticality. A sociolinguist may define fluency in terms of style-shifting ability and linguistic and paralinguistic appropriacy in interaction. An educator may focus instead on formal accuracy and style for the skill areas of reading, writing, speaking, and listening. No matter what the perspective, native-ness is categorically different from fluency because it is an essentially social construct. It defies definition and operationalization because its essence lies in our individual and collective judgments. Davies offers this amusing metaphor as a counter to the often-sober discussions on the issue:

> The Native Speaker, like Lewis Carroll's *snark*, is a useful and enduring linguistic myth; again, like the snark, itself a product of the debate over idealism in philosophy, it must be taken with a large pinch of salt. (Davies, 2000: 92)

Regardless of some reservations as to its (prescriptive) relevance, the native speaker ideal is very real, referenced as a measure of comprehensibility, if not acceptability and belonging. As the discussion here confirms, attaining to a native level may be relatively unusual, though not altogether impossible. It is fair to say that the mechanisms behind late learner attainment are multi-variate and complex, leading to great variation in outcome. At the same time, the linearity of the age–outcome relationship fades with maturation (around puberty), suggesting that any decline in language learning after that point is determined by factors other than age. This chapter has reviewed research on socio-psychological and cognitive concerns, universal and developmental processes, and possible neurological limits on development as they are confounded with maturation. Taken as a whole, the data show wide variation across individuals, indicating a cluster of operative influences – some of which have yet to be identified, many of which are difficult to measure. This does not relieve our task of investigating the nature of this confluence. An integration of perspectives will surely lead to a more thorough account of this interplay of neurobiological, cognitive, and socio-psychological elements in attainment.

Notes

1. Studying aphasics, Lenneberg discovered that linguistic recovery was highly successful if the aphasic patient was under the age of 10 years. Simply put, if certain grammatical and semantic functions already located in the left hemisphere could be 're-assigned' to the right hemisphere, language processing could be recovered. In short, 'plasticity,' or flexibility of hemispheric specialization was thought to end by early puberty (in line with animal imprinting behavior research that supports a strict critical period for certain behaviors – for discussions, see Long, 1990; Newport, 1991; and Oyama, 1976). Later research suggested that hemispheric specialization (lateralization) exists as early as birth, and does not develop further. What appears to be further lateralization may actually be a manifestation of the 'increasing cognitive and behavioral repertoire of the child' (Witelson, 1987: 653). Thus, a debate was created that is ongoing, having generated a good deal of controversy in the SLA literature (Krashen, 1981; Long, 1990; Munsell *et al.*, 1988; Obler & Gjerlow, 1999; Scovel, 1981; Seliger, 1978; Seliger *et al.*, 1982).
2. Munro and Derwing (1999) report that heavily accented speech results in fewer problems with intelligibility than speech with errors in prosody. Taken with Moyer's (1999) findings for more native-like ratings for participants with suprasegmental training, it could be that native speaker interlocutors allow for more phonetic variation, but perceive intonation and stress as fundamental to comprehensibility.
3. Interestingly, Oyama's (1976) study showed that 'casual' story telling demonstrated less non-native accent than the more formal paragraph recitation.
4. Schiffler (2001: 328) reports that Broca's area (responsible for vocal recognition and articulation) is 20% larger in women than in men, and that Wernicke's area (responsible for syntactic and logical processing) is 30% larger on average, which he interprets as consistent with findings that women have better verbal skills than men, and do better in formal foreign language instruction on average.
5. The experience factor deserves to be clearly operationalized in research on phonological acquisition (see Flege & Liu, 2001). It has typically been defined as length of residence, a rather vague measure of direct exposure and interaction, showing a range of strength in impact on ultimate attainment (see Bohn & Flege,

1992; Oyama, 1976). More recently, it has been investigated as previous experience with the target language as that impacts on perception and production (Flege *et al.*, 1997).

6. However, Müller (1996) cites animal studies that identify sound-processing capacities in birds, rodents, monkeys, and apes (see also Kuhl, 1986). On this basis, Müller argues that phonological processing, per se, is not a species-specific function. On the other hand, 'there is evidence for some degree of specificity of phonological versus non-linguistic auditory processing in humans ... [which indicates] different neural activation patterns for phonetic as compared to nonverbal auditory stimulation' (Müller, 1996: 615).

7. The hierarchy idea means that for any given language, the existence of final voiced obstruents 'implies' the existence of devoiced ones as well.

8. An interesting finding is reported in Major's 1993 study of American learners of Brazilian Portuguese. Of five participants, the one with the most native-like phonetic accuracy claimed to pay close attention to forms even within informal (uninstructed) contexts. Major speculates that overt monitor use benefits long-term acquisition, and that phonetic mimicry is somehow integrated in a circular fashion with socio-psychological factors of confidence, motivation, and willingness to engage in authentic interaction.

9. Aptitude is still not well-researched, although several test batteries exist for its measurement, beginning with the Modern Language Aptitude Test (MLAT), developed by Carroll and Sapon (1959). The MLAT tests four basic types of ability: phonetic coding ability, grammatical sensitivity (or ability to distinguish grammatical functions), inductive language learning ability (how one generalizes patterns), and rote learning ability for words and phrases. This test is only one device for determining specific underlying abilities that may or may not be operative and critical to SLA.

10. Phonology and pronunciation have not been emphasized in any method since the Audio-Lingual heyday of the 1960s and 70s, and it could therefore be observed that there is little to study regarding the treatment of phonology in the classroom these days. More recent communicative approaches focus on functional and communicative accuracy. Native-level pronunciation is not an established goal, particularly for lower levels of proficiency. It is also not expected of superior level proficiency (see ACTFL guidelines in Omaggio, 1986). At this point, there is simply no consensus on appropriate objectives for phonological instruction. In Leather's (1983) view, part of the reason for the lack of a method is that we still do not understand how new phonetic systems are acquired, what the relationship of perception to production is, and whether these skills develop independently or affect one another's development simultaneously.

11. Others have similarly advocated an emphasis on prosody as a tool for accurate perception and production (Boyle, 1987; Cessarius & Bolinger, 1991; Chun, 1988).

12. Technological tools have been criticized for appealing to rote, discrete-point items, so meaningful contexts should be incorporated whenever possible to enhance learning.

13. The current study findings, presented here in Chapters 3 and 4, confirm this position.

14. MacIntyre *et al.* (1998) underscore the importance of internal predispositions and

abilities *against the backdrop of the target language community,* i.e. acknowledging language use in its natural socio-cultural context (see MacIntyre & Charos, 1996).

15. To further complicate the measurement issue, it is likely that motivation works in a circular way, feeding success, which in turn contributes to higher levels of motivation (see Dörnyei, 1994a; Strong, 1984). If motivation is dynamic, one-time measures may be inappropriate if they do not address the long term.

16. It is worth noting that Gardner's first description of the construct originated from studies on immersion learning, where cultural and social concerns of belonging and identity are undoubtedly much more intense than in a foreign language classroom. Gardner's 'socio-educational model' of language learning was novel in that it attempted to account for the cultural and social setting in which language training takes place (see Gardner, 1985b, 1988).

Chapter 3
Verifying the Relative Strength of Maturation, L2 Experience and Psychological Orientation: The Quantitative Findings

Introduction: Purpose and Approach to the Current Study

As the previous chapters have emphasized, the immigrant language learning situation inherently brings social, cultural, and political pressures to bear on the language acquisition process. These pressures color the learner's experience, particularly that of late learners, but also of children whose families may not be accepted into the mainstream. The empirical study described here provides a context for these issues based on a sample of immigrants to Berlin. It is the goal of this investigation to explore the significance of social-cultural and psychological factors, such as identity and milieu, in relation to frequently cited neuro-biological and cognitive influences in SLA. By incorporating data on contact with native speakers and on opportunities to build L2 experience, we may better understand how acquisition proceeds, plateaus, or stagnates on the path to native-like competence.

With these broad objectives in mind, this chapter presents a descriptive and inferential analysis of immigrant learners of German, emphasizing the interrelated nature of psychological, social, biological, and experiential factors in their language learning over time. These interrelationships are validated statistically, and their relative strength to ultimate attainment is compared as well. The findings presented support the position that a theoretical re-orientation of the critical period paradigm is necessary to best appreciate the social-cultural context of SLA. Following the descriptive and statistical analysis, the discussion is expanded in the next chapter through qualitative interview data.

The following broad issues are explored through this holistic investigation of the individual learner's L2 experience:

- What is the relative significance of factors deemed influential to ultimate attainment, especially in the phonological realm (e.g. factors such as age

of onset, length of residence, concern for accuracy, motivation and acculturation concerns, and formal and informal learning opportunities that
could mitigate possible transfer effects)?
- How do social-psychological orientations and attitudes influence
specific behaviors and goals (such as the pursuit of greater contact
with native speakers, formal language instruction, etc.) that may
determine ultimate attainment?
- What roles do cultural and linguistic identities play in language
acquisition in the long term, especially as they may impact on access
to and pursuit of authentic input?

Given that critical period effects appear to be most robust in the phonological realm, the data here emphasize judgments on the authenticity, or
native-ness, of task performance. These tasks concentrate on phonology,
although morphology, syntax, lexicon and pragmatic skills are represented
to varying extents throughout. The fundamental theoretical points
addressed by this methodology are simply stated below:

- *If biological factors indeed exhibit the strongest influence on language abilities,
especially as assessed across tasks, confidence in more traditional critical
period accounts of maturational effects may be appropriate. Alternatively, if
these biological influences are inextricably related to other (non-biological)
realms, particularly if these prove to be more significantly correlated to
outcome, such confidence is unwarranted.*
- *If quantitative and qualitative data confirm the interrelationships between
biological, experiential, and social-psychological realms, a new model of
critical period research in SLA should be considered; namely, one that does
not attribute primary significance to age of exposure, apart from its
concomitant factors.*

Secondarily, I hope to discover learners who flout predictable age
effects, attaining to a native level in spite of later exposure (beyond the age
of 9 or 10 years). If any such 'exceptional' learners appear, it may be possible
to understand their success as a function of optimal milieu, including
optimal attitudes and opportunities for developing authentic L2 experience, in the same way that deficits in these realms may help explain
non-native outcomes.

Research hypotheses

As stated, this study departs from existing work by integrating quantitative and qualitative data in order to examine the connections between
maturation and social context, personal interaction, and psychological

orientation as they impact on access to formal and informal opportunities to interact in the second language. In keeping with this grounded theoretical approach, the following hypotheses guide the methodology and analysis:

(1) Age of onset will correlate negatively to ultimate attainment (the earlier the exposure, the higher the level of attainment), *but not in isolation from concomitant aspects of maturation, i.e. social-psychological and experiential variables such as duration of exposure, perceptions of oneself as a speaker of L2, etc.*

(2) Other biological-experiential factors such as gender, native language(s), other languages known, and length of residence in Germany will not correlate significantly to higher levels of attainment.

(3) Affective and instructional factors will demonstrate significant inter-relationships with one another (especially to age of onset and length of residence – the two variables most often cited in critical period and ultimate attainment research) – as well as to linguistic outcomes. For example, interactive experience will correlate significantly and positively with attainment, as well as to social-psychological orientations such as self-perceptions of native-ness, motivation, and identity. At the same time, there may be fundamental conflations between factors that are difficult to tease apart through quantitative analysis, requiring other data sources and instruments to get at its functional significance for ultimate attainment.

Data and instruments

Data for this integrative study were gathered from three main instruments:

(1) a questionnaire surveying biological-experiential, social-psychological, instructional-cognitive, and experiential-social data, according to both scalar and open-ended formats (Appendix 1);

(2) a set of controlled and semi-controlled production tasks (Appendix 2);

(3) a semi-structured interview reiterating and expanding upon issues addressed in the first instrument (Appendix 5).

Through this balance of instruments, linguistic performance data may be assessed and statistically correlated with individual, non-linguistic factors. Moreover, relationships between realms of background variables may be revealed as an integral basis for understanding the dependent variable: linguistic performance. Most importantly, statistical results may be more appropriately interpreted through information provided by the questionnaires and interviews. Table 3.1 lists the variables surveyed by these instruments according to the categories mentioned.

Table 3.1 NNS variables surveyed* (*n* = 25)

Biological-Experiential:
<ul><li>Gender</li><li>Native language(s)</li><li>Bilingual vs. monolingual childhood</li><li>Other languages known through passive exposure</li><li>Age of first exposure to German</li><li>Length of residence in Germany</li><li>Level of education completed thus far</li></ul>
Social-Psychological:
<ul><li>Intensity of motivation to learn German</li><li>Consistency of motivation to learn German over time</li><li>Necessity of German language for future career plans</li><li>Desire to improve German for personal reasons</li><li>Behavioral changes to initiate more contact with German speakers</li><li>Satisfaction with phonological attainment</li><li>Self-rating of spoken German</li><li>Importance of sounding native</li><li>Identification with German language and community **</li><li>Consistency of attitudes toward Germany **</li><li>Primary social contacts (Germans vs. non-Germans) **</li><li>Cultural affiliations (informal or through official organizations) **</li><li>Future plans to stay in Germany</li></ul>
Instructional-Cognitive:
<ul><li>Instructional years in German language itself</li><li>Instruction in German but for subjects other than German language</li><li>Primary focus/approach of instructional methods for learning German</li><li>Formal feedback concentrations (phonology, lexicon, etc.)</li><li>Strategies for improving pronunciation</li><li>Formal phonological instruction</li><li>Level of informal feedback on pronunciation (e.g., segments vs. intonation)</li></ul>
Experiential-Interactive:
<ul><li>Context for initial exposure to German</li><li>Primary contacts to NS of German</li><li>Consistency of contact with NS</li><li>Frequency of spoken interaction with NS</li><li>Frequency of writing in German</li><li>Frequency of non-interactive contexts for German</li><li>Consistency of feedback received from NS</li><li>Formality of contexts that rely exclusively on German language</li></ul>

* all variables measured in surveys were verified in interviews
** not treated in the statistical analysis (see Chapter 4)

Participants

The non-native speaking (NNS) participants for this study are all immigrants to Berlin (*n* = 25), between the ages of 25 and 35, who currently study at various institutions of higher learning in the area. The average length of residence (LOR) in the sample is 6 years, with a range of just over 22 years. The range of AO is 31 years across the sample, but the mean is 12. Thus, the average AO is past the critical period for language learning if we apply the strict 9-10 cut off point.[1] Because of their educational pursuits, all had passed the *Abitur,* the equivalent of a college entrance exam given at the conclusion of *Gymnasium.* Some had also finished a Master's level of study, or *Magister.* Given the nature of their academic work and degree of language preparation enabling them to take on advanced study in Germany, this group is arguably in good stead to defy the critical period. To be specific, most have experienced considerable instruction, along with informal exposure in numerous contexts, either exclusively in the target-language country or in combination with home-country exposure to German. It is fair to say that this combination of formal instruction and informal exposure qualifies their language learning experience as optimal, possibly allowing them to overcome predicted, age-related constraints.

Almost without exception, the research on German as a second language focuses on immigrants with little, if any, access to education in German (with the exception of some school-age children). There is little research on adults in general, especially those with a strong desire to acquire German to a native level. This is clearly an area ripe for study, especially as these advanced learners differ from native speakers of German in terms of language experience and identity (see Moyer, in press, for review). Some arrived in Germany only a year or two before this study took place, and are still struggling with issues of acceptance and belonging, not to mention the occasional problem with linguistic accuracy. In any case, there is no serious disparity in socio-economic or educational level that could indicate real social disadvantage. If native and non-native performance do not overlap, these instruments and analyses may capture the essential realms of explanation for those differences.

General procedure

Responding to an advertisement placed at several institutions of higher learning in the Berlin area for a study on advanced speakers of German, volunteers identified themselves as native or non-native by telephone interview with a research assistant.[2] All participants completed each portion of the study in a quiet, secluded room, and non-native participants for the study additionally filled out the background questionnaire (Appendix 1). All aspects of the study were conducted entirely in German. For the linguistic audio recordings, subjects were asked to complete the tasks at a pace that was natural for them, in immediate succession, with all tasks together taking about 20–25 minutes (Appendix 2). They were not allowed to re-tape any portion, but some did self-correct specific words during recording. (Audiotapes were later collected and remixed, with individual speech samples placed on a master in random order for the native speaker judges – for details see 'Procedure for linguistic tasks,' below.) Interviews were conducted after the linguistic tasks by a research assistant with a similar background to that of the participants, i.e. also a non-German, international student of similar age pursuing an advanced degree (Appendix 5; more information on the interview protocol is found in Chapter 4).

Descriptive and Statistical Analysis of Non-Linguistic Data

In this section, background information gleaned from the questionnaires is described for the sample, and some initial bivariate correlations between realms are given to demonstrate the interconnectedness of these background variables.

For each item on the questionnaire, responses were coded as continuous, integral, or categorical, depending on the nature of the question (numerical, scalar, open-ended, etc.). Descriptive statistics on these data are presented in Tables 3.2–3.5, and several of the more interesting correlations between variables are presented later under 'Relationships between background variables'.

Biological-experiential factors

Of these non-native speakers (NNS), 10 are men and 15 are women. Their mother tongues represent diverse heritage backgrounds, including Polish, Russian, Ukrainian, French, Turkish, British, and American. Approximately one third of the sample was raised bilingually (most often Russian and another Slavic language); five had occasional, passive exposure to German growing up; two grew up in households where one parent spoke German[2]. There were also nine native speakers (NS) who participated as controls for all the speech tasks. Table 3.2 outlines the background variables termed 'biological-experiential' for the NNS.

As shown in Table 3.2, two-thirds of the sample were raised monolingually, learning German as adolescents or adults. Native language was spread out among a number of languages from different families. Only 32%

Table 3.2 Biological-experiential factors (*n* = 25)

Gender	Native languages*	Bilingual childhood	Other languages known*	Age of onset (years)	Length of residence (years)	Level of education
M 10 F 15	Belorussian 1 Polish 4 Russian 7 Slovak 1 Ukrainian 1 Rumanian 1 French 4 English 5 German 5** Turkish 2	Yes 8 (32%) No 17 (68%)	Russian 3 Polish 1 Hungarian 1 Persian 1 French 3 Italian 2 Spanish 2 English 9 German 6 NNS with multiple languages 8	Mean 12 Range 31 Min 0** Max 31 SD 7	Mean 6 Range 22.3 Min 0.7 Max 23 SD 8	Abitur*** 11 (44%) MA degree 14 (56%)

* some participants reported more than one native language and more than one language known other than the native language, so the totals in these columns are higher than 25

** see Note 2, at end of chapter

*** equivalent of college entrance exam

of the sample were raised bilingually, and those same participants tended to arrive in Germany early in life. Most who were raised as monolinguals learned German upon arrival, or studied it for a few years before coming to Germany as adolescents or young adults.

The mean AO for this sample is 12 – past the critical period for language learning; however, the range is wide at 13 years (therefore, age effects might be expected to appear, and indeed they do). Of interest here is the fact that earlier AO correlates to factors in all of the realms tested. (A fuller exploration of evident age effects is found later in the chapter, and the particulars of individual backgrounds are more fully compared in Chapter 4.) Similarly, length of residence shows a wide range, at 22.3 years, with the minimum at less than a year and the maximum at 23 years. (As with AO, effects for LOR might be expected to appear with such a range, and this is borne out in the statistical analyses.) Finally, this sample is well educated, with 56% having already completed a master's program, and 44% in their early stages of university study.

Social-psychological factors

This sample of learners can only be described as highly motivated and intent on improving their language abilities in German – an ideal sample to potentially defy predicted age effects if social-psychological factors are of utmost importance.

The non-native speakers express an overwhelmingly strong interest in the language – 88 % at strong or very strong. Only 3 of 25 were neutral (and these 3 scored in a solid 'non-native' range in performance – see 'Correlations of linguistic and non-linguistic data' section below). The consistency of that motivation is high – 72 % reported no change since arriving in Germany. Those who did report a change indicated that their perceptions of the importance of the language have shifted over time. For instance, two participants report a greater urgency to acquire German given their recent decision to stay in Germany. Two others describe a similar shift in their attitude toward German fluency; they see it as necessary, but describe the language as a 'tool' for survival.

Some gender differences are apparent in the area of motivation. Women reported significantly higher motivational levels, and as a behavioral response to increasing motivation, they tended to take coursework in German more often than their male counterparts did.

The majority of the sample expressed the need for German language fluency in their professional futures; only two say it is not crucial to their professional development. (This particular factor showed surprisingly little strength in relationships to other factors, recalling the controversial evidence both for, and against, the importance of a professional or 'instrumental' orientation to language learning motivation – see Moyer, 1999.) The desire to improve German fluency for personal reasons is keenly felt among this sample, with 84% reporting strong desire, and only 16% saying they are neutral, or have no particular desire to attain native-level status in German.

Along with these orientations, participants report initiating their own opportunities for greater language contact through both formal and informal channels. Of those who reported in this category (52% of the sample), most either took more courses in German (16%) or combined coursework with ways to increase time spent with Germans, either in personal or work-type settings (12%). The implications of these findings are explored in much greater detail in subsequent sections.

It is interesting to note that 40% of the sample labeled their speech as identifiably accented (significantly overlapping the raters' judgments, in fact). At the same time, 32% thought that they sometimes sound native, and

Table 3.3 Social-psychological factors ($n = 25$)

Intensity of motivation to learn German	Very strong 11 (44%)	Strong 11 (44%)	Neutral 3 (12%)	Weak 0	
Consistency of motivation over time	Definite change 5 (20%)	Partial change 2 (8%)	No change 18 (72%)		
Necessity of German for future career plans	Yes, definitely 20 (80%)	Not sure 3 (12%)	Not needed 2 (8%)		
Desire to improve German for personal reasons	Definite desire 21 (84%)	Neutral 2 (8%)	No strong desire 2 (8%)		
Behaviors to initiate more contact to German speakers *	No particular changes made** 4 (16%)	Spend more time with Germans 1 (4%)	Look for work in German business 1 (4%)	Take more courses in German 4 (16%)	Several options at once 3 (12%)
Satisfaction with attainment in German thus far	Strongly agree 6 (24%)	Agree 3 (12%)	Neutral 9 (36%)	Disagree 5 (20%)	Strongly disagree 2 (8%)
Self-rating of spoken German	I sound native 4 (16%)	I sound mostly native 3 (12%)	I sometimes sound native 8 (32%)	I have a definite accent 10 (40%)	
Importance of sounding like native speaker	Very important 14 (56%)	Important 8 (32%)	Neutral 3 (12%)	Not important 0	

* not all participants reported this category, therefore % does not add up to 100
** usually reported as such because motivation has remained consistent over time, according to the survey data

a combined 28% reported sounding native some of the time, or a great deal of the time. This may have some connection to satisfaction with their attainment, which also covers the spectrum: 36% are satisfied with the level they have reached in German. At the same time, the importance of sounding native is high – 88% rate it as important or very important. (This feature did not figure prominently in the performance ratings, in contradiction to several studies on phonological attainment.)

Instructional-cognitive factors

The factors representing formal, overt, and corrective feedback and instruction include: duration and types of German language instruction, exposure to formal German through other instructional contexts (e.g. through other subject areas with German as the language of instruction), phonological instruction and feedback, and self-initiated learning strategies for improving pronunciation.

For this sample, the amount of direct language instruction is impressive, with a Mean of 6.7 years. For subject areas other than the language itself, but taught in German, the Mean is 7.5 years. This formal instructional experience varies in the sense that some instructional methods encountered have relied on different approaches. Most of the participants in this study (72%) had received both grammar-translation and communicative instruction, and reported consistent access to these approaches over their cumulative language learning experience. The feedback received in class was of a varied nature, usually consisting of lexical, grammatical and some phonological feedback. No one cited any pragmatic or interactive skills, per se, as the subject of any instruction or feedback.

Phonological instruction was surveyed in order to discover whether formal training in pronunciation might influence performance abilities, as well as self-perceptions of fluency or motivation to improve. These survey items revealed very little emphasis on pronunciation in the classroom overall. Some 63% experienced only occasional or no overt instruction, while the remainder had received formal practice on segmental and/or suprasegmental discrimination. Surprisingly, 24% reported some informal feedback from native speakers on their suprasegmental production, either for stress or intonation at the word and sentence levels. (Both formal and informal feedback and instruction in German phonology did not, however, appear to correlate with persistent phonological difficulties, nor to performance ratings in this analysis – see the section on 'Correlations of linguistic and non-linguistic data', and Moyer, 1999.)

This sample does cite various, persistent difficulties with German phonology, even at the advanced stage of learning. The problems cited

Table 3.4 Instructional-cognitive factors ($n = 25$)

Instructional years in German language	Mean = 6.7 yrs	Range = 19 yrs	Min = 1 yr	*Max* = 20 yrs	SD = 5
Instruction in German for other subjects	Mean = 7.5 yrs	Range = 15 yrs	Min = 1 yr	Max = 16 yrs	SD = 5
Primary focus of German instructional methods	Grammar/translation 5 (20%)	Communicative 1 (4%)	GT+communicative 18 (72%)	GT + phonology 1 (4%)	
Formal feedback concentrations (in class)	Phonology feedback 1 (4%)	Lexical/semantic 3 (13%)	Grammar 3 (13%)	Pragmatic/Interactive 0	Several concentrations 17 (71%)
Formal phonological instruction	No overt correction 8 (36%)	Occasional correction 6 (27%)	Drills 5 (23%)	Suprasegmentals 2 (9%)	Drills + suprasegmentals 1 (4%)
Level of informal phonological feedback*	No consistent feedback 6 (24%)	Segmental feedback 2 (8%)	Suprasegmental feedback 6 (24%)	Lexical or other 7 (28%)	
Strategies for Improving pronunciation	No particular strategy 1 (4%)	Reading aloud only 0	Imitating NS 13 (52%)	Both reading aloud and NS imitation 9 (36%)	
Continued phonological problems*	Segmentals 6 (24%)	Stress/intonation 2 (8%)	Segmental + suprasegmental 7 (28%)		

* some participants did not report this category, therefore % do not add up to 100 include word and sentence- or discourse-level difficulties, such as intonation, vowel length and height (umlauts), phonotactics (not specified), and segments such as /a, i, œ, u, ng, x, R/. In addressing these difficulties, and overall pronunciation, many cite radio as most helpful – they imitate broadcasters out loud, and occasionally practice certain words and sounds with friends.

Experiential-interactive factors

In describing L2 experience, two primary areas have been noted in SLA research: classroom (or formal, instructional experience), and residence in the target language country, expressed as length of residence (LOR). These descriptions of experience do not reflect the learner's participation in any way. This is especially clear if we consider the significance of consistent access to authentic, personal interaction over time. Surely, access to spoken interaction affects the quality of one's fluency in profound ways. Similarly, an instructional focus on communication and interaction is undoubtedly more effective for developing interactive skills than a focus on grammar translation. Perhaps because *experience* is multivariate and dynamic, it has hardly been addressed in empirical studies as such. Still, specifics must be accounted for if we are to understand the relevance and value of experience for SLA.

To this end, the questionnaire includes a number of items designed to specifically target the learner's cumulative L2 experience. Special attention is given to contexts for interactive experience, as well as what could be termed passive, or indirect, exposure, in order to look at the possibly differential impact of these features. With those objectives in mind, the categories of experience are listed in Table 3.5, with a brief discussion following.

As with the other realms outlined above, the interactive experience is significantly correlated to every other realm (biological-experiential, social-psychological, instructional-cognitive) in a number of interesting ways. A large percentage of the sample was initially exposed to German through formal channels: 72% at either school or university, an additional 12% by private tutor. As for current contact with native speakers, 44% report having very consistent interactive opportunities currently, while others report initial difficulties making new friends with native Germans (*Einheimische* or *Muttersprachler*). Those who had lived in Germany longest had more close, personal relationships with Germans, and 32% overall reported multiple sources of native speaker contact, such as personal and professional acquaintances, or having a German boyfriend or girlfriend in addition to acquaintances with colleagues.

These participants showed an enormous range of interactive time, ranging from 0 to 84 hours weekly (Mean = 20 hours). They averaged more

Table 3.5 Experiential-Interactive factors ($n = 25$)

	Home/family	School	University	Tutor	Work
Context for initial exposure to German	4 (16%)	16 (64%)	2 (8%)	3 (12%)	0
Primary contacts to native speakers of German	Several sources of contact 8 (32%)	German relatives or parent 2 (8%)	Friends and acquaintances 14 (56%)	Professors or colleagues 1 (4%)	No consistent sources 2 (8%)
Consistency of contact with native speakers	Very consistent 11 (44%)	Consistent with some people 6 (24%)	Not very consistent 5 (20%)	Not at all consistent 3 (12%)	
Frequency of spoken interaction (hrs per week)	Mean = 20 hrs	Range = 84	Min = 0 hrs	Max = 84 hrs	SD = 21
Frequency of writing in German (hrs per week)	Mean = 25 hrs	Range = 49	Min = 1 hr	Max = 50hrs	SSD = 17
Frequency of non-interactive contexts*	Mean = 19 hrs	Range = 100	Min = 0 hrs	Max = 100 hrs	SD = 22
Consistency of feedback from native speakers**	Consistent feedback 1 (4%)	Occasional feedback 6 (24%)	Inconsistent feedback 4 (16%)	No feedback available 2 (12%)	
Formality of contexts using German exclusively*	None require German 5 (20%)	Formal (University) 4 (16%)	Informal (friends) 3 (12%)	Both formal and informal 11 (44%)	

*TV watching, email, letter writing, etc.
**some participants did not report this category, therefore percentages do not add up to 100

time writing in German, at a mean of 25 hours weekly (this correlated, perhaps not surprisingly, to persistent difficulties with pronunciation). The balance of spoken to written use of the language is interesting, as it may reflect highly variable access to personal interaction for the remainder (56%) of the sample, with some participants reporting almost no situations in which German is used exclusively. Given this range in day-to-day target language experience, the importance of access to L2, particularly over time, can hardly be overstated.

In order to expand the theoretical and empirical framework for critical period studies, I have argued that multiple factors co-vary with age, notably: social-psychological, instructional and experiential or interactive experience. This theoretical position is validated by the numerous interrelationships evident between major realms examined here, and is summarized briefly in the following section.

Relationships between background variables

The complex relationships between realms underscore the fact that learning circumstances are highly variable across individuals, yet some predictable connections between factors are evident. Table 3.6 depicts some of the most statistically significant connections between select background variables.

A simplified schema captures these interrelationships in another way, with *all* statistically significant interrelationships accounted for.

Table 3.7 shows that the highest number of significant correlations occur in the following patterns:

(1)   the biological-experiential realm (including AO, LOR, native language) correlates most to the social-psychological realm (various motivation and self-perception measures); and
(2)   biological-experiential and experiential-interactive factors (native speaker contact, consistency of access, informal feedback on language fluency, etc.) are also highly correlated.

At the same time, the other realms are also closely linked to one another through at least 6 significant interrelationships. Some of the most interesting relationships are summarized below (all references to correlations are statistically significant at $p < 0.05$ or less):

• Appreciating being (mis)taken for a native speaker correlates to one's access to multiple L2 contact sources, indicating a connection between language identity and increased contact. Those with a stronger sense

Table 3.6 Significant correlations for selected background variables ($n = 25$; only p values at ≤ 0.05 are provided)

	A	B	C	D	E	F	G	H	I	J	K	L	M	N	O	P	Q	R	S	T
T								0.03								0.008	0.008			
S																0.04	0.04			
R			0.03													0.0009				
Q	0.03	0.04	0.03	0.02			0.04	0.009												
P			0.02	0.03																
O					0.02		0.008	0.03												
N		0.04		0.04							0.02									
M							0.04	0.04												
L		0.05																		
K			0.03				0.03													
J	0.001		0.007					0.003												
I	0.0009	0.001	0.0009			0.009	0.0009													
H	00.03	0.04	0.02		0.03															
G			0.003																	
F		0.04																		
E	0.04		0.04																	
D	0.03																			
C	0.01	0.004																		
B	0.003																			
A																				

Key to Table 3.6

Biological-experiential:	**Instructional-cognitive:**
A Age at first exposure to German	J Length of instruction in German (in years)
B Bilingual childhood	K Approach of instructional methods for
C Length of residence in Germany (years)	learning German
D Level of education completed thus far	L Formal feedback concentrations
	M Strategies for improving pronunciation
Social-psychological:	N Formal phonological instruction
	O Continued phonological difficulties
E Intensity of motivation to learn German	**Experiential-social:**
F Consistency of motivation over time	P Primary contacts to NS
G Personal desire to improve German	Q Frequency of spoken interaction with NS
H Satisfaction with phonological attainment	R Consistency of contact with NS
	S Formality of contexts that rely exclusively
I Self-rating of spoken German	on German
	T Consistency of feedback from NS

Table 3.7 Significant correlations between language learning realms*

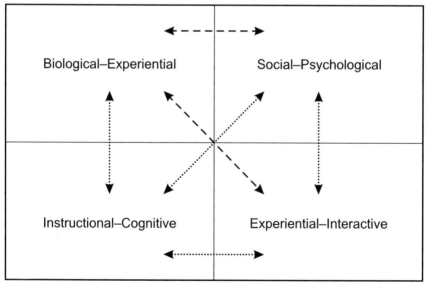

◀┈┈┈┈▶ 6 correlations   ◀ ─ ─ ▶ 8–9 correlations

*significant at $p<0.05$; correlations between factors within 4 major realms not shown

of self in German tend to actively pursue opportunities to enhance their own language development.
- Similarly, those who are relatively dissatisfied with their German tend to do little overtly to improve it. They also tend to have less frequent contact with native speakers.
- Perhaps not surprisingly, infrequent contact correlates to lower motivation, while consistent contact correlates to high motivational intensity, and to self-perceptions of native-ness.
- The intention to use German in one's professional future correlates to greater reliance on German across domains (as opposed to using, or switching to, L1 in certain domains).

Individual participants experience a range of access to native speakers, usually improving with longer residence and greater confidence in one's language abilities. These relationships may be circular in nature. For example, the anxiety experienced by a few has prevented them from seeking personal relationships with Germans, and their sense of self in the language is much less developed than for those with more contact. It is also interesting to note that self-initiated strategies for linguistic improvement are most common for those with the highest levels of motivation. Thus, higher confidence, greater contact, and language fluency seem to reinforce one another.

In sum, the connections between access and affect are noteworthy. In developing authentic, communicative experience with native speakers, an individual acquires a stronger sense of linguistic identity, as well as a stronger motivation to pursue to higher, (i.e. more native) levels. These connections are dealt with in greater detail in subsequent sections.

Of special interest are two factors that contract the greatest number of significant relationships to factors beyond their own realm: *age of onset* (AO) and *length of residence* (LOR). The nature of their covariance with other factors may account for their traditional strength in explaining acquisitional outcomes. Therefore, in the interest of better understanding the influence of these factors, their correlation to experiential factors is noted below (all references to correlations are statistically significant at $p < 0.05$ or less).

Age of onset correlates to multiple variables, across realms, with *early L2 exposure* correlating to:

- native language, bilingual childhood, longer residence, and gender (more women arrived earlier, or began German study earlier in their lives for this sample);
- greater satisfaction with one's attainment, higher self-assessment of

linguistic fluency, higher intensity of motivation, and stronger tendency toward professional motivation;
- greater instructional experience in the language; greater indirect instructional experience (i.e. through other subject matters with German as the language of instruction);
- greater opportunities for informal contact with native speakers,
- greater access to informal feedback from native speakers on fluency/ authenticity.

Length of residence correlates to a number of the same variables, with a few differences. These connections between *longer residence* and other experiential variables are noted below (again, with p at <0. 05 or less):

- greater satisfaction with one's attainment, higher self-assessment of linguistic fluency, stronger tendency toward personal orientation of motivation;
- greater instructional experience in German; greater indirect instructional experience, types of formal classroom feedback, instructional methods used in the language classroom, types of phonological training in the classroom;
- greater opportunities for informal contact with native speakers.

These measures of target language exposure arguably predict a number of important opportunities for building language experience. Simply put, the longer, or more extensive, one's exposure, the more positive an impact this seems to have on orientation to the task (not to mention actual attainment, see next section). Thus, these connections support the position that AO and LOR should not be isolated from their related factors. In reality, the nature of their impact may lie in several realms: affective, interactive and instructional. These realms represent opportunities to increase language fluency across a range of means – direct and indirect, formal and informal.

Table 3.7 represents multi-directional connections between multiple aspects of L2 experience. Since each learning situation is unique, and the balance of factors shifts as circumstances change, it is no wonder that SLA is marked by such variation across individuals. With this in mind, my objective is not to favor a simple model for outcomes at the risk of ignoring key elements. Rather, I hope to describe significant factors as adequately and accurately as possible given this variability. Thus far, it is clear that predictable patterns of interdependence exist between influences. Their significance for attainment further confirms the relevance of multivariate *experience,* set forth here as key to the process and its outcomes, as the following sections show.

Results of the Linguistic Performance Data

In this section, correlations of factors to linguistic performance are presented, beginning with a description of procedure, tasks, raters and ratings, differences between native and non-native participants, and differences in performance across tasks. The focus for the subsequent discussion will address these findings, along with the patterns found among background variables.

Procedure for linguistic tasks

As mentioned earlier, participants were given four basic tasks for the linguistic data instrument (see Appendix 2, adapted from Moyer, 1995 and 1999):

(1) First, participants read aloud 38 words in list format, chosen for their inclusion of frequently-cited difficult sounds in German: /y, u, ø, œ/ contrasts; final devoicing of /b, d, g/ and /g/ in final position; contrastive vowel length, glottal stop, and initial consonant clusters, such as *ps-*. Compound words were chosen for difficulty in stress patterns. In this way, speakers would be required to accurately and naturally produce sounds and sound sequences that are typically difficult for learners of German.

(2) Participants were then asked to read a paragraph at a natural tempo. This task was meant to target assimilation, elision, intonation, and other segmental and suprasegmental features beyond the word-level. It also targets some level of lexical knowledge, in that unfamiliar words may be read with an unnatural pace or degree of segmental accuracy.[3]

(3) The next task was spontaneous speech, elicited by a list of possible topics of a personal nature. Each informant was asked to choose one of several possible topics: an important event in their lives: a difficult or embarrassing situation, a provocative theme or very significant person for them, etc. This task was intended to represent casual, informal speech. Participants were asked to speak for no more than two minutes. Because this task is a reflection of the learner's natural speaking style, the ratings for it are assumed to cover suprasegmental, grammatical, and certainly lexical and pragmatic features that may not be exhibited in the other, more controlled tasks.

(4) The fourth task was to recite a list of 10 short sayings or proverbs in German (between 5 and 12 words long). These sayings rely strongly on intonation for getting their meaning across, and for this reason, unfamiliar ideas can lead to awkward delivery.

Each in its own unique way, these tasks were designed to test advanced ability in the sense that they require phonetic, suprasegmental, lexical and syntactic fluency for effective delivery. The possibilities of error and hesitation in the extended and uncontrolled task put the global abilities of the speaker up for close examination. Because of the breadth of these tasks, and their inherent difficulty, this instrument is considered an effective test of ultimate attainment – emphasizing, but not restricted to, L2 phonology (see Moyer, 1999).

Raters and ratings

Three native-speaker judges (two from Germany, one from Austria), all university students in the US, volunteered to listen to all speech samples. For the analysis, the speech samples were randomly mixed so that the raters would not recognize any particular speaker across tasks. Furthermore, tasks could then be objectively compared for possible formality or length effects (see 'Analysis of task differences' later).

Each rater was asked to determine for each item whether the speaker was native or non-native, and to assign a level of confidence to this rating according to a 3-point scale. When the binary variable (native versus non-native) is combined with the 3-point confidence scale, a 6-point rating scale results, as follows: 1 = definitely native, 2 = native, 3 = perhaps native, 4 = perhaps non-native, 5 = non-native, 6 = definitely non-native. Each participant was then assigned an overall performance mean based on the average of judgments across all raters for all 4 tasks (reported in the next section). While raters listened to each speech item, they were encouraged to write any notes regarding their criteria for judgment, discussed in greater detail later in the chapter. Given the nature of the tasks, i.e. some are more controlled than others, it is evident that pure phonetic accuracy is not isolatable. Therefore, the Mean ratings are a measure of overall fluency, given that extended discourse abilities are required.

The consistency of these judgments is borne out among the raters, according to a Kappa analysis of inter-rater reliability. Kappa allows for a more rigorous test of agreement than correlation or chi-square analyses, but these coefficients are also included in Table 3.8 below.

In the table, the first column gives the relevant figures for each rater as compared to reality, i.e. whether the participant is indeed native or non-native. The bottom half of the column lists the figures for the actual inter-rater reliability. This table shows that Rater 1 has the lowest correspondence to reality, but that his judgments are reasonably reliable when combined with the other two raters. The highest Kappa is found in the pair of Rater 2 and Rater 3, i.e. these two raters are in reliably consistent agree-

Table 3.8 Kappa test for rater and inter-rater reliability

Rater	χ^2	Pearson's r	Kappa	T	Sig. of T for Kappa
1	20.38	0.40	0.29	4.51	0.0009
2	25	0.44	0.44	5.0	0.0009
3	42	0.57	0.52	6.47	0.0009
Rater pairs					
1:2	23	0.42	0.32	4.7	0.0009
2:3	59	0.67	0.62	7.6	0.0009
1:3	43	0.58	0.54	6.6	0.0009

ment with each other (Kappa of 0.50 is considered reliable). These findings reflect a point well worth noting: the raters are, in a sense, supposed to be 'fooled' if possible, into believing that a NNS is possibly native, given the hypotheses of this study. Perfect correspondence to reality is therefore not the sought-after finding for this sample of advanced learners who have benefited from both formal and immersion-type exposure to German, and who exhibit such strong motivation toward not just learning the language, but improving their proficiency in it. This combination of optimal experience and psychological orientation should set these learners up for a possible refutation of predicted age effects, if the hypotheses are borne out by the analysis (which follows in the next section).

Group differences between native and non-native speakers

For the entire sample of 34 (NNS = 25; NS = 9), clear, significant differences emerged in performance ratings for native speakers versus non-native, at $p < 0.0009$ ($r = 0.67$). This means that the raters were indeed able to discern qualities they judged to be native rather than non-native. Moreover, the ratings themselves corresponded significantly with the ratings that the participants gave themselves ($p < 0.0009$) (Table 3.9 shows a t-test comparison of group means.)

As for the NNS, Chart 3.1 represents the breakdown of ratings categories (definitely native, native, etc.) assigned per individual, accounting for all four tasks. The shaded portions of the pie show the non-native labels (definitely non-native, non-native, perhaps non-native), contrasted with the unshaded portions, which denote native-level categories of judgment.

As the chart shows, 36% of the participants were judged to be on the native side of the 6-point scale, while 64% were identified as non-native.

Table 3.9 T-test comparing NS and NNS performance (*n* = 34; all subjects included)

	Group Mean	*SD*	*SE*	*F*	*Sig. of F*	*T*	*Sig. of T*
NNS	4.4	1.5	0.29	6.3	0.02	-5.1	0.0009
NS	1.8	0.64	0.21				

Thus, although group differences were statistically significant overall, there were a number of NNS who rated consistently in the native category, exhibiting some overlap with NS participants. Going in the other direction, no NS landed in the NNS side of the rating scale. However, a few were not rated as 'definitely native,' indicating some level of uncertainty. Three NS scored at 2.44, 2.58 and 2.9 respectively – a Mean rating that was surpassed by several of the NNS. In short, a small zone of overlap is apparent – an issue that is revisited in the chapter conclusion.

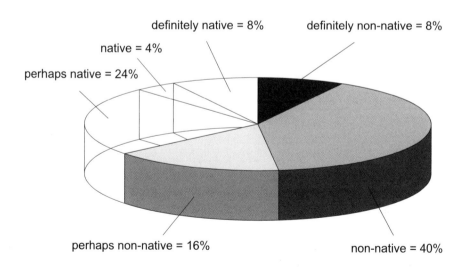

Chart 3.1 Mean rating groups, non-native speakers only (*n* = 25)

Analysis of task differences

In addition to comparing group performance, a separate analysis looked for differences in Mean ratings across tasks. Table 3.10 shows the ANOVA analysis comparing task performance Means for the entire sample ($n = 34$) and the NNS group alone ($n = 25$).

While task differences are not significant for the entire sample, nor for the NNS as a separate group, there are some interesting trends. For example, when task Means are compared for the entire sample, the third task (extemporaneous speech) averaged closer to native than any other

Table 3.10 ANOVAs: Comparing task means

Entire sample ($n =34$)

Task	Mean	SD	SE	Min. Mean rating	Max. Mean rating
1	4.0	1.8	0.31	1	6
2	4.02	1.7	0.30	1	6
3	3.68	1.8	0.32	1	6
4	3.7	1.9	0.34	1	6

	SS	df	MS	F	Sig
Between groups	3.17	3	1.06	0.33	0.80
Within groups	398.14	125	3.19		
Total	401.3	128			

NNS only ($n=25$)

Task	Mean	SD	SE	Min. Mean rating	Max. Mean rating
1	4.65	1.4	0.28	1	6
2	4.62	1.4	0.28	1	6
3	4.23	1.7	0.34	1	6
4	4.09	1.8	0.35	1	6

	SS	df	MS	F	Sig
Between groups	6.0	3	2.0	0.80	0.49
Within groups	237	96	2.5		
Total	243	99			

task, including the isolated word list. In fact, the isolated word list and the paragraph task had the poorest Mean scores (i.e. most *non-native*). This indicates that informal speech, perhaps reflecting a more natural rhythm and individual style, brings out the best performance for both the native and non-native speakers. However, when the non-natives were tested as a separate group, it is the sentence-length task that evoked the best scores (i.e. closer to *native*). While these differences are not statistically significant (all task Means ranged from 4.09–4.65 for the NNS), the isolated word list and paragraph recitation showed the poorest performance on the scale. Thus, while these tasks may have offered the greatest level of control over articulation (and presumably greater monitor use), this may not have led to greatest precision. On the other hand, these tasks were designed to include challenging segmental and phonotactic features, whereas the free speech task was uncontrolled, and thus allowed for avoidance, (especially lexical). From another viewpoint, however, it is also possible that the free speech and the sentence-length tasks are judged as much on rhythm and stress as on segmental precision.

In sum, the presumed formality of a task may not be the salient factor in performance accuracy. It is far more likely that native-like delivery is a matter of suprasegmental and even pragmatic features, such as tempo, rhythm and style as well as linguistic control, or accuracy. The extent of contextual isolation, or even text type itself, may evoke varying degrees of naturalness in style, and therefore fluency. Reading aloud, especially isolated items, may be the least reliable indicator of actual fluency. If so, more natural texts, especially extemporaneous ones, may lend themselves to better performance (particularly in terms of suprasegmental precision – a factor found to be significant in judgments of native-like fluency – see Moyer, 1999).[4]

Correlations of linguistic and non-linguistic data

In examining the bivariate relationships between background variables and Mean ratings, significant correlations were evident in every L2 experiential realm tested in this study. Table 3.11 lists the results of the correlation analysis.

To summarize the general findings, each realm tested contained at least one factor that appeared significant to performance results, with 3 realms exhibiting several such correlations. The most significant relationships appeared between Mean Rating and the social-psychological realm. Using Table 3.7 as a model, and including Mean Rating, Table 3.12 provides a visual depiction of these interrelationships, described in greater detail below.

Table 3.11 Correlations between background variables and Mean ratings
($n = 25$)

	p value	r
Biological–Experiential		
Gender	0.38	0.18
Native language	0.26	0.24
Bilingual vs. monolingual childhood	0.01	0.50
Other languages known	0.20	0.26
Age of exposure	0.0009	0.72
Length of residence	0.0009	0.67
Level of education	0.23	0.25
Social–Psychological		
Intensity of motivation	0.18	0.27
Consistency of motivation	0.03	0.44
Professional need for German	0.42	0.17
Personal desire to acquire German	0.01	0.48
Behavioral changes to increase exposure	0.95	0.02
Satisfaction with phonological attainment	0.0009	0.74
Self-rating of spoken German	0.0009	0.89
Importance of sounding native	0.42	0.17
Instructional–Cognitive		
Instructional years in German language	0.004	0.57
Indirect instruction (subjects other than German)	0.002	0.67
Primary focus/approach of instructional methods	0.06	0.38
Formal feedback concentrations	0.59	0.11
Strategies for improving pronunciation	0.08	0.38
Formal phonological instruction	0.85	0.04
Level of informal feedback on pronunciation	0.35	0.22
Continued difficulties with German phonology	0.09	0.45
Experiential–Interactive		
Context for initial exposure to German	0.12	0.32
Primary contacts to NS	0.74	0.07
Consistency of contact to NS	0.27	0.23
Frequency of spoken interaction	0.0009	0.73
Frequency of writing in German	0.84	0.05
Frequency of non-interactive contexts for German	0.52	0.14
Consistency of feedback received from NS	0.26	0.32
Formality of contexts relying exclusively on German	0.97	0.008

Significance of biological-experiential factors

- The finding for bilingual as opposed to monolingual childhood is clarified thus: performance ratings are significantly higher when one is raised as a bilingual, and it does not seem to matter what the native language is (no significance for this particular factor was found). A task-by-task analysis shows that significance for bilingualism appears across tasks. This evidence in support of the significance of bilingualism in early childhood is revisited in the following sections.
- Age of exposure to German is indeed significant for Mean rating, demonstrating a powerful relationship, but possibly not an altogether direct one. At the same time, age of exposure contracted highly significant relationships with numerous other background factors, possibly indicating *indirect*, as opposed to direct, influence, assuming the prominence of these other factors upon (and after) puberty (see chapter conclusion).
- The underlying significance of length of residence is not clear, as mentioned previously. It could represent any degree of passive exposure or high level of engagement with L2. Like AO, LOR correlates to

Table 3.12 Language learning realms to performance*

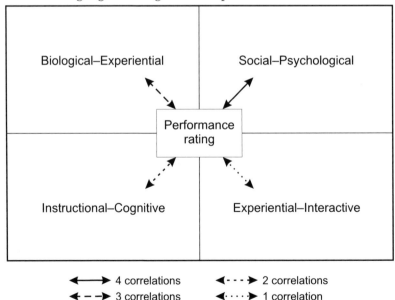

*significant at $p < 0.05$

numerous other factors. Therefore, its significant relationship to attainment here could be more a function of its relationship to (or even determination of) other experiential factors. Some of those significant relationships are outlined in the conclusion to this chapter.

Significance of social-psychological factors

- Motivation indeed exhibits powerful ties to outcome. Here, the *consistent* force of motivation to pursue German over the long-term indicates more native-level attainment. Moreover, the perception of that motivation as personal, as opposed to professionally-oriented only, is also of great importance to outcome (These findings will be discussed at greater length in the discussion and conclusion sections.)
- Two other factors in the social-psychological realm are highly significant to attainment: satisfaction with one's phonological fluency, and self-rating of one's own German. These two factors may simply be realistic assessments of one's current abilities, and therefore not particularly informative or of great explanatory value. On the other hand, they are both connected significantly to specific opportunities for contact and interaction with NS, as well as to other factors that may be tied to intention to pursue the language. Therefore the meaning of these correlations requires more careful consideration.

Significance of instructional-cognitive factors

- Instruction in the language, specifically the extent of the learner's instructional background, is highly significant to attainment. This finding is not surprising, given a growing body of evidence on the importance of instruction for long-term attainment (Moyer, 1999; see Chapter 2 discussion). Both direct and indirect *formal* experience are reflections of time spent in-country and age of onset in the sense that younger learners obviously enrolled in German schools. At the same time, direct instruction in the language, also available to the late learners, may be uniquely effective in advancing language fluency.
- The substantial finding for instructional method ($p < 0.06$) indicates that language instruction, per se, plays an important role in attainment. Specifically, exclusive emphasis on grammar or translation leads to poorer fluency in speaking across a variety of tasks.
- Strategies for improving pronunciation are of marginal importance (at $p < 0.08$) as follows: the more strategies undertaken (self-initiated), particularly where overt imitation of NS is involved, the more native-like one's attainment. This implies that conscious effort and attention to task have a positive impact.

- Continued difficulties are also of marginal significance ($p < 0.09$): some entrenched problems, on both the segmental and supra-segmental levels combined, correlate to a less-than-native rating, as opposed to having difficulties only with certain segments. This is in line with earlier research on the importance of suprasegmental fluency for judgments of native-ness (Moyer, 1995, 1999).

Significance of experiential-interactive factors

- Finally, the opportunity to engage in authentic communication with native speakers is highly significant. This finding confirms that the amount of active participation in spoken interaction plays a key role in performance abilities.
- Other factors measuring formality and consistency of feedback, context, and mode of engagement with German (written, passive listening, etc.) did not appear statistically significant to outcome (though they were significantly related to factors in other realms, especially the social-psychological cluster of factors).

As previously mentioned, two participants had grown up speaking German (with a German parent), but identified themselves as non-native speakers for personal reasons. For instance, one woman has traveled back and forth between England and Germany throughout her life, and sees English as her dominant language. In the interest of verifying the correlations without these two potential outliers (they were the only NNS who scored below a 2.0 for a Mean Rating), the analysis was re-run without them, and some slight changes appeared:

- Intensity of motivation shows up as significant to outcome at $p < 0.04$.
- Personal motivation becomes even more significant, from $p < 0.01$ to 0.001.
- Bilingual childhood slips to a marginal significance of $p < 0.09$.

All other factors noted in Table 3.11 remained statistically significant, though some of the actual p values shifted slightly (e.g. AO slipped from $p < 0.0009$ to 0.002). Most importantly, frequency of spoken interaction lost its previous significance (from $p < 0.0009$ to 0.14), leading to the conclusion that these two participants indeed skewed the correlation between hours of interaction and language outcomes. Perhaps these two were truly indistinguishable from native Germans in their social opportunities. For the other non-German NNS, alternate aspects of experience could possibly fill the gaps characteristic of late arrival (i.e. the necessary acculturation and social adaptations) and allow for eventual native-level attainment.

Indeed, it is possible to become fluent at that level without much interaction with native speakers, as is the case with one participant here who spends an average of only 5–6 hours a week speaking to NS, yet scored just within the native side of the scale at 3.8 (this in spite of an AO of 12 years – beyond the critical period). What this woman did have was 20 years of formal language study, 6 years residence in-country (LOR), and the highest intensity and breadth of motivation reportable in the survey. Perhaps this combination of long-term experience, formal and informal realms of contact, and extensive motivation led to such an impressive level of attainment (see Chapter 4). The bottom line is that opportunities to engage in spoken interaction were highly variable across the sample, but those with such access were much more likely to have a native-level rating.

Multiple regression tests for comparative factor strength

Apart from testing simple, bivariate relationships, one of the primary objectives of this study is to examine the relative strength of several key factors in attainment, such as AO, LOR, motivation, etc. The two outliers were therefore removed for the regression analyses given their impact on the correlations between outcome and several factors (noted above). A simple linear regression analysis of the most significant factors revealed the following top five variables[5] for performance outcomes (Table 3.13).

Given the strength of these linear relationships, several multiple regression analyses were undertaken in order to find the maximum possible prediction of the variance, and the relative contribution of each factor to the model. Statistical Package for the Social Sciences (SPSS, version 10.0 for Macintosh) performed all analyses, with 95% confidence intervals for each regression coefficient. Tables 3.14–3.17 present four of these models (in increasing order of predictive strength with the fewest variables).

Table 3.13 Top five variables for performance outcomes, in order of descending strength ($n = 23$)

	r	r^2	Significance
1. Satisfaction with own phonological attainment	0.71	0.51	$p < 0.0009$
2. Length of residence	0.68	0.46	$p < 0.0009$
3. Personal motivation to acquire German	0.66	0.44	$p < 0.001$
4. Age of onset with German	0.61	0.38	$p < 0.002$
5. Indirect formal (instructional) experience	0.60	0.36	$p < 0.008$

Table 3.14 Regression model #1

	r	r^2	r^2 change	F change	Sig of F change
LOR	0.68	0.46	0.46	18	0.0009
AO	0.75	0.56	0.10	4	0.05

Table 3.14 lists only LOR and AO, the two most cited factors in critical period and ultimate attainment studies, in order to show how well they may, together, predict individual variation in outcome. In regression model #1 (stepwise), the addition of AO does not add impressively to the explanation, at an r^2 change of only 10%. When AO is the first variable entered in the analysis, its strength is more apparent, at $r = 0.38$ ($p < 0.002$). Given the stronger presence of LOR, it was then entered as the first variable in a second stepwise model with social-psychological variables *satisfaction with attainment* and *personal motivation to acquire fluency in German*, as Table 3.15 shows.

Table 3.15 Regression model #2

	r	r^2	r^2 change	F change	Sig of F change
LOR	0.68	0.46	0.46	18	0.0009
Satisfaction	0.83	0.68	0.22	14	0.001
Personal motivation	0.87	0.76	0.08	6	0.03

According to regression model #2, LOR accounts for 46% of the variance in outcome ($r^2 = 0.46$), *satisfaction* adds 22% to the explanation (r^2 *change* = 0.22), and *personal motivation to improve German* adds another 8% (r^2 *change* = 0.08), weaker than AO's contribution in model #1. Now, the total variance accounted for is 76% – an impressive finding.

When AO takes the place of LOR as the first step (regression model #3), the totals end up the same (76%), but both *satisfaction* and *personal motivation* become more powerful in their contributions to the explanation (Table 3.16).

In essence, whether LOR or AO is the first step, the addition of the psychological variables *satisfaction* and *personal desire to improve German* bring the total predictive strength of these models up to 76% ($r^2 = 0.76$).

Table 3.16 Regression model #3

	r	r^2	r^2 change	F change	Sig of F change
AO	0.61	0.38	0.38	13	0.002
Satisfaction	0.78	0.62	0.24	12	0.002
Personal motivation	0.87	0.76	0.15	12	0.o03

Without those psychological variables, the model remains at 56% (Table 3.14). As noted above, the significance of F change increases substantially in regression model #3 for *personal desire to improve German*, indicating that in model #2 LOR may account for some of its significance – consistent with the claim above that LOR seems to be a more powerful predictor, and consistent with the idea that LOR may be a measure of experience and orientation to L2.

In the interest of exploring the most economical model possible, two final regression analyses were undertaken. In the first of these (model #4), a predictive value of 68% was discovered with just 2 variables: LOR and *satisfaction with attainment*, as shown in Table 3.17.

The fact that only two variables account for such a high percentage of the variance in outcome is noteworthy. The combination of duration of L2 experience/exposure and the psychological perception of being satisfied with one's attainment provides a strong indication of long-term acquisition success – or lack thereof. It is true that the group Means between native and non-native were significantly different (Table 3.9). Even though overlap was evident, on average, these NNS were, on the whole, perceived to be NNS. Their reported *satisfaction* may be a function of some kind of plateau effect, or stagnation in L2 development. In other words, high satisfaction may indicate some kind of acceptance of the status quo, though that may be recognizably non-native. Given the fact that the majority of participants rated their own speech as sounding non-native, perhaps this explanation is fitting. (Their self-ratings corresponded to the raters' judgments at a highly significant level at $p < 0.0009$.)

Table 3.17 Regression model #4

	r	r^2	r^2 change	F change	Sig of F change
LOR	0.68	0.46	0.46	18	0.00092
Satisfaction	0.83	0.68	0.22	14	0.001

While participants were not overwhelmingly satisfied with their attainment (a total of 36% agreed or strongly agreed that they were), they rated concern for pronunciation accuracy rather high (88% said it was important or very important). Still, this factor was not of great significance to outcome (see Chapter 2). In fact, some participants reported 'giving up' their earlier drive toward perfect mastery, more due to a shift toward setting up a life in Germany, rather than any loss of interest in the language, per se. (These points receive prominent focus in Chapter 4.)

As in earlier models, the same results were not manifest when AO was coupled with the satisfaction variable; a slightly weaker 62% was the total r^2 (not shown). When AO was added to model #4 as either the second or third step, SPSS automatically eliminated it on the basis of poor significance (i.e. once *satisfaction* and LOR were accounted for). A reasoned interpretation of these combined results suggests that AO loses much power as a predictor of L2 attainment when it is measured against other concomitant variables of experience and orientation. Particularly for a sample of learners with appreciable in-country experience, AO's effects may be inextricable from those of LOR. The correlation between these two variables is significant at $p < 0.01$, and their strength in the various regression models appears to closely overlap.

Model #5 examines the relative power of the two most significant social-psychological variables: *satisfaction* and *personal desire to improve German* (Table 3.18).

Table 3.18 Regression model #5

	r	*r²*	*r² change*	*F change*	*Sig of F change*
Personal motivation	0.66	0.44	0.44	16	0.001
Satisfaction	0.86	0.74	0.30	22	0.0009

This final model accounts for 74% of the total variance in outcome, with just two variables, *and without either LOR or AO*. Based on these results, it is clear that social-psychological variables are as strong (or stronger) in their predictive power as are AO and LOR *combined* (at 56% – see model #1), leading credence to the position that narrow analyses cannot capture the *relative strength* of factor influence. More will be said about these issues in the conclusion section.

Discussion of Statistical Analysis Results

Validation of hypotheses

The objective of this analysis is to statistically validate multiple influences on attainment, and to further explore how these influences may be conflated with one another. Statistical analyses confirm two of the original hypotheses; one was not upheld. These results are explained below:

> *Hypothesis 1:* Age of onset will correlate negatively to ultimate attainment (the earlier the exposure, the higher the level of attainment), but not in isolation from concomitant aspects of maturation, i.e. social-psychological and experiential variables such as duration of exposure, perceptions of oneself as a speaker of L2, etc.

Indeed, age of onset holds a significant, negative correlation to outcome, such that earlier exposure is indicative of attainment that is closer to native level. Early onset also appears to impact on all realms, with three statistically significant correlations to the social-psychological realm: motivational intensity; satisfaction with attainment; self assessment of L2 ability; and the experiential-interactive realm (consistency of feedback from native speakers, frequency of spoken interaction with native speakers, and contexts for initial exposure to German). In addition, AO correlates to instructional experience and indirect formal instruction/exposure.[6]

The breadth and strength of these interrelationships substantiate Hypothesis 1, particularly as five of the above-mentioned correlations are also highly significant to outcome (see Table 3.11). Earlier exposure is typified by greater access to both formal and informal channels of L2 contact, and may lead to a stronger sense of L2 ability as well. As for the *intensity of motivation – age of onset* connection, it is the late learners who feel the motivational drive most acutely; early exposure appears to ameliorate the urgency to attain to a native level. The underlying reasons for this are not readily apparent from these data. It may be that early learners have already reached their language learning goals and are more concerned with the real-life functions served by the second language within the target language community. (More is said about this in the following section, and in Chapter 4.)

> *Hypothesis 2:* Other biological-experiential factors such as gender, native language(s), other languages known, and LOR will not correlate significantly to higher levels of attainment.

Length of residence and a bilingual upbringing were definitely shown to correlate significantly to higher attainment levels. Therefore Hypothesis 2 is not upheld as stated, though gender, native language, and other languages known were not found to be significant to performance ratings.

Here, a picture emerges of bilingual childhood and its concomitant factors, summarized briefly as follows: a bilingual childhood is most likely to correspond to greater length of residence, earlier onset with L2, more interactive opportunities with NS, greater consistency in motivation toward L2, greater satisfaction with attainment in L2, a higher self-assessment of L2 abilities, and more traditional types of phonological instruction and feedback, such as drills. By contrast, participants raised as monolinguals had none of these clear advantages in L2 experience.

While replication is needed to verify any possible universal patterns, the relationships found here are in keeping with the principled approach of this methodology: *Earlier exposure to L2 may coincide with multiple avenues of access and reinforcement in the language, e.g. greater opportunities for contact with NS, greater opportunities for both formal and informal instructional formats, etc., thus providing some level of explanation for age effects in L2 performance outcomes.*

One way to understand the influence of early onset requires closer examination of the LOR factor. I noted earlier that LOR is one of two variables with the highest number of significant relationships to other experiential factors. Most of these relationships involve instructional-cognitive features, e.g. duration of formal instruction, indirect formal language instruction, focus of classroom feedback, instructional method, and focus of phonological instruction (the last two are marginally significant at $p <$ 0.07 and 0.08, respectively). One such relationship was apparent for the experiential-interaction realm: frequency of spoken interaction with NS. The remainder appear in the social-psychological realm: personal desire to acquire German, satisfaction with attainment, and self-rating. Of these nine factors noted, six are also highly significant to outcome (see Table 3.11).

Altogether, these findings paint a complex picture of the learner with greater residential experience. The strong connection evident between longer residence and earlier exposure deserves closer examination; those with longer residence, and from an earlier age, benefit from more formal instruction, more indirect formal instruction, and more opportunities to interact with native speakers. They also exhibit greater satisfaction, and assess their L2 abilities at a much higher level.

Hypothesis 3: Affective and instructional factors will demonstrate significant interrelationships with one another (especially with AO and LOR –

the two variables most often cited in critical period and ultimate attainment research) – as well as to linguistic outcomes. For example, interactive experience will correlate significantly and positively with attainment, as well as to social-psychological orientations such as self-perceptions of native-ness, motivation, and identity. At the same time, there may be fundamental conflations between factors that are difficult to tease apart through quantitative analysis, requiring other data sources and instruments to determine the significance for ultimate attainment.

Hypothesis 3 is also upheld by the analyses presented: Affective, instructional and interactive factors all demonstrate significant correlations to linguistic attainment, as well as across experiential realms. Below, I clarify a few points regarding the significance, and limits, of these findings.

First, the experiential-interactive realm shows less of an influence than expected, with the exception of frequency of contact with native speakers. This corroborates recent evidence for *interaction* as key to language attainment (though true long-term studies have been notably scarce). More study is recommended for future studies, as this area has received so little quantitative investigation in SLA research.

Second, the significance of the spoken contact variable is obviously skewed by the two participants with a German parent (as noted previously). Undoubtedly, they function as native speakers, even if they label themselves 'non-native' for reasons of language affiliation. Taking their home environment into account, they have enjoyed greater linguistic exposure, and from very early childhood, in comparison to the others. This has impacted their attainment positively, as the statistical correlation verifies. Thus, their formal and informal exposure to German could arguably be described as optimal throughout their early language development. This is not so for the culturally and ethnically non-German NNS participants who had had very different backgrounds in terms of access to native speakers (not to mention schooling).

Third, it is clear that opportunities for interaction vary greatly across individuals; most have either very minimal access or quite a lot – there is little middle ground. With more even distribution across the spectrum, this factor may have maintained its significance even without the two outliers.

Rater criteria for judgments of native-ness

As noted above, any task beyond isolated production of words inherently provides information of a grammatical, pragmatic, and lexical nature. Raters were first asked to identify which criteria they felt were most important for their own judgments of native-ness for speakers of German (Appendix 3), based on the broad categories of:

- *pragmatics:* style, coherence/ organization, fluency, appropriateness
- *grammar:* word order and morphology
- *pronunciation:* accent, stress and rhythm, intonation and pitch; vowel and consonant precision
- *lexicon:* breadth and idiomatic language
- *'other:'* speed/tempo, hesitation, comprehensibility

The category with by far the highest rankings across the board for importance in judging native-ness was pronunciation[7] (one rater further differentiated priorities within phonology, such as stress and vowel/ consonant accuracy, etc.). The importance assigned to phonology reiterates the point made in the conclusion of Chapter 2 that pronunciation is likely the most salient feature for determining native-ness. Certainly the actual notes made by each rater confirm this position.

Raters were given space to write comments for each task item regarding the features that influenced their ratings (Appendix 4). Of 143 total 'errors' cited (some raters made several comments per item), 113 (79% of the total) are based on phonological criteria, verifying the significance of pronunciation for determinations of native-ness. These tallies are given in Table 3.19.

Specific segments are noted most often, with unspecified 'foreign accent' a close second. Suprasegmental features also figured prominently in the assessments, with intonation, speed, stress and hesitation together totaling 37% of errors noted. Several segments are also cited as problematic (along predictable lines), including: final stops /b, d, g/, uvular /R, x/,

Table 3.19 Criteria for ratings

Phonological criteria	*n*	*% of all errors noted*	*Non-phonological criteria*	*n*	*% of all errors noted*
Specific segments	39	27%	Lexicon/word choice	19	13%
'Foreign accent'	37	26%	Morphology	7	5%
Intonation	16	11%	Syntax/word order	4	3%
Speed/tempo	10	7%			
Syllable stress	7	5%			
Hesitation and rhythm	4	3%			
Total	**113**	**79%**	**Total**	**30**	**21%**

initial /h-/, and all umlauted vowels. Participants themselves cited some of these same segments as problematic. In fact, one participant wrote that he could not distinguish certain sound contrasts in spite of overt instruction on those distinctions. Additionally, some Polish and Russian participants noted their difficulties with vowel length, and some native English speakers cited problems with uvular /R/ and /x/. These self-reports indicate that there is some remaining influence of a contrastive nature. Those sounds that do not exist in L1 may still cause difficulty in L2, despite targeted instruction in some cases. A number of participants address these phonological difficulties overtly, through imitation and reading aloud in hopes of ameliorating their inaccuracies. These issues are discussed at greater length in Chapter 4.

Conclusion: Theoretical Implications

The fundamental objective of this study is to examine the relative strength of factors deemed significant for ultimate attainment. The instrument therefore includes measures of L2 contact and experience, as well as social-psychological factors – a more holistic approach than is characteristic of critical period studies. Based on the analysis here, four major realms of language learning are significant, with interconnections in many directions. Below, I summarize the issues brought to light by these analyses, according to each realm investigated.

Balance of biological, social, instructional, and experiential factors

The biological-experiential realm, as conceived here, includes age of onset and length of residence, as well as native language, other languages known, gender, educational level, and bilingual versus monolingual upbringing. The quantitative analysis points to the statistical prevalence of both AO and LOR in comparison to these other factors. The linear relationship of both AO and LOR to attainment is represented in Graphs 3.1 and 3.2.

The regression lines depict the following relationships: the earlier the onset with L2, the more native one's attainment; the longer the residence, the more native one's attainment (though there are several here who defy those predictions). In Graph 3.1, there is a surprising range for those exposed before the age of 10. In addition, it appears that the greatest regression from the Mean coincides with age 10–11, and most important, the linearity continues into adulthood (unlike the Johnson & Newport 1989 findings – see next section for more discussion).

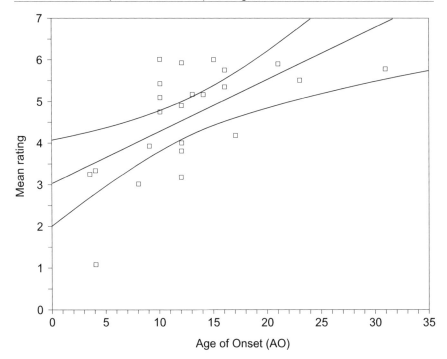

Graph 3.1 Age of onset (AO) to attainment ($n = 23$, $r^2 = 0.38$)

As for the linearity in relationship between LOR and attainment, Graph 3.2 shows a great range around two years' residence (several NNS have native-like ratings in spite of short residence). Still, the relationship is more powerful here than that for age, at $r^2 = 0.46$; therefore residence may be a stronger predictor of outcome than age.

Even though LOR appears to have a clearer connection to attainment here, whether it exerts dependent or independent effects is unclear, as is also the case with AO. The multiple regression analyses indicate that AO and LOR exert similar influence on outcome, and contract relationships with many of the same variables. Moreover, 6 of these 9 overlapping correlations are highly significant to attainment. Table 3.20 lists those factors exhibiting statistically significant correlations to *both* AO and LOR.[8]

Given these overlapping correlations, AO and LOR were tested for interaction effects. If interaction is not significant, both variables can be assumed to exert some main, independent effect on outcome. Two-way ANOVAs

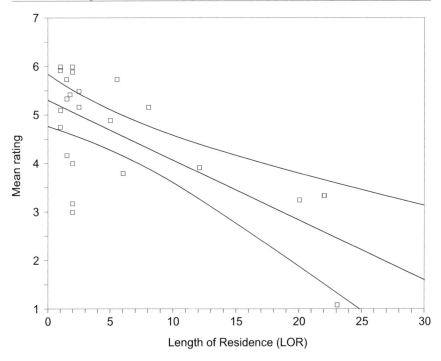

Length of Residence (LOR)

Graph 3.2 Length of residence (LOR) to attainment ($n = 23$, $r^2 = 0.46$)

Table 3.20 Overlapping correlations of AO and LOR

	Age of onset		*Length of residence*	
	r	*p value*	*r*	*p value*
Biological-Experiential				
Bilingual childhood	0.58	0.003	0.56	0.004
Native language	0.44	0.01	0.43	0.03
Socio-Psychological				
Satisfaction with attainment	0.52	0.007	0.47	0.02
Self-assessment of fluency	0.78	0.0009	0.79	0.0009
Instructional-Cognitive				
Duration of instruction	0.53	0.008	0.54	0.007
Indirect instruction	0.69	0.001	0.77	0.0009
Experiential-Interactive				
Frequency of NS interaction	0.51	0.03	0.51	0.03

(not shown) found no significant interactions between AO and LOR groups, specifically: age effects were similar across LOR groups and these two variables have some independent impact on attainment. To go a step further, two-way ANOVAs were computed for both AO and LOR groups against all of the variables shown to be significant to attainment (Table 3.11), and no significant interactions were found. Finally, significant background variables were tested against one another, also with no significant interaction effects at $p \leq 0.05$. This means that *all factors accounted for as significant in Table 3.11 exert main effects*. It is true that they are also highly correlated to one another in many cases, but their significance to attainment is not necessarily obscured or inflated by their associations to one another.

From a theoretical standpoint, these findings are of great importance, stated simply as follows: *Variables of a socio-psychological nature, a biological-experiential nature (describing conditions of L2 exposure), and variables of an instructional or cognitive nature all contribute to a model of SLA, with both independent power and important interconnections.*

Given the theoretical import of these results, the role of age alone should be neither overestimated, nor dismissed. As discussed in Chapter 2, age effects may be neurological in nature, e.g. directly influencing the likelihood of developing accurate perceptual and/or articulatory targets in L2 phonology (though that level of interpretation cannot be supported by these data and instruments). However, from a neuro-cognitive point of view, the connections between AO and overt practice and feedback are worth serious consideration. According to these data, early exposure is significantly tied to duration of instruction – the earlier a participant begins learning German, the more years accrued of formal instruction (direct and indirect). *Thus, early learners experience more direct or overt practice, reinforcement, and feedback aimed at improving language development.* This formal quality of L2 experience is surely an advantage in the long-term, shown to be significant to attainment (both with and without the outliers).

From another perspective, age is clearly tied inextricably to social-psychological influences. Without the two outliers, AO becomes even more highly correlated to social-psychological variables, such as: intensity of motivation, personal motivation, satisfaction with attainment, and self-rating of fluency (and these are all highly significant to attainment here). Later exposure is indicative of greater personal motivation and intensity, but lower satisfaction and self-ratings. In addition, later exposure holds marginally significant relationships to the greater importance placed on sounding native and the greater likelihood of a professionally-oriented motivation. The final regression model (#5, Table 3.18) shows that psychological factors, such as *personal interest in improving fluency* and *satisfaction with attainment* account for 74% of the variance in outcome – a stronger prediction than that offered by the combination of AO and LOR (Table 3.14). Considering these findings, length of residence and age of onset should continue to receive attention, but not without a consideration of learning circumstances and opportunities as well as learner attitudes.[9]

As for the statistical importance of length of residence, it is significant for formal instruction, both direct and indirect formats, as well as classroom feedback. It is further related to instructional method and phonological feedback. Thus, longer residence implies a spectrum of contexts for formal language experience and specific emphases on L2 skill development. This insight points to a serious gap in the SLA research regarding the need to understand the nature of LOR's statistical significance, i.e. whether the underlying mechanisms of its influence are of a cognitive or psychological nature. It may be both, as the number of correlations of LOR to these other language learning realms is so high, and its independent strength is not impressive, especially when psychological factors are adequately accounted for (Table 3.18).

In comparison to the biological-experiential realm, social-psychological factors demonstrate impressive strength based on the statistical correlations and multiple regression models (Tables 3.11–3.18). Socio-psychological factors are addressed here not just in stationary, quantifiable terms; their dynamic aspects are also considered. Motivational orientation, intensity, consistency, and perceptions of attainment are all significant to outcome. These results underscore the need to study motivation's role in ultimate attainment, particularly for older learners. Apparently its intensity and consistency are highly influential, regardless of whether the learner's orientation is personal or professional in nature. As an example, even when the functional significance of L2 changes in the eyes of the learner, it is the steadiness of his or her intention to pursue fluency that is important in the long run. In a sense, personal versus professional, or integrative versus instrumental orientations of motivation may be less important than the qualities of intensity or consistency.

Of interest is also the extent of connections between the social-psychological and other language learning realms (Table 3.7), as well as the connections across social-psychological factors themselves. For instance, the learner's appreciation for sounding native, while not significant to outcome, does correlate to self-initiated behaviors to increase L2 contact – a reminder of the connections between attitude and concrete, goal-driven actions. These connections deserve much greater empirical focus in SLA research.

To summarize the social-psychological profile of this sample, these learners enjoy a combination of great personal desire and perceived need to attain to native-like levels in German for professional reasons. For those whose motivation has shifted, most report an increase over time, especially with regard to long-term goals that require excellent language abilities. These goals have often developed since arriving in Germany, in response to completing some level of academic study, or in response to forming more and deeper personal relationships (or both). For some, German as a second language takes on new significance over time as a central means to long-term integration, not just successful communication.

Perhaps not surprising, the desire for formal language study wanes as more time is spent in-country. Personal contacts become the greatest area of growth or change reported, and the primary means for achieving greater language fluency, according to the surveys. Even for those who report difficulties forming new friendships, such personal connections are seen as most beneficial to linguistic and cultural integration. In the absence of personal interaction, many learners work on their language through more passive means. Over time, opportunities to build close friendships tend to increase, as participants gain more confidence and seek out these opportunities. *All these findings confirm the connections between motivation, goal-setting, and concrete actions undertaken in pursuit of native-level attainment.*

As for instructional-cognitive factors, long-term language instruction plays a significant role in attainment, as does the learner's cumulative, indirect classroom experience in L2, even when it is not the subject of study, per se. These less direct but formal opportunities to reinforce learned structures apparently benefit the acquisition process as much as direct classroom instruction. While all participants enjoy a combination of direct and indirect language instruction, some rely strongly on formal practice in the absence of native speaker contacts. These findings, along with the marginal significance found for self-initiated strategies to improve pronunciation, suggest the importance of conscious practice and self-monitoring in reaching a native level. In fact, learner strategies are highly correlated to self-rating and to sense of satisfaction with attainment, substantiating the interconnectedness of cognitive and affective concerns.

Regarding the efficacy of certain types of instruction – marginally significant to outcome – communicative methods were more indicative of native levels of fluency, especially in combination with phonological emphases. Participants cite communicative approaches as most beneficial to language acquisition, and an important factor in motivation. (One respondent even remarked that she would not have continued learning German if the instructional focus had not shifted to a communicative approach after the first few years.) Heavier grammar or grammar-translation focus in early classroom experience seems to have led to uncertainty and hesitation in speaking, according to several reports. For these learners, it took several years of in-country experience, often limited to contact with other foreigners, to turn this hesitation around.

The importance of formal phonological instruction for long-term attainment is unclear from these data. Here, few subjects report any such training, and statistically significant relationships to outcome are not evident for such a small number. On an informal level, most acknowledge receiving some corrective feedback from native speakers, though inconsistent, on both segmental and suprasegmental levels. Such corrections typically occur during the early phases of learning when non-native accent is easily identifiable. Seldom is corrective feedback given at the advanced stages, even if learners ask for it. Some speculate that friends and acquaintances have simply stopped correcting for 'affective' reasons. Where communication gaps still occur, errors (usually lexical) are corrected. For this sample, this kind of informal feedback from native speakers shows a strong, if not significant relationship to outcome.

In the current study, L2 experience is purposefully described in terms of interactive as well as 'passive' engagement – a distinction in information processing that has been called into question, yet not completely dismissed. Here, this distinction is useful since passive, or non-interactive, activities do not appear in the list of statistically significant factors for attainment. At the same time, however, interactive factors appear weaker overall than expected. It is uncertain whether the instrument itself failed to capture the import of this realm, or whether these particular aspects of experience truly are weak, or indirect, indicators of attainment (especially in comparison to other factors tested). The experiential-interactive realm did exhibit numerous relationships to the other realms tested, and its relevance for attainment should not be disregarded.

As noted earlier, the range for interactive contact is high (50 hours weekly), with a Mean of 14.5 (SD at 14 is also very high). This range and SD indicate a wide degree of individual variability in access. A closer focus on interactive experience is suggested for future study, perhaps with an experimental design to more closely capture and isolate various aspects of this construct.

For this sample, clear support emerges for authentic communication as the most important means for strengthening fluency, eliciting needed feedback, and receiving spontaneous correction. Over time, the amount of German spoken seems to evolve as a measure of the relative strength and number of friendships with Germans. As discussed earlier, contact with native speakers does impact the learner's sense of satisfaction with attainment, degree of motivation, and perceptions of native-ness. Still, it does not appear that a relative lack of native speaker contact precludes an excellent, even native-like level of attainment, based on the performance of at least one participant. In her case, experience with the language through formal channels, and outstanding levels of motivation, may have somehow fostered the ability to attain to such a level.

All of these points must be considered against the general issue of the impact of age. Age of onset is shown here to connect impressively to experiential, instructional, social, and psychological variables, bringing us back to the question of the *nature* of maturational influence. According to traditional accounts, age holds a direct (and independent) level of explanation for late language learning. Yet even conservative viewpoints must acknowledge that age is not isolatable from its concomitant influences. The evidence and analyses presented here indicate that the directness and independence of age effects may be weaker than many earlier studies suggest. Moreover, optimal experience could mitigate maturation's negative influence. It is therefore reasonable to assert that the ultimate attainment 'story' is told as much by factors *coinciding* with maturation, such as motivation, access to instruction, sufficient authentic input, etc. These factors are all shown to exert their own independent effects here. In short, if maturation does influence SLA, this may be due as much to changes *beyond* the neuro-cognitive realm, as to those within it.

Throughout this work, I have argued that attainment relies on multiple factors, with the balance of each factor's strength highly variable across learners. Acknowledging the dynamic nature of these factors, it may not be possible to develop a simple model of late SLA, i.e. one that pinpoints the relative impact of any one factor or cluster of factors. Perhaps one cannot describe, much less *prescribe*, what *works* beyond individual cases. Nevertheless, the cumulative evidence presented here points to one firm conclusion:

While age of onset may exert independent influence on attainment, it does not provide a satisfactory explanation for non-native outcomes in SLA.

Its influence may be largely indirect, related to opportunities to build L2 experience, for example. After puberty, one's *intention* to achieve a certain status in the target language may ultimately influence the process, even constraining it in predictable ways. These possibilities receive greater attention in Chapter 4.

Age versus maturation

The issue has been raised whether age effects in SLA are tied to maturation itself, in which case the linear relationship between age and outcome would show a sudden or marked decline around puberty, or whether SLA is characterized by a more gradual decline indicative of general age effects (Birdsong, 2002; Johnson & Newport, 1989). If linearity appears to shift dramatically at maturation, this could indicate some developmental change, probably neurological rather than social-psychological or cognitive in nature. Alternatively, age effects may be relatively smooth, with no obvious 'flattening' or discontinuity of function (Birdsong, 2002; see Flege *et al.*, 1995 – cited in Birdsong, 2002).

In the previous section, I noted a continuation of linearity between age of onset and attainment beyond the age of 15 (Graph 3.1), the age at which linearity appeared to drop off dramatically in the Johnson and Newport study (1989). However, in both the current study and the Johnson and Newport study, no one with an AO beyond 15 reaches a native level. This suggests a shift in age effects around the 10–12 year range. To plot these possible changes more accurately, groups of AO were tabulated and graphed, initially with only three distinct groups: 0–10 years, 11–14 years,

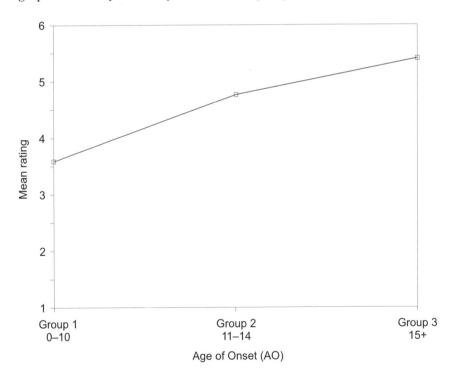

Graph 3.3 Mean rating according to AO group (*n* = 25)

and 15 and beyond. ANOVA analysis confirmed the significance of these group differences (F at $p< 0.03$). This is shown below in Graph 3.3.

According to Graph 3.3, age effects look steady: the older the learner at initial onset with L2, the higher (less native) the mean rating (1 = definitely native, 2 = native, 3 = probably native, and so on up to 6 = definitely non-native). These results could be interpreted as proof of general age effects, but some information may be lost in the large range of ages in each group. To check the validity of this slope, a more narrowly defined range of ages per group was set up, graphed below as follows: 0–9 years, 10–12 years, 13–15 years, and 16 and up. ANOVA confirmed a higher significance for the F value ($p < 0.0009$) assigned to these group differences (Graph 3.4).

Graph 3.4 more clearly shows a steep and steady slope from birth to the age of 10, then a less dramatic (but clearly identifiable) slope from 10 (Group 2) to approximately 13 or 14 (Group 3). By the time the learner is 15, linearity appears to cease altogether, and individual variability takes over. It seems that age effects are not strong across the entire spectrum of AO, as

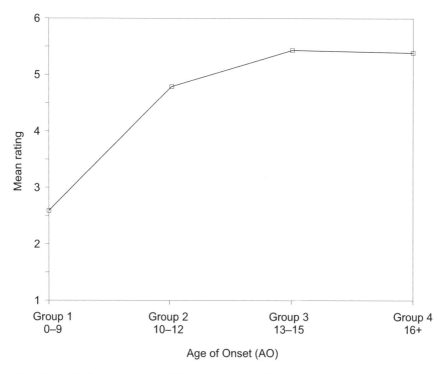

Graph 3.4 Mean rating to AO group, revised ($n = 25$)

some studies have shown (Patkowski, 1980; Oyama, 1976 – cited in Birdsong, 2002), but are somehow bound to maturation, yet continuing for several years beyond it. Continuing declines beyond age 12 indicate the possibility that something other than maturation is at play. Though maturation implies a host of changes (including, but not restricted to, neurological ones), a general age effect may continue until early adulthood. Thus, the influence of age comes into play well before maturity, appearing from earliest childhood, and continuing, though with less predictive strength, throughout puberty and for several years beyond.[10] These shifts in linearity support the argument that other factors play increasingly important roles in language acquisition as certain neurological changes stabilize at puberty.

Exceptional learners

With few exceptions, immersion-type empirical studies do not account for exposure through long-term instruction and multiple contexts for interaction. As noted earlier, this sample of learners could be described as optimally oriented to SLA. They are highly motivated, interested in developing native-level fluency for both personal and professional reasons, and they have benefited from language experience across a range of formal and informal contexts. As such, they may be considered exceptional in comparison to many late learners. Still, the group differences between native and non-native speakers were strongly and significantly apparent; only a few non-native speakers cross the boundary into native-level performance. Who are these few, and which aspects of their experience or orientation may account for their exceptional abilities?

Exploring these questions is the focus of the next chapter, where age of onset's influence is treated as essentially connected to psychological, social, and instructional aspects of the learner's experience. The issue of the relative strength of the various factors is especially important for understanding special cases: those who appear to defy critical period predictions. Through a careful, qualitative analysis, the relative impact of age, motivation, instruction, cultural affiliations, etc. may become clearer. Accordingly, the next chapter emphasizes individual opportunities for personal contact, senses of belonging and cultural identity, as well as attitudes toward the target language and its culture.

Notes

1. Krashen (1981), among others, has argued for an earlier close of the critical period, and Long (1990) has posited multiple critical periods for various subsystems of language, e.g. younger for phonology than for morpho-syntax (see Chapter 1).

2. Two participants had a German-speaking parent but classified themselves as non-native speakers of German because, according to their own reports, the other language was emphasized in the household and their identities were more firmly rooted in the other language. Nevertheless, because their AO was effectively 0 (they were consistently exposed to German and grew up speaking it simultaneously with the other language), they were removed from the regression analyses to prevent skewing these tests, and the correlation analyses were rerun to compare results without them. These differences are noted throughout the discussion.

3. One word on the paragraph reading test caused problems: a borrowing from English, 'service,' which is commonly used in German, but would presumably be unfamiliar to those with little or no experience with English. Several of the non-native speakers from Russia and Poland stumbled on this word and had to repeat themselves as they tried to approximate the sounds accurately. This may have contributed to a more non-native rating .

4. In a correlation analysis between task ratings and background variables, all tasks confirmed the correlations presented below for Mean Rating overall, meaning that the same variables were found to be as significant for individual task performance as overall. However, two additional findings are worth mentioning. First, the word list task performance was substantially tied to the context in which the learner was first exposed to German ($p < 0.06$) in the following relationship: the more isolated and formal the first exposure, the poorer the performance – tutors and later exposure at university in particular indicated more non-native ratings. For the third task (free speaking), consistency of motivation was significant at $p < 0.04$ as follows: shifting motivation was indicative of poorer performance. These two findings could be tied to AO in ways that will be discussed in the following sections.

5. The regression analyses experimented only with the first four variables (Table 3.13) of the highest significance, in order to maximize the r^2 values of each model.

6. These findings hold when the outliers are excluded, except that frequency of spoken interaction loses its statistical significance, as noted.

7. Pragmatics was the lowest reported priority among the raters; grammar was second to phonology/pronunciation.

8. Without the two outliers, results were the same, with two exceptions: frequency of spoken contact with native speakers lost its significant (mentioned previously), and personal motivation to improve German appears significant at $p < 0.04$ for AO and at $p < 0.0009$ for LOR.

9. Since participants' discussion on identity issues and cultural belonging do not lend themselves well to quantitative measures, the connections between AO and social-cultural issues will be taken up in the next chapter.

10. It should be noted that no distinctions were made to separate groups from one another, for example into 'early' versus 'late' learners, thereby showing disaggregated samples.

Chapter 4

Understanding Identity, Intention, and Opportunities for L2 Contact: The Qualitative Findings

The analysis presented in Chapter 3 introduces empirical evidence challenging the notion that age of exposure is primarily responsible for outcomes in late language learning. In cases of later exposure, psychological factors, contact opportunities, and intention to become native-like may play the greatest roles in attainment. Similarly, in the face of inadequate linguistic input, targeted practice and feedback may be necessary to develop this level of fluency. These concerns all point to the essentially personal and unique nature of language learning. Even where opportunities for contact and authentic input abound, individuals exercise some measure of choice, meaning that their decisions and actions vis-à-vis the target language (TL) and its community of speakers play a significant role in ultimate attainment.

Such ideas are not new, yet they have hardly been explored in the research on age effects in SLA. *Intention*, in some ways similar to Norton Pierce's (1995) idea of *investment*, may drive the learner's eventual attainment by profoundly impacting engagement with the target language. Thus, how effectively and consistently the learner utilizes available linguistic resources, may be a deciding factor in *constraints* on attainment. Those who consistently pursue native-level status may have the greatest success toward that goal, regardless of age of onset. The converse can also be reasonably assumed. In short, we may better understand the developmental process (and ultimate attainment) by exploring how the learner 'enters into the conversation,' or engages with those external opportunities (Norton Pierce, 2002). This chapter explores such issues for these advanced learners, emphasizing how a sense of self in L2 emerges in response to both internal drives and developing experience.

As pointed out in Chapter 3, the age factor may pertain to access, as well as to a sense of determination to pursue native-like fluency. Understanding these connections may be best served through qualitative methods, such as introspection and interview techniques. Additionally, qualitative data are invaluable for studying special cases – learners who impress by exceeding expectations (and even those who fall short of native-ness in spite of optimal experience and orientation). I have maintained throughout that the nature of significant relationships can only be illuminated when the individual learner's experience is taken into account.

The objective of this qualitative analysis is therefore to explore: (1) how L2 development is supported through external resources and opportunities; (2) how long-term attainment is influenced by the learner's socio-psychological orientation to the target language and its community of speakers, and (3) how a sense of belonging develops in that linguistic and cultural context. Several broad questions guide this inquiry:

(1) Which aspects of L2 experience should be considered fundamental to ultimate attainment?
(2) How do psychological orientations and experiences in the target-language country influence specific behaviors and goals in the process?
(3) How do constructs such as linguistic identity and belonging connect to other potential influences on attainment, such as intention to reside and/or affiliate with the target language culture?

To address these questions, interview data will be presented according to thematic content on learner attitudes, goals, and opportunities to develop L2 experience. Comparative examples will enhance this discussion, and one special case will follow the thematic sections. I conclude with a section on the importance of the intention to reside in-country as it relates to language attainment and sense of belonging in the target language.

Instruments and Procedure

As mentioned in Chapter 3, non-native participants agreed to an interview immediately following the linguistic tasks. A near-native speaker of German (L1 English) conducted the interviews entirely in German. Because the interviewer was also non-German, as well as an advanced student with connections to these institutions of higher learning, no particular features of social distance or disparity in language abilities were predicted (or apparent). Following a warm-up phase, participants generally described how they came to Germany, under what circumstances, what their programs of interest were, etc. As the interview questions gradually probed areas of greater introspection, participants were forthcoming about personal experiences that had colored their attitudes toward both the German language and culture. Because the interviews were semi-structured, participants recounted their impressions freely. Each interview took a natural, conversational course at its own tempo (see Appendix 5).[1]

Thematic Presentation of Results

Throughout the interviews, several themes emerged as significant to target language development, including:

(1) opportunities for L2 contact;
(2) attitudes toward L2 and the target language community;
(3) sense of self in L2, particularly in reference to motivation and perceived functions of L2; and
(4) issues of cultural affiliation and identity.

These considerations reveal that experience and perceptions together contribute to the learner's sense of self in the target language.

Opportunities for contact with native speakers

Some of the strongest evidence for the influence of personal contact comes from the German studies on immersion, or primarily uninstructed, language acquisition. In the earliest phases (1970s), researchers were forced to acknowledge the difficult socio-political situation of most immigrant learners of German. Though the various strands of the German as a second language research (GLA) vary greatly in both theoretical stance and empirical method, on the whole, there is strong evidence for the significance of personal contact to native speakers for ultimate (and short-term) attainment (see discussion, at the end of the chapter).

Because there is such strong evidence for the centrality of contact, this construct was addressed in the written survey and discussed at length in the interview. Participants were asked about contact with Germans in the context of describing their work, study, etc., any connections they had to their home country, whether their living situation brought them into contact with people from other places, and so on. Contact opportunities varied markedly across individuals, with about half reporting sufficient access to native speakers of German, and the same amount reporting minimal contact. What stands out from the interviews is a pervasive sense of difficulty in making new friends (though a few do not report any unusual difficulty in this area). Those who have lived among other foreigners in student dorms, for example, generally report greater contact with other foreigners. One Polish student describes it thus:

I feel good here, but the problem is that I have so little contact with

Germans, even in the dorm here. I would like to ... see if I could do better if I were in a different situation socially, where I wasn't just among foreign students who are here [temporarily]. I would like to see if I would be accepted for myself.

Another Polish woman reports similar disappointments:

At the university, I got to know fewer people than I expected to or wanted to because of the nature of the university here – one comes and goes as one pleases. In Poland you have to show up to class and get to know others. Here, you have no obligation to talk to others, so it was harder. It took me longer to get to know people.

These remarks reveal that difficulties with acceptance may be anticipated to some extent, especially regarding encounters with the general public. (Those who consider themselves to be identifiably 'non-German' or physically 'foreign' looking report more unpleasant encounters.) Expectations for easy contact may also differ appreciably according to cultural background. One Russian immigrant notes his desire for greater frequency of contact and more emotional intimacy than he has thus far experienced in Germany. At the same time, this does not prevent him from adapting to those differences and pursuing new friendships. Another immigrant from Slovakia, Belinda, recognizes the element of mutual responsibility in forging personal contacts:

Belinda: ... The point is [that] if I seek out contact, I can get it. The question is [then] about maintaining those [friendships] ...

Interviewer: Is it important for you to have those kinds of contacts?

Belinda: That has more to do with the person. Many people say it is hard to get to know Germans, and it's really a problem for them. But it hasn't been for me. If you aren't really proficient with the language or you have a strong accent, it's probably true that it's harder to make contacts, but for me, I don't differentiate between Germans and others. I'm open to making all kinds of friends.

Belinda's comments underscore the negotiative nature of social assimilation. Contact must ultimately be welcome on both sides, and maintaining such connections may become more difficult as one gets older – a phenomenon several participants confirm. Maturation can thus be seen as related to social adaptation, in mutually constitutive ways, impacting access to quality linguistic input. This recalls Pavlenko's recent suggestion that factors traditionally described as 'individual' (such as age, gender, ethnicity, and even psychological factors) are also 'socially constituted ... [they] have clear social origins, and are shaped and reshaped by the contexts in which the learners find themselves' (2002: 280f).

Reconciling early expectations with reality often leads to the need to adjust plans of action, according to these learners. Across all the interviews, patterns of individual adaptation strategies emerge. Certain strategic behaviors target the specific need to enhance language skills, others combine language exposure with social engagement. These patterns of behavior are activated from the earliest stages after arrival. For some who began with a primary emphasis on study, close relationships end up taking the place of formal instruction over time, and friendships become the primary source for real language input. Where specific courses of action become established (e.g. through work, assistantships, or independent projects), overt instruction often becomes an endeavor that requires too much time and energy. In general, the perceived need for overt instruction lessens as language fluency and social stability are strengthened. For those with fewer personal contacts, formal or even 'passive' sources of language input compensate for lack of direct interaction. Several participants frequently read and listen to the radio to reflect consciously on language structures, phonological features, etc. For instance, they read aloud or imitate native speakers on the radio, pushing themselves to approximate a native sound (88% of the sample report engaging in these kinds of strategies consciously).

Another common strategy for linguistic development is actually avoiding speakers of their own mother tongue to ease linguistic (if not cultural) assimilation into the target language. One Polish immigrant woman, who had lived in Germany since the age of 14, describes how her avoidance of other Poles has served an important purpose for her:

> From the very beginning I wanted to speak as much German as possible ... then I got to know my best friend ... and gradually I had to speak more and more German as I got to know people, and Polish was just the language I spoke with my parents.

These remarks serve as a reminder that, for each immigrant, the balance between mother tongue and target language shifts as the function of each language changes. A daily reliance on L2 necessarily leads to a loss in the communicative function of L1. These shifts, in turn, impact on linguistic identity. Several participants commented on their efforts to either avoid mother tongue speakers, or to initiate conversations with them *in German*. They see this as important for maintaining consistency in their linguistic input and practice. Undoubtedly, their willingness to consciously (even doggedly) pursue interaction in German, and even to ask for overt feedback, has had a measurable impact on their fluency as well as on their linguistic identity over the long-term.

Most study participants take proactive steps to increase contact, for example to follow up informal acquaintances in the hopes that deeper friendships will develop. Accordingly, such friendships become more meaningful over time, leading to greater confidence in the language as breadth and depth of self-expression increase. As noted in the last chapter, many participants say that personal contact has been the most effective and important aspect of their experience in-country for developing near-native fluency. This importance is based on a combination of authentic input and feedback on lexical, syntactic, and especially suprasegmental skill. Many participants often say they wish for more direct feedback from friends and acquaintances.

As reported, interactive contact is significantly correlated to perceptions of fluency, sense of satisfaction with language attainment, and intensity of motivation toward L2. While it is important to note that multiple sources of language contact do not, by themselves, ensure native-level attainment for anyone in this sample, it is evident that consistent contact significantly correlates to higher intensity in motivation. In turn, motivation significantly correlates to strategies for improved fluency (especially phonological accuracy). In addition, learners who view German as essential to their futures pursue more contact domains, and use German exclusively in those domains. They also report greater satisfaction with their own attainment. (Those with lower satisfaction reported engaging in fewer such behaviors.)

Personal contact with native speakers has not been adequately or consistently addressed up to now in the empirical research on ultimate attainment (see discussion at the end of the chapter). The essential nature of its contribution to acquisition is not completely clear. High levels of contact may lead to certain social and cognitive strategies that directly impact language attainment, not to mention affective orientations to the task, such as motivation. The strategies reported here show some sensitivity toward (and ability to adapt to) shifts in language contact, especially in terms of intensity and consistency. It is possible that contact influences motivation, sense of self in L2, etc., leading to specific strategies to enhance access and experience. These relationships are surely circular in nature: if motivation and confidence lead to greater contact, contact must also lead to greater confidence, etc. This idea is supported here by participant comments. As their confidence in the language increased, they felt able to seek closer connections to native speakers. (This issue is highlighted in the following sections and revisited in the chapter conclusion.)

Attitudes toward the target language culture

Attitudes toward L2 have long been thought to contribute to SLA, though definitions of the construct itself have been difficult to come by, and methodological approaches are inconsistent (Baker, 1992; see Skehan, 1989; and chapter conclusion for more discussion). For this study, attitudes were ascertained through questions on whether participants felt 'at home,' and whether any in-country experiences had led to changes in attitudes. By asking about real experiences, attitudes were contextualized, and individual perspectives on cultural difference emerged. Across these interviews, similar impressions of 'the German mentality' emerged. Of greatest interest for this study are the psychological and social adjustments made as learners reckoned with those cultural differences.

In these interviews, attitudes toward cultural differences are usually expressed with some measure of distance and neutrality. Differences are either accepted at face value, or else learners learn to see them as potentially positive. In essence, they tend to negotiate awkward gaps in perspective, values, etc., with an eye on the bigger picture: the opportunity to live in Germany. Since their appreciation for this opportunity is often expressed in these contexts, I assume that the symbolic function of Germany (as land of opportunity, future plans, etc.) overrides most negative evaluations. Below, excerpts illustrate how individuals adapt to potential conflicts, and even convince themselves to turn them into opportunities for personal growth.

Numerous accounts of a German emphasis on 'correctness,' and 'precision' are often associated with verbal directness. (Several even note that German acquaintances have urged them to be more assertive verbally.) A few report feeling either intimidated by this quality or resistant to accepting it. In terms of adaptation, many had turned this initial intimidation around; they now see directness as a reflection of greater self-confidence and self-reliance – a 'German' attribute to emulate. One Polish immigrant, Dora, remarks:

> At the beginning I was shocked at how things were – that weeks would go by and no one would speak to me. And [later] I thought maybe I would get to know people at the university, but that wasn't the case. That was shocking for me. I found Germany to be cold and profit-oriented. But with time, the older I got, the more I thought it could be pleasant to just live my own life without worrying about others. This perspective I learned to see as positive instead of negative. I guess I've become half-socialized in this way ...

Many of the interviewees report occasional, negative experiences, usually in retail stores, post offices and other administrative offices. One question raised by a number of participants was whether unfriendly treatment was specifically targeted at them as foreigners. However, most say they have adopted a philosophical approach to such difficulties. Alex, an immigrant from Russia says, 'Over time you learn that it does no good to do anything back. You learn that you can just as easily make friends as enemies here.' A Frenchwoman, noting that her foreignness is much more of an issue in Germany than in France (she is part Indian), describes the problem as partly mutual:

> One feels like a foreigner when one is partially foreign, but here you have the feeling that people are noticing it [more]. But then, if you have the impression that you're a foreigner, you'll have the impression that others are noticing that.

This sense of personal responsibility, and its accompanying psychological flexibility, is a striking adaptive feature among this group. It may rely, in part, on their excellent linguistic abilities in German. In difficult situations (especially among strangers or civil servants), only one person reported being reluctant to speak up in her own defense. For the most part, few say that personal experiences have led to lasting negative impressions. (The only serious complaint for many is homesickness.)

In mentioning individualism and self-assertiveness as German attributes, participants say it is important to understand both sides of that coin. On the one hand, greater self-reliance is necessary in a culture that expects you to make your own decisions; on the other hand, it is not always easy to connect to others, or even to get help when you need it, according to some. The Polish immigrant, Dora, illustrates the problem as follows:

> What I don't like I have long since learned to live with, and that's the fact that you don't ask people for help here. I know that is not done. When you do, they will probably help you, but next time they avoid a person who needs help ... Relationships are based on the understanding that you must fend for yourself. I don't really like that, but I've learned to live with it.

Some describe the relative lack of psychological and social dependence as liberating. In particular, those from Eastern European countries and the former Soviet Union report great appreciation for so much personal freedom relative to their home countries. They enjoy coming to their own decisions regarding their future plans, career paths, etc. Dora describes this freedom in terms of greater privacy:

I'm free-floating [here] and don't belong anywhere in particular ... the mentality is of course, different, so I have some difficulties with that. Because I'm 33 [years old] and doing things on my own, where in Poland everyone expects me to get married – no one expects that here and that's exciting and liberating, the fact that you don't owe anyone any explanations here of what you are: gay, pregnant, old, young, or whatever you are, you don't have to explain it to anyone here.

In many cases, greater personal freedom has led to greater self-reflection and emotional maturity. One woman says, 'I trust myself here, I'm self-reliant and that plays a big role in how I feel here.' Another immigrant describes how the desire for self-reliance actually motivated her move to Germany:

I wanted to test myself, to see if could bear up in a strange place, someplace interesting, and whether I could master another language, and I wanted to see how I am on my own, because we are influenced by others, by our environment, and I wanted to find out what part of me comes from [just] me, and what part is from others. I wanted to test myself and maybe change myself somewhat ... I have already changed, but I'm not yet satisfied.

These learners may be 'exceptional' in their attitudes; most of them hold German society in high esteem, aspiring to absorb as much of the culture and language as possible. Mara, a Russian immigrant remarks:

Sometimes I make a conscious effort to remind myself what I have in common with Germans when I come across a situation where I might react negatively as a Russian ... I don't have to react ... if I understand how and why a German is doing something.

These comments reveal a conscious effort to control negative reactions, which is not always easy. In principle, any feature attributed to the 'German mentality' can be understood from both positive and negative angles. For example, several mention a strong tendency in German culture to engage in socio-political and philosophical debate. One consequence of this is that Germans often compare their cultural practices with those of other countries, 'requiring' the interlocutor to 'take the other side.' While this often leads to valuable new perspectives, according to these comments, it can also cause 'mental fatigue,' when one feels obliged to (falsely) defend the home country. Those specific examples aside, there is a widespread reluctance among these immigrants to criticize cultural differences. 'It isn't a question of whether I like it,' says Alex, 'it's just that we have other mentalities. These cannot be judged.'

It is clear that the 'foreigner' concept is a salient aspect of everyday life in Germany. For most immigrants, this is not a positive experience. At the same time, feeling like a foreigner has often led to new insights that may not otherwise be possible. The subsequent adjustments in perception and understanding, while positive on the whole, are highly idiosyncratic. Not all wish to view their own cultures so critically, nor do they wish to fully adopt German culture. One of the Americans, Drew, is especially blunt in his remarks:

> There's a paradox, namely, that I have to get clear with this country, with these people, this city, and try to lead my day-to-day life with some kind of pleasure. On the other hand, I don't want to fit in to this kind of stiff-necked – no more than I already am [laughter] – idea that I am not loud enough, not insistent enough, even in the simple things like buying fruit [from a vendor] ... I'm tired of being told that I'm not confrontational enough ... I just have no desire to act like that.

Such a conscious resistance to acculturate may have had profound consequences for Drew's language acquisition. Although he has five years' experience in-country and considerable German instruction as well (also five years in-country), he says he feels 'alienated' – a feeling he says has caused him to reflect a great deal on his sense of belonging in Germany. Although he has several acquaintances, he has not assimilated to any great extent. The linguistic task ratings confirm that he is nowhere near native; his fluency was judged at the 'definitely non-native' level (Mean Rating 5.75). How may these potential connections between attitudes and language acquisition be understood in the context of his overall experience?

Drew began to study the German language at the age of 30 – definitely a late learner. While an argument could easily be made for neuro-cognitive constraints with such a late AO, socio-psychological considerations may be equally strong in his case. His conscious disdain for German culture, reinforced through personal experience with the general public (and even through his study of German history and culture, he says), has led to very negative impressions that color his day-to-day existence. His investment in the German culture is arguably quite low. If anything is emphasized in his interview, it is personal disappointment and discomfort during his residence in-country.

Drew's story illustrates the negative impact that age and experience can have on language attainment. His language experience might otherwise appear optimal, with its combination of naturalistic (immersion) experience and formal instruction. However, his psychological orientation to the culture, his perceptions of everyday experiences, and an emphasis on his own shortcomings in the language resonate clearly throughout.

The importance of attitudes is underscored throughout his interview. He tends to openly reflect on his weak potential (and low desire) for native-level linguistic assimilation (not to mention cultural). Drew admits he has fossilized in certain areas of German phonology and morphology. At the same time, he disregards feedback on those features, even though German is important for his future, according to his comments. Drew's writing is marked by ungrammatical and incomplete sentences (he wrote extensive comments on almost all of the survey items). His spoken language is often difficult to understand owing to his fragmented and somewhat incoherent style. His accent is recognizably foreign, though he speaks without hesitation and has an impressive vocabulary. Drew has clearly accepted his non-native status, and does not seem to want to surpass it at this point.

Though Drew's approach to language learning is difficult to unravel here, it is clearly marked by ambivalence and contradiction. In terms of motivation, he does not place himself in the highest category, but says German has become increasingly important for him over time. (This calls to mind the issue of *intention* toward linguistic fluency, *as separate from cultural or social investment* – see Norton Pierce, 1995, 2000.) As Drew's case shows, one does not imply the other. He needs the linguistic fluency for his future career, but rejects the culture. Living in Germany forces Drew to maintain a kind of psychological schism: the language and culture must be separate. In this way, he preserves his (non-German) identity and can continue to prioritize the language. Certainly in his case, *intention* is a complicated matter: Drew says he never 'feels German,' nor does he wish to be taken for a native speaker. Still, he wishes for more contact with Germans; his current level of isolation is something he would like to see change for the better.

One of the most interesting insights gained from this interview is that survival strategies may allow a learner to reconcile negative experiences and attitudes with long-term goals. However, such negative orientations do appear to impact linguistic attainment, even demonstrating that fossilization can be a matter of conscious choice.

Sense of self in L2: motivation, behavior, and language function

For a language learner living in-country, the connections between attitudes and experience may constitute a sort of psychological 'feedback loop.' Positive attitudes may enhance or encourage positive experiences, and vice versa. At the same time, the story above illustrates the degree to which the language may be viewed as separate from its cultural framework. Several participants experience a similar schism, though of a decidedly more positive nature. For them also, the language is a goal in and of itself. Of those interviewed, 80% point to German language fluency as necessary for future professional plans; 84% express a personal desire to achieve greater fluency, and this drive is remarkably consistent – two aspects of psychological orientation significantly correlated to outcome. In practical terms therefore, these drives may constitute a base of support that positively influences L2 experience and eventual attainment.

The analysis in Chapter 3 reveals that high satisfaction and motivational intensity are connected to individual strategies initiated to improve language fluency, as well as greater contact. Based on these findings, along with the existing research (see discussion in Chapter 2), I have argued that motivational intensity and consistency, self-perceptions of language ability, and concrete behaviors are connected in essential (and possibly circular) ways. The excerpts below illustrate how specific attitudes and behaviors may reflect such a cluster of factors. The individual strategies cited seem to emerge when learner expectations and real experience do not neatly synchronize. Where social and psychological adjustments are needed, a fundamental connection to the language per se may be the steadiest aspect of the learner's approach.

These individuals develop a sense of self in German in some common ways. Reflecting on one's own strengths and goals seems to feed the determination to work toward native-like attainment. As an example, Anja, a Polish immigrant, has consistently made an effort to speak as much German as possible since arriving in Germany eight years ago. She quickly made close friends with a native speaker, consciously reaching out to others in order to get past her 'overly formalized German' from earlier school days. Several others report proficiency in the language upon arrival, but quickly discover awkward gaps in linguistic and pragmatic knowledge. As a result, they were forced to acknowledge that their 'classroom German' was insufficient, particularly for conversational fluency. This realization caused them early on to seek out more domains for interaction in German.

Many describe how they came to rely on the German language as essential to survival and self-sufficiency; the mother tongue was thus maintained only through contacts with friends and relatives back home (depending on the age at immigration – early immigrants still speak the mother tongue at home). Several report this shift in balance between L1 and L2 as a conscious decision. Anja, for example, has enthusiastically pursued multiple avenues for language contact from the very beginning. Today, she speaks Polish only with her parents. Dora (also Polish) has similarly relied on German from her earliest stage of arrival, yet continues to be reluctant to seek contact. Dora spends fewer than 10 hours per week actually interacting with native speakers – most of her language input is 'passive' as she describes it, e.g. through television, radio, etc. Nevertheless, her motivation to learn the language has been consistently strong. She describes her fundamental connection to the language thus:

> I love the language. It's the only thing I can do well. If I go a few months without speaking German I feel very nervous … I actually speak very little from day to day, but I just need to hear television or people talking on the street, and if I forget something [in German] it's as if someone has taken away a part of myself. The loss of any part of the language is traumatic for me.

Dora has clearly incorporated the language as an essential part of her identity. This strong connection to German has carried her through difficult transitions in the early phases after arrival, and continues to help her to cope with the social distance she still experiences, even after six years. Dora, by her own admission, has not striven to change her social circumstances. Instead, she frequently imitates native speech to improve her fluency, particularly her phonological authenticity. Dora scored within the native speaker range, despite her relative social isolation, and perhaps largely due to an embrace of the language as essential to her identity.

Almost without exception, these participants say they have struggled to develop a sense of self vis-à-vis the language and the culture. In spite of frequent setbacks socially, the overwhelming majority expresses a consistent drive toward native-level language acquisition: 80% say they definitely need it for their future careers (mostly *in Germany*); 84% persist for personal reasons. For this sample, a strong combination of motivational forces influences their pursuits. The sense of importance and prestige afforded the language itself comes through clearly in the interviews. Many simply enjoy the challenge that relying on a second language presents.

Learning to rely on the target language may be a relatively smooth transition when learners consciously regard this process as a means to greater personal growth. In fact, this is the most common characterization among these learners. The German language serves communicative functions as well as a symbolic one: it represents the locus of the culture where they hope to find acceptance. In essence, its value is interwoven with a very real sense of self and place, now and in the future. Since many hope to settle permanently in Germany, near-native status is key to a greater sense of belonging and acceptance.

As noted in Chapter 3, stronger language ability implies increased confidence. Dan, an American, says, ' I do ask questions, or start to talk, and I notice that after awhile I feel a little better, a little braver, that I can do this, so I start to slowly feel good.' Another immigrant from Great Britain remarks, 'Things have got better with time as I've got better with the language and I've become more self-confident.' Citing Clément's earlier work, Noels *et al.* (1966) describe the development of confidence as essential to developing social contacts, not to mention an identity in L2:

> Aspects of contact with the second language group, such as the frequency and quality of contact, lead to variations in the individual's level of linguistic self-confidence. Self-confidence, defined as self-perceptions of communicative competence and concomitant low levels of anxiety in using the second language, leads to an increased usage of, and communicative competence in, the second language. (Noels *et al.*, 1996: 248)

Thus, a circularity (like that posited for motivation) is operating here, according to these researchers. Based on the results of their study, self-confidence in L2 leads to higher quality contact, less contact with L1 speakers, and more involvement overall in the L2 community (Noels *et al.*, 1996; for the relationship between motivation and self-confidence, see Labrie & Clément, 1986). One participant in this study puts it succinctly: 'The better one's language abilities, the easier it is to develop good contacts.'

Confidence may be an underlying aspect of the 'satisfaction with attainment' factor found to be so significant in the quantitative analysis (Chapter 3). From this instrument, it is difficult to say. In any case, satisfaction and confidence are two important aspects of a developing sense of ability in German – noted by these participants in interesting (and unexpected) ways. Neither the interview protocol nor the written survey pointedly ask about 'sense of self,' yet this information was spontaneously offered in the context of questions about course of study, contexts for using German, and attitudes about connecting to the L2 community.

Two points are worth reiterating with regards to positive attitudes and developing L2 experience. First, a positive assessment of one's own language abilities significantly correlates not only to actual outcome (at $p < 0.0009$), but also to numerous other factors, including motivational consistency and frequency of spoken interaction with native speakers. (Again, a circularity of related variables seems likely here.) Arianne, a Frenchwoman, describes connecting to L2 as her ultimate reason for residing in-country. 'I don't learn to speak so that I can stay, rather, I stay so that I can continue to speak German. It's backwards, I guess.' Second, motivation may not suffer from the 'reality' of non-native status. This sense of the language as a worthwhile endeavor in and of itself is underscored by this fact: most participants believe they do not consistently sound native, if at all, yet their motivational intensity is quite high (88% report it as strong or very strong). (Only 24% report strong satisfaction with their current language abilities, and just as many are not satisfied). The fact is, these learners are realistic about their own attainment and this does not deter their desire to sound native (88% say it is important or very important to them). This begs the question: *what social and psychological functions are served by the target language, and what impact could these have on attainment?*

The transition to exclusive reliance on German has been difficult for some. Those who still feel unable to express themselves as clearly in German (as compared with L1) say they appreciate any opportunity to use their first language. For them, language choice is clearly linked to instrumental and symbolic functions. For example, the mother tongue may represent a 'return' of sorts to an earlier time in life, a previous identity, as well as a symbol of intimacy or shared understanding. By contrast, German is often described as a 'tool' for communicative and professional purposes, but also as a language with symbolic value – as an endeavor in itself, as a representation of German literature, history, etc. These functions are salient and significant in the experience of these learners – they are not mere abstractions. Depending on the context, the choice of German over Polish, or Russian over German, etc., demonstrates solidarity or distance to the learner's interlocutors. These ideas recall Norton Pierce's (1995), assertion that identity is multiple and contradictory and the post-structuralist idea that L2 users are 'agents in charge of their own learning' (Pavlenko, 2002: 293). L2 learners are aware of the various struggles and conflicts they face, and the role that language plays therein. Their engagement in the process is both active and marked by self-reflection.

An unexpected twist on language choice is also revealed in several interviews. Some informants describe how they 'play' with language identity, i.e. purposefully misrepresenting their national heritage for their own amusement, as they put it. This usually takes place when traveling to other countries (or even when traveling back home!) among strangers. Those who engage in this kind of play say they enjoy the fact that their German is so advanced that they can 'fool' others into thinking they are 'really German.' This may be an important manifestation of 'integrative motivation,' if indeed these learners really hope to appear German in foreign contexts. (There is a subtext here, namely, that it would be harder to convince Germans of their native-ness.) The fact that these stories were not unusual shows that identity represents a conscious choice, that it is flexible, and that there may be some special purpose in passing for a native speaker, particularly as a temporary performance (see Davies, 2003; Piller, 2002).

Perceptions of foreignness and belonging

Given the growing body of research on the significance of identity and belonging in SLA (see chapter conclusion for discussion), these issues are addressed here through questions on cultural affiliation, sense of well-being (*wohl fühlen*), and sense of identity in Germany. According to these data, each participant defines these issues in unique ways. For example, Alex offers this simple description of belonging: 'Sometimes you ask yourself where home is, and what home is, and it's really a question of where you feel most secure, and that's what I feel right now in Berlin.' At the same time, Alex refers to everyday reminders of his 'foreignness' (such anecdotes were the rule, not the exception). Although a sense of well being is widespread for these learners, notions of belonging are much less generalizable. For example, Anja and Dora, two Eastern Europeans who arrived in German in early adolescence, have very different accounts of Germany as home:

> I see myself as someone who belongs here. I don't feel different here. When people say 'we' I know that they don't include me, but I can join in … I belong to the society here … and I can get around very well here, but I definitely don't have a patriotic feeling about Germany, as if it were my 'home,' absolutely not. (Anja)

> My home is here, and I actually feel much more at home here than I do in Poland. I would really like to stay. (Dora)

In terms of national affiliation and identity, participants differ in the emphasis they place on heritage:

> I've never had such a situation where I've felt strongly like a Ukrainian … I mean, to feel like that I would have to identify with the Ukrainian people. Till now I haven't had any desire to do that. I'm Ukrainian according to my passport, and according to my background, and I can certainly speak the language well, but that doesn't mean that I have such a national awareness that I would proclaim my Ukrainian identity … There are certain things that one can think of which make one proud, or make one want to be identified as Ukrainian. Soccer, for example [laughter], but otherwise the most important thing is to simply feel that you identify with others … (Alex)

Identity may overlap with a sense of belonging, but it should be understood as a distinct construct. Some learners describe a sense of belonging and comfort in Germany, even though their essential identity does not come into question, for example:

> I'm Polish, and that's how it is ... I would always be aware of my Polish heritage, no matter how good I felt here, and even though I might feel better here than in Poland. So I could see myself as both in a sense, or as belonging to a European sense of identity. If I lived in England, I would eventually feel like I belonged there too! (Anja)

Perceptions of foreignness are not always cast in a negative light. However, some ambivalence is common to the experience of many:

> I don't think I could ever really feel like I belong here, or like a German. It has something to do with character, humor, worldview ... a kind of attitude I believe I'll always have ... In society at large, I've sometimes had the feeling that I'll never be able to completely mix in here, or the Germans will never understand me and it's either about the language or the mentality. (Jeff)

> When I first arrived, I was constantly comparing things, how things were done, and now much less so, and I don't assume that the French way is necessarily the best way. Now these differences still occur to me, but not in the same way ... I feel much more like a European and [no longer] like I'm French. I don't think about specific nationalities anymore. I think as Europeans we have to find a compromise ... I find this old allegiance idea outdated. (Arianne)

While each person makes unique psychological and social adjustments to immigration, when taken together, their stories reveal interesting similarities. The struggle to find a sense of belonging typically refers to past, present, and future affiliations. In negotiating such affiliations, most emphasize their willingness to find new ways of being, and to help themselves through the process by utilizing all available resources for greater contact. For instance, domains of friendship, recreation and entertainment, formal study and coursework, and even jobs in German businesses are all sought after as ways to access and affiliate with native speakers. The balance of these domains for any individual naturally changes over time, as opportunities and priorities change. Many refer to future (projected) plans of action or intention toward closer contact with the surrounding native speaker community – this is seen as beneficial to their language fluency as well as to their sense of belonging.

While most learners here take a consciously positive approach to potentially difficult transitions, not all experiences have been painless. In this regard, the stories of two ethnic immigrants are remarkable in their contrasts. Korech and Ahmet are Turkish-Germans who arrived in Germany as young children (AO 4 and 3.5, respectively). Both have strong connections to their Turkish heritage, but very different attitudes toward their place in German society. Both men have gone through the German school system and made it through the *Abitur* – a cumulative final exit exam based on a rigorous, college preparatory high school program. This is a highly valued accomplishment in Germany, and leads to greater opportunities for a professional career (other school programs emphasize technical training, for example). Over time, Ahmet has integrated his Turkish heritage with his life in Germany, valuing both cultures as contributing positively to his self-image. Ahmet says he is privileged to see life through two languages and cultures – an advantage he believes he shares with all second-generation immigrants:

> At some point, you grow up, discover your identity, and at that point you realize that this split that you've grown up with is an advantage. You recognize both sides, the positive and the negative, and you can go forward without difficulties.

As for how he feels in Germany now, Ahmet says:

> Germans ask me what my identity is almost every day [laughter]. For example, 'Do you feel more like a German or more like a Turk?' and I've sometimes said that I know I have two sides in me. What did Faust say, 'Two hearts beat in my chest'? ... I have to say very openly, 51% goes to the Turkish side, I mean, this heritage from my family, my parents, that lies very deep and that's how it will be for my entire life. I know my German identity, but the background is Turkish.

Ahmet has 'countless' German friends and spends most of his free time engaging in social activities with them. For all intents and purposes, he seems comfortable with a dual sense of identity. He mentions nothing specific regarding his acquisition of the German language in his interview, except to say that he was fluent before entering primary school, and was therefore integrated into regular German classes. Ahmet received no instruction in Turkish at all except for a short period of one hour per week after school – he says he did poorly in that class. He was positively disposed to German from early childhood, and his German is much stronger than his Turkish (even though he does try to consciously work on his Turkish with friends). He was frequently told as a child that his German language skills were excellent.

By contrast, Korech has no German friends to speak of, in spite of also growing up in Germany and speaking fluent German. As a child, he could speak no German before entering school other than a few 'playground' phrases he had picked up. In primary school, he had 12 years of German language instruction. His instructors emphasized pronunciation for the first few years before focusing more exclusively on grammar. In *Gymnasium*, Korech chose German as one of his curricular emphases, hoping it would eventually secure him a better job. He even opted for a German passport, giving up his Turkish citizenship. Despite his early exposure, extensive instruction and professional interest in acquiring native-level German, Korech has a self-described, noticeable accent in German (see Pallier *et al.*, 1997 for similar findings), and a self-described identity conflict as well.

There are two obvious discrepancies in the backgrounds of Korech and Ahmet. First, their German language abilities at the onset of primary school were dissimilar (though according to the critical-period literature, this should have had no lasting impact on their attainment, especially considering vast instructed and un-instructed exposure well before puberty). Second, they express noticeably different attitudes toward German society as a whole, and their discrepancies in identity are also remarkable.

As Korech describes it, his identity struggles and a low resolve to connect with Germans seem to go hand-in-hand. He says he has 'no mother tongue,' because German is not spoken at home, and his Turkish literacy is very poor. Korech therefore lacks confidence in both languages; his *linguistic* identity is weak, and this troubles him to no small degree. As for social contact, Korech works, studies, and plays soccer with Germans, but says he 'avoids them whenever possible' because of their negative attitudes toward foreigners. His social identity, like his linguistic identity, is thus marked by conflict.

Much like Drew, Korech has largely separated the language from the culture. He expresses pride in his linguistic accomplishments in German. On the other hand, he focuses on the negative aspects of German culture, intentionally closing off opportunities for closer contact:

Korech: There are people that I simply can't understand, and people that I don't want to understand. Then I really don't want contact ... I never feel like a German. I always feel like a Turk. I can't feel like a German. As long as things are the way they are here, I don't want to feel like a German, I don't want to be seen or identified as a German, I don't want to be held responsible for the way things are here.

Interviewer:	What is it like here?
Korech:	I mean look at how it is with politics about foreigners. Look at how they talk about us. Even if I were a German I couldn't change things. I could possibly change one person, but not 60 or 70 million.

Korech clearly does not wish to affiliate himself with Germans or German culture. On whether he feels Germany is 'home,' Korech points to the irony of the question:

Interviewer:	Are you ever asked whether or not you feel 'at home' here?
Korech:	How could I feel anything but 'at home' if I grew up here? When someone asks me this question it's obvious they think of me as a foreigner ... When I'm in Germany, I cannot identify myself as German because I'm not accepted here. Every time they look at me, they see the Turk, the foreigner in me, instead of the German.

Korech's impressions have become more acutely uncomfortable over time. He sees himself as never being able to feel fully Turkish or fully German: 'I'm caught between two cultures and two languages.' He steadfastly holds onto his Turkish identity in defiance of his belief that acceptance in Germany depends upon his giving it up:

Korech:	... I mean, integration yes, assimilation no.
Interviewer:	How do you mean?
Korech:	I am ready to integrate myself here in Germany, but I'm not ready to be oppressed or made to feel inferior. I'm not prepared to give up everything that matters to me so that I'll be accepted.
Interviewer:	What do you think Germans expect of you?
Korech:	They expect me to assimilate. They expect me to give up anything that connects me to Turkey. I don't want to give that up.
Interviewer:	What does that mean for you, to assimilate?
Korech:	Of course there are positive and negative things, but I'm so fixated on the negative that I can't think of anything positive. Let's see, positive ... that they send help if there's a catastrophe in Turkey, or when we travel, they are hospitable ...

For Korech, his Turkish and German identities are apparently incompatible; there is a sense that he feels it is hopeless to try to be 'German' if he wants to maintain his sense of Turkishness. Ahmet, on the other hand, has found a way to reconcile these dual affiliations. Both men say they are 'rooted' in Germany, but they clearly have different approaches to the question of 'investment' – a point that will be revisited in the chapter conclusion.

One of the objectives of this study is to examine issues such as identity in the framework of maturational constraints. Because these two immigrants were exposed so early in life to German as L2, issues of identity would not be predicted as important influences on language attainment. Therefore, the social-psychological factors in general would be predictably much less important for them than for late learners.

As noted earlier, perceptions of belonging and identity, constructed on both individual and collective levels, have everything to do with a personal sense of history, comfort, adaptation, and acceptance. As a postscript of sorts for the stories of Korech and Ahmet, it is important to note that the idea of *Heimat* is poignantly relevant for younger immigrants (especially *Migrantkinder* born in Germany) who wish to feel part of a culture that understands them. Stories and personal interviews abound on the juxtaposition of impossibility and necessity underlying this desire (see Harnisch *et al.*, 1998; Tan & Waldhoff, 1996). If the expectation to be *either* German *or* Turkish is too confining, many endorse the development of a young, Turkish-German culture that is flexible enough to allow for an integration of both. Horrocks & Kolinsky (1996) reason that new, cross-cultural identities are more the rule than the exception for the second and third generations of Turks in Germany, and in turn, these social changes impact trends in bilingualism. Tan & Waldhoff (1996) describe a generation of Turkish Germans whose abilities in both languages are impressively strong. In this study, immigrants from Turkey, Poland, Russia, France, the UK, and the USA all exhibit similar linguistic strengths, and express their own concerns for finding a sense of belonging in Germany.

An Exceptional Learner

In the quest to understand why some learners exceed expectations, we frequently attribute their 'success' to special neuro-cognitive abilities or talents, though there is little conclusive evidence to sustain that assumption at this point (see Chapter 2 discussion). The question of access to Universal Grammar (UG) after puberty versus the possible predominance of general processing strategies is also quite abstract; we may never be able to determine the answer confidently. However, assuming the predominance of cognitive processing allows for a great deal of individual variability – an undeniable characteristic of late SLA. An alternative interpretation supported by the theoretical stance of this work is that *engagement* with the target language is key to variable outcomes. By exploring how learners *engage* in the learning process, we may understand 'exceptional learning' as a combination of highly optimal orientations along with optimal experience (i.e. consistent, authentic, interactive, etc.). In this section, I explore these issues in-depth through the story of one learner whose attainment could be described as exceptional (she scores within the native-speaker range on all tasks). She not only defies predicted critical period effects, she does so under less-than-optimal circumstances.

Dora, a Polish immigrant, arrived in Germany as a young adult. She had studied German in a Polish classroom from the age of 12, and has lived in Berlin for 6 years. Her mother and brother also live in Berlin, and she speaks Polish with them. Dora describes her exposure to German as 'passive' in the early phase of her immigration because she had very few opportunities for direct, interactive contact with Germans. She gradually developed enough confidence to pursue a few friendships, and to speak up in her university classes. After six years, Dora still has relatively little contact with Germans, calculating that she spends an average of 7–8 hours per week in conversation, but about 30 hours a week engaged in passive activities such as reading, seeing films or television, or simply listening to the language around her. She does not mention any specific close friends, and describes her interactions in German as primarily involving work or study, as opposed to leisure. Most of her social contacts are limited to the university environment, and further limited to a specific topic: German studies. She has had even fewer social connections from various work environments than from the university:

Interviewer: What about your contacts with Germans? Do you know many, uh ... [Germans]?

Dora: No, I'm afraid I'm a disappointment there [laughter]. I'm a person you can come to, but I don't really seek or create personal contacts. Sometimes it happens, for example, in a seminar when you have to work together, but people I know from there, whom I then meet again in another seminar maybe 15 or 20 people I know that way we just don't get together often. I mean, they would say 'hello' to me on the street, but [laughter] I just don't have many acquaintances here. Maybe with folks I've worked with, employers, yes, but I don't really meet up with them, not on purpose. It's just [that] I don't really know ordinary Germans[2] except for a few people at work. I mean it isn't a real relationship. I work for them. They pay me, so we know each other, but we don't get together or anything.

Dora maintains that she does not pursue greater contact per se, but has come to know more Germans over time. Her lack of close personal contact is somewhat remarkable in light of her advanced language abilities, though not surprising given similar experiences of isolation among many immigrants. How can we understand Dora's 'exceptional' attainment if not from the position of optimal contact, i.e. direct interactive experience?

As noted earlier, Dora claims the highest levels of motivation, and that has been consistent over time. She sees herself as personally and professionally invested in German, and these orientations have been consistent throughout her residence in Germany. I also noted earlier that Dora's strong connection to the language may account for her desire to attain to such an impressive level. At the same time, Dora's confidence in her language abilities frequently wanes, depending on her opportunities to interact in German. She enjoys being surrounded by the language, and feeling that she is constantly learning more: 'If I forget something [in German] it's as if someone has taken away a part of myself' (quoted above).

Dora has clearly developed a strong sense of identity based on her mastery of the language. She believes this mastery is the only employable skill she possesses. In fact, Dora repeatedly says with regret that she will likely have to return to Poland to put her 'only practical skill' to use. Even so, she hopes to find a way to stay in Germany for good reason: 'My home is here, and I actually feel much more at home here than in Poland. I would really like to stay, but I probably won't be able to.'

It is difficult to know how Dora's affiliation with the language developed, though it is likely that German culture is a comfortable 'fit' for her as an adult. I noted that she enjoys the relative lack of expectations placed on her: she feels free to lead an independent life now, as she puts it. Based on her comments, it is fair to say that Dora's investments in the language and culture have much to do with self-image. This vital connection between language and sense of self is arguably a cornerstone of her overall experience in Germany.

Dora's motivation to study German was predicated on her desire to succeed *at something*, she reveals with a laugh. She committed to German as her focus of study at the university because, 'I thought to myself, what can I actually succeed in? Not psychology! But German, I could do.' She based this conclusion on her own classroom experience, where instruction in grammar and translation came easy, though she apparently left high school with weak conversational skills. She reports very little exposure to authentic German before arriving in Germany. For Dora, this meant she spent months just listening before attempting to speak.

According to her written survey comments, Dora still has difficulty with some linguistic features – all phonological: rounded and unrounded /o/ sounds, /e/ and /i/ (perhaps because of their long, tense qualities). She also maintains that her sentence intonation is not consistently authentic. Rater assessments confirm these self-evaluations. The isolated word and paragraph tasks were the least native-sounding of all her four tasks, according to the raters. The isolated word task elicits consonant and vowel allophones that are notably difficult for non-native speakers; some items emphasize vowel length and quality, some emphasize consonant clusters in various environments, or in rapid succession, etc. Therefore, Dora's inconsistent ratings for the word list may not be surprising. Two of the three raters apparently changed their minds while listening: one raised her estimation, another lowered it, indicating a high degree of uncertainty, the third thought she was definitely native on that task. For the paragraph recitation, one rater remarked that Dora's intonation sounded non-native. However, the open-ended task and the sentence-length recitation brought her Mean Ratings much closer to native (3.33 and 2.67 respectively), overlapping with several of the native-speaker controls. When the raters' comments are carefully considered together, they coincide with Dora's own perceptions: she sometimes sounds native (and is assumed to be native), though not consistently. In the last two or three years, Dora has begun to consciously imitate native speakers in the hopes of improving her pronunciation, but there is no way to know how successful those specific efforts have been.

The connections between Dora's pride in achievement, sense of linguistic identity, and language ability are prominent throughout her interview. She is proud of her attainment, and feels strongly that her linguistic endeavors have been worthwhile. Still, while her enthusiasm for German is clear, her confidence is more tenuous. When it comes to characterizing her potential 'German-ness,' as opposed to her 'Polishness,' some measure of discomfort is clear:

Interviewer: There's an incredible number of Poles here in Berlin, right? Do you have any connections there?

Dora: Yes, I know, but I said that, in principle, I don't want to know them. I mean, Polish immigration [to Germany] is like, well, first there are the political refugees, artists and so forth, those who are already well established and have integrated with the Germans. They don't seek contact with other Poles. The ones who do seek contact are a certain kind of people. They need assistance or are looking for advantageous connections for jobs and so forth, and I don't want that, I don't want to know them. I have my own problems I'm dealing with, and I'm not interested. Maybe that's wrong of me, I could have found a good job with a Polish cultural institute or something in a similar circle, but I don't want to ask anyone for anything, and secondly, I doubt they would be interested in me! I really have no contact with Poles here.

Dora preserves her independence by intentionally distancing herself from other Poles, yet she does not reject her heritage at all, saying she 'understands the Polish mentality much better than the German.' Her descriptions of visits to friends or relatives in Poland are quite interesting, because she notes that she often feels the need to 'defend Germans against negative stereotypes of them.' In these situations, she sees herself as out-of-place, slightly different from her Polish interlocutors, but not fully German either. In Germany, she is similarly split between two identities:

I feel myself to be Polish here [in Germany] – how do you call it, schizophrenia? A split of consciousness – that's it. It often happens, the fact that I feel Polish here often comes from the fact that I am asked where I come from, and then I have to say ...

Could Dora feel herself to be 'German' if not for such questions? It is not likely. Her sense of belonging is also colored by the perception that her Polish identity is devalued in the German, even European, context:

I don't really have so much to offer here as a Pole. I haven't experienced the other half of the world, so I'm less attractive maybe. I'm limited to an Eastern European experience, and therefore you become really aware of your identity, and that you're foreign, and that you can't simply be so accepted here. I have a split identity I guess, with a tendency to feel foreign here, but it's okay.

Taken together, these observations are a reminder that identity may be *contradictory,* but not ambivalent. When in Germany, Dora's identity is influenced by a perception of low prestige vis-à-vis her Polish heritage. By contrast, she says her bilingualism, as well as her experience in Germany, is highly valued in Poland. These contradictions may be uncomfortable, but Dora describes them with some measure of acceptance; she repeatedly says she has adapted to certain shortcomings or disappointments by re-interpreting the 'negative' versus the 'positive.' By changing her evaluation, she feels a greater sense of comfort as someone who must move within and between two cultures.

Several conclusions may be drawn from Dora's experience that could apply to other exceptional learners. First, it seems critical that Dora has constructed a sense of identity around her language achievements, and that she sees herself as a successful learner of German. Furthermore, her rewards for her efforts appear to be internally generated – she provides her own positive feedback. Second, this language-oriented identity may be the foundation that anchors her psychologically as she accommodates and adapts to new, and sometimes difficult, situations. Third, Dora has received extensive instruction and feedback over a period of many years. Her language acquisition is therefore characterized by plenty of formal and informal experience. Finally, she has constructed a home for herself in Germany, emotionally, socially, and professionally, as well as linguistically.

To summarize, Dora's language learning experience underscores the importance of optimal *investment* and *engagement* in the target language. This exceptional learner has pursued native-level attainment in German as an endeavor unto itself. Her commitment to highly advanced language skills is fundamental to her sense of long-term accomplishment and reward. Moreover, Dora's pursuits can only be characterized as both conscious and directed. She has consciously structured certain attitudes and opportunities for herself in the interest of achieving her goals. I would argue further that these psychological orientations have influenced certain cognitive approaches to the process. For example, we know that Dora has adopted certain strategies to address weaknesses in her phonological fluency. Socially, she has adapted to certain limits in the environment by seeking other sources of language input. She has emphasized her own strengths as she has made up for weaknesses in actual experience. She has shown flexibility in that she has re-evaluated old-standing views in order to accommodate a new lifestyle – a change that she sees as highly positive. Psychologically, there is little doubt that she is optimally oriented to the task. Dora reports the highest levels of motivation toward language acquisition, and expresses pride in the fact that she sounds native, even if that is less consistent than she would like.

In spite of a relatively late start, and a rather isolated social situation,

Dora's psychological approach, together with her active pursuit of input and feedback, illustrate *optimal engagement* – something that has surely led to such an exceptional end-state.

Conclusion

At the conclusion of Chapter 2, I argued that relying on just one realm of explanation for age effects is too narrow; neuro-cognitive, psychological, and social factors must be considered together in late language learning. The statistical analysis in Chapter 3 highlighted multiple significant factors in end-state attainment. To understand how internal and external factors *interact* in the process, however, a qualitative approach is needed. The integrated methodology presented in this study provides group (quantitative) and individual (qualitative) data *for the same learner population*, allowing for clearer interpretations of this balance of multiple factors. This chapter has therefore presented individual accounts of language acquisition experiences *in the context of the target language community*. The themes outlined in this chapter, pertaining to psychological and social influences in this experience, are summarized briefly below:

Opportunities for contact

Contact opportunities vary widely among individuals, partly due to living conditions or circumstances, and partly due to personality or attitudinal factors. Although personality is not targeted or tested here specifically, it is understood that each learner has unique social and psychological approaches to immigration, and to language acquisition. For example, one person whose risk-taking tolerance is low, and who believes that forming personal friendships with non-Germans is difficult, may have little inclination toward seeking new contacts. These individual variations notwithstanding, consistent patterns emerge from the qualitative analysis that point to common approaches to the language acquisition task:

- Social strategies help the individual adjust to disappointed expectations for personal contact. Formal language input contexts, or even 'passive' ones, may make up for these gaps between expectation and reality.
- Personal contact may be the most effective context for improving language skills, according to these learners. Almost without exception, overt feedback is appreciated and actively sought, even in informal contexts.
- Contact correlates to greater satisfaction with L2 abilities, as well as motivational intensity and closer-to-native attainment.

These patterns are not revelations; some are substantiated in the research on German as a second language. Studies investigating developmental phenomena from cognitive and modular viewpoints verify the impact of personal contact *on par with the significance of age of arrival and length of residence* (Dittmar, 1979; Dittmar & Klein, 1975; Meisel & Clahsen, 1985; Rieck, 1989). Actual physical isolation (e.g. ghettoization of ethnic populations), poor input (e.g. foreigner talk), and pervasive social discrimination all are treated in the literature as negative influences on language acquisition. Sociolinguistic research devotes more attention to these problems as they impact long-term social integration (Barkowski *et al.*, 1976; Buss, 1995; Clyne, 1968 as cited in Pfaff, 1981; Götze & Pommerin, 1988; Horn, 1996; Kolinsky, 1996; Meng, 1995a; Pfaff, 1981; Rosenberg, 2000; Sayler, 1986; Worbs, 1995). As is reiterated in much of this research, only language proficiency can lead to greater personal contact with native speakers – the basis for real social integration. The circularity is obvious: without authentic input, language proficiency suffers, leading to lower chances of personal connections with native speakers. Many have called for a greater emphasis on overt instruction to ease this problem in the early stages of immigration.

Building on the recognition that language proficiency is important for social assimilation, more recent work examines the connections between contact, attitudes and actual progress in L2. One example comes from Frischherz (1997), who explores conversational fluency for Kurdish and Turkish immigrants to German-speaking Switzerland. In this study, Frischherz relates fluency to three main factors: (1) attitudes toward the language and culture, (2) opportunities to form friendships with Germans, and (3) instructional experience. Frischherz concludes that acquisitional sequences are directly linked to the quality and consistency of interactive opportunities. Though these conclusions are arguably weakened by his methodology (he offers no formal correlational analysis), they are confirmed in other studies. Röhr-Sendlmeier (1990) uses language assessment instruments, surveys, and interviews with participants and their families and teachers. Her multi-variate analysis illustrates that contact with German peers both in and out of school is the most significant factor correlating to gains made over time based on a repeat measure of various aspects of language fluency. Duration of instructional experience and time spent beyond the classroom on activities conducted in German are also highly significant (though nothing is more significant than contact).

Based on the available evidence, personal contact with native speakers appears to exert profound influence on attainment. How the contact variable actually operates in the learner's experience is unclear. Perhaps contact increases motivation, and deeper motivation leads to the pursuit of stronger contacts (the circularity has already been noted). I argued previously that contact may lead to certain cognitive strategies as well – these would have to be examined on a case-by-case basis. Methodological hurdles notwithstanding, these data depict psychological orientations as dynamic, responding to external feedback and opportunities. Two findings from the Frischherz (1997) study are worth bearing in mind here – participants with the most native negotiation skills are most likely to *create* opportunities to interact with native speakers. They also express more positive attitudes toward the TL itself, and see fluency as critical to self-reliance. These patterns are confirmed here, and deserve greater empirical examination in future studies.

Attitudes toward the target language culture

Throughout these interviews, references to a 'German mentality' abound. A handful of 'German' qualities commonly stand out in the learners' experiences as potential sources of difficulty. To a large extent, these remarks provide a context for understanding how similarly individuals adjust to such cultural differences. These necessary adjustments are accompanied by plenty of self-reflection on what it means to be 'Polish,' 'French,' 'American,' etc., as opposed to 'German.' In hindsight, some of these differences are experienced as challenges, but they are rarely overwhelming:

- Cultural differences initially seen as negative are often recast as positive, or neutral, as immigrants adjust psychologically and socially.
- Attitudinal shifts often lead to self-reflection and a new sense of self, with *greater self-reliance* (perhaps an inherent aspect of immigration) the most common result of such a shift.
- Attitudes toward the target language and its culture may be maintained separately in the mind of the learner, allowing for a continued commitment to language fluency in the face of negative perceptions toward, and experiences in, the target language community.

Perhaps most notable are the tendencies toward conscious self-reflection as well as psychological flexibility. Most participants describe negative experiences early on that could have predicted a sense of *anomie*. Instead, most see such episodes as opportunities for self-reflection – they rarely see cultural differences as actually preventing them from achieving their goals. This reveals a psychological flexibility that may be unusual for adults and adolescents. These learners appear to keep their eye on the prize: linguistic assimilation, if not cultural. Even those few who know they will not stay permanently are motivated to leave Germany with native-level language abilities.

The view that attitudes are inherently connected to identity, as well as to motivation, is upheld in the relevant literature (Cargile & Giles, 1997; Gardner & Lambert, 1959, cited in Gardner *et al.*, 1997; Labrie & Clément, 1986; Schumann, 1994). The fact that I arbitrarily separate them here from *identity, belonging, sense of self*, etc. should not imply that these are essentially separable constructs. The nature of their connectedness, unfortunately, is rather like their impact on acquisition: it cannot be directly observed. Nevertheless, the data here suggest strongly that attitude is connected to outward behaviors, as well as to internal orientations such as motivation.

As noted earlier, the construct 'attitude' is fundamentally difficult to define and measure (Baker, 1992). Baker (1992: 10f.) describes 'attitude' as a 'hypothetical construct used to explain the direction or persistence of human behavior' – not directly observable, but often inferred by outward behaviors. According to Baker, one critical aspect of attitudes is their *task-specific* or *goal-specific* nature. The evidence here supports this assumption. Positive attitudes may account for the persistence of these learners in the face of socio-psychological difficulties. Perhaps the goal of language mastery keeps them on track – their efforts almost seem impervious to external setbacks. It must be noted, however, that these learners have options when it comes to access, probably owing to their language proficiency and educational level.

There is little doubt that attitudes play a role in SLA, though the directness of that role is questioned. From the earliest research in this area, Gardner and others (Gardner, 1985b; Gardner *et al.*, 1985) have asserted that language attitudes are less directly involved in language attainment than is motivation, for example. Taylor (1977: 72) takes a similar position, but notes that negative attitudes can 'provide a poor basis for bilingualism.' In other words, if attitudes are negative, especially between the host language community and the immigrant community, attainment will predictably suffer. The murkiness of any *causal* relationship between attitudes and actual behaviors is intensified by Taylor's assertion that *behaviors* likely influence *attitudes*, and not just the other way around (1977: 72). Acknowledging the murkiness problem, it may not be possible to ascertain exactly how attitudes influence the language learning process. Nonetheless, their increasing importance after puberty is assumed. For this reason, they are an important consideration for current and future SLA research.

One of the fundamental premises of this work is that age effects may be less of a direct predictor of ultimate attainment than other, less observable, factors in the socio-psychological and experiential realms. This view is not unfounded. Spolsky (1989), for instance, connects attitudes directly to age effects. Referring to Taylor's (1977) comparison of child and adult learners on 'non-cognitive' grounds, he writes:

> The question of attitude may provide an explanation of the age differences ... An emphasis on affective factors, like attitude and personality, offers an alternative hypothesis to ... the explanation of differences between children and adults [as] a critical period, biologically determined. It [affect] has the decided advantage of taking a factor considered true of all children (for example, language ego-permeability as in Guiora) and suggesting that it is *differentially* true of adults; this is surely more easily credible than the notion of a language acquisition device that sometimes does not decay but usually does. (Spolsky, 1989: 157; *italics mine*)

Baker (1992: 42) takes a similar position, maintaining that 'age is an 'indicator' or 'holding' variable that sums up movement [change] over time, and does not reveal the underlying reasons for that movement.' In Baker's proposed model, age may influence attitudes as it impacts on *experience* with the target culture. Experience may, in turn, influence attitudes. Age may therefore be only *indirectly* involved in language acquisition. This position is not really falsifiable, because age is always a player in the equation. Nevertheless, based on the evidence presented here, it should not be ruled out as plausible.

Sense of self in L2: Motivation, behavior, and language function

The learner's motivation toward the target language may be closely tied to its perceived functions. For these individuals, German serves communicative and practical functions as well as symbolic ones: it is the cited means to long-term assimilation potential and professional success. For the most part, these learners have high motivation, both personal and professional in nature, and this is not only strongly significant to their attainment (see Chapter 3), but is also key to how they negotiate external opportunities and even constraints:

- Those who see German as symbolically relevant (e.g. to their future success) tend to seek language input from multiple sources. These same learners report greater satisfaction with attainment thus far.
- Motivation toward native-level attainment can sustain a sense of well-being when other positive (external) reinforcements are lacking. This indicates a high level of perceived prestige for the TL.
- Through language choice, certain communicative and symbolic functions relevant to the context are reinforced. For example, L1 may be

used only with relatives (at home), while L2 is a practical 'survival tool' to be used everyday in the TL community.

This qualitative analysis shows the relevance of language function, perceptions of prestige, and motivation to real courses of action. These influences deserve a much closer look, as connecting points between internal orientation and outward behavior. The intersection of social and psychological forces is key to understanding how individuals try to further language contact. For example, many learners describe how their own social strategies, and cognitive ones, have increased as their L2 fluency advanced. This is a reminder of the causal impact of greater fluency: it seems to lead to higher levels of confidence, as well as greater contact.

The points above reiterate the connections between psychological factors and actions taken *in context* and *throughout the language acquisition process*. The fact that satisfaction with language ability, motivation, and frequency of contact are statistically linked here validates earlier research, and supports Pavlenko's position that we should ask 'more nuanced questions about the ways in which the L2 user's investment in a particular language was shaped, and the ways in which it is being reshaped by his or her present engagement with the language and its speakers' (Pavlenko, 2002: 294). To this end, these qualitative and quantitative methods *combined* provide greater insight into how learners strategically affiliate themselves linguistically (and culturally) with the TL community.

Perceptions of foreignness and belonging

Each participant has devoted some amount of conscious attention to the question of identity, struggling with perceptions of foreignness and belonging in Germany. Identity is never described as static, and certainly not as unquestioned – it often implies contradictory affiliations:

- A non-German identity does not necessarily lead to a weak sense of belonging or acceptance in Germany. However, many feel that their foreignness is an obstacle to greater social integration.
- Low-level language abilities correspond to a greater sense of social distance and isolation. Those with stronger foreign accents in particular say that much is made of their foreignness.
- A sense of identity as non-German does not necessarily hinder a motivation toward native-like fluency in German.

These patterns demonstrate that identity is not necessarily conflated with investment in the target language (see Norton Pierce, 1995), or intention toward native-like attainment. *Intention* can still be quite strong even when identity in the target language is weak; it is quite like motivation in that sense, which can be high even when language abilities are relatively low. This is an important point, because it means that identity need not be a causal factor in ultimate attainment, though it may nevertheless be a powerful influence for some learners. A drive toward the language itself seems to operate, somewhat regardless of circumstance, such as when TL serves significant functions for future well-being.

Motivation, attitude, sense of belonging, and identity are all potentially critical to ultimate attainment, though not in the same balance across learners. This may depend upon perceived rewards and likelihood of success as much as anything else. As an example: if only minimal communicative fluency is needed to survive in a new society, why push beyond that unless some other mechanism dictates the need? That mechanism could be the desire to affiliate (or integrate), or it could be an investment in language attainment itself. (These possibilities are illustrated in the previous sections.)

As mentioned, the relationships between motivation, attitude, and identity are widely cited in the literature. Gardner (1979, as cited in Dörnyei, 2003) first described motivation in complex terms, as a possible reflection of the individual's desire to connect to the target language community and culture, rather than a more practical orientation (see Chapter 2 discussion). Such desires are undoubtedly connected to expectations for rewards, thereby influencing behaviors perceived likely to bring about such rewards. I note in Chapter 2 that the desire to acculturate, or to sound native, is an especially potent indicator of phonological attainment according to several studies (Grosskopf *et al.*, 1996; Guiora, 1992; Guiora *et al.*, 1972; Major, 1993; Stokes, 2001 – see Piske *et al.*, 2001). Dora's story certainly offers a glimpse into how these connections may function in actuality. The possibility that acquiring a new language can, in itself, impact identity is not just an anecdotal truism, though more study is needed to clarify the nature of its impact on attainment (see Buss, 1995; Gardner *et al.*, 1999; List, 1989).

How the individual interacts with the TL community and gradually develops a sense of identity, in conjunction with greater TL experience, has been noted in the Canadian SLA literature in particular (Clément & Kruidenier, 1983; Genesee *et al.*, 1983; Lantolf, 2000; Noels *et al.*, 1996; Norton Pierce, 1995, 2000; Pavlenko & Lantolf, 2000). The importance of language abilities for developing identity is perhaps a less-well-known feature of language acquisition research in Germany. Meng's (1995b) report on *Aussiedler* families suggests that weak language skills are typically associated with a weak German identity. Moreover, predictable communicative difficulties between native speakers and non-native speakers with poor language skills reinforce negative stereotypes of foreignness. Social and linguistic adjustment strategies among Turkish immigrants, even in the second and third generations, have been noted as well (Abali, 2000; Hinnenkamp, 2000; Kallmeyer *et al.*, 2000). Taken together, these studies show that non-nativeness is an uncomfortable status, sometimes transcended by those who construct an identity as 'pan-European.' Others adopt the German culture as primary, or embrace a dual identity – a topic of great public interest in Germany.

What do such patterns actually mean for language attainment? A sense of the significance of these behaviors, especially as they reflect *active engagement* in the process, is offered by Buss (1995). This study is based on a biographical sketch of a Turkish woman who moved to Germany to join her *Gastarbeiter* (guest worker) father. Along with her increasing language fluency, she recounts several life-altering decisions based on professional disappointments as well as fortuitous opportunities. Had her skills in German been a low priority for her, i.e. had she not pursued the language with such enthusiasm (and success), these opportunities for upward mobility would not have been extended to her. Over time, German became increasingly important as she began to see herself in a new light: as bicultural and bilingual. This new identity fitted neatly with her early ambitions for greater self-reliance. Viewed in retrospect, the choices she made were directly based on her long-term intentions to move into a middle class existence in Germany. Buss concludes that whether or not such processes are conscious, they are 'active.' The learner shows interest in communication, and even feedback, thereby influencing and 'structuring' her own language input (Buss, 1995: 268f). This position is similar to Van Lier's assertion that consciousness and social interaction go hand-in-hand, that interaction offers opportunities for conscious learning, and that learners are *actively engaged* in these opportunities (Van Lier, 1998, 2000). Buss also emphasizes that the acquisition process relies on a positive self-image in the target language. In other words, a strong sense of self in L2 is necessary for linguistic assimilation.

As a final note on identity, the 'foreigner' label is a salient aspect of everyday life for these learners. Nevertheless, identity is not always such a serious matter. As mentioned previously, several participants report playing with this notion. As Alex puts it: 'You have to have a little fun in life, create some stories for yourself!' This sentiment is echoed by a woman who grew up in Germany in a French-speaking household. She was schooled in both German and French, and holds dual German and French citizenship. When traveling back to France, she pretends to be a 'very studious learner of French' in order to get special accolades for her 'language talent.' Within her own family, she says she has taken on the role of 'the German,' amidst her parents and younger brother who assert their steadfast 'Frenchness.' In another anecdote, an American tells of traveling with several Germans and another American into Turkey, pretending to be German throughout the trip. He surprised himself later by re-reading his diary entries from the trip. There he discovered his own references to himself and his companions as a 'bunch of Germans.' The fact that he did even not notice this at the time indicates that he may have a 'permeable ego' – a quality cited as beneficial to phonological authenticity (see Chapter 2).

Intention to stay

One possible reflection of engagement that has received no specific attention in the SLA literature to my knowledge is *intention to reside.* The personal decision to permanently reside in-country could reasonably exert strong influence on language attainment. In the interest of investigating this assumption, each interview was carefully reviewed for information regarding the informant's intention to stay in Germany. Responses reveal a spectrum of projected permanent versus temporary plans to reside (Table 4.1).

According to Table 4.1, those who intend to stay permanently appear to have been in Germany longest. Indeed, LOR and intention have a marginally significant correlation to one another ($r = 0.4$; $p < 0.07$). That same group (#1) also exhibits a closer-to-native Mean Rating on average, borne out by another marginally significant correlation ($r = 0.37$; $p < 0.08$). A one-way ANOVA tested the statistical significance of intention groups for Mean Rating. Indeed, significant effects are evident, as shown in Table 4.2.

These results indicate that, for this sample, *projected* residence has some

Table 4.1 Intention to reside in-country ($n = 25$)

Groups according to 'intention to reside'	*n*	*M of LOR*	*M of Mean Rate*	*Range*	*Min/ Max*	*SE*
1: Intention to stay permanently	7	9.8	3.63	4.1	1/5.1	0.5
2: Intention to stay for 2–5 years	5	2.3	5.54	1.1	4.9/6	0.2
3: Unsure about permanence	7	5.7	4.65	2.6	3.2/5.8	0.4
4: Certain to leave (within 1 year)	4	1.5	5.17	2.0	4/6	0.5

significant bearing on language attainment (we already know that *actual* length of residence is significant – see Chapter 3). This could be interpreted as follows: *intention* to settle in-country is, in fact, a pivotal factor in ultimate attainment. On the other hand, its effect could be conflated with the effects of an already-established, long-standing residence. The question is thus: Are those with longer residence already simply more likely to intend to stay permanently? Could the effect of *intention* be, in other words, an indirect influence, more aptly (or directly) reflected in *length of residence?* In order to rule out a possible conflation, a two-way ANOVA test examined possible overlapping effects for length of residence groups and intention groups (Table 4.3).

Table 4.3 shows that there is no significant interaction between *length of residence* and *intention to stay*, meaning that *both factors exert independent influence on language attainment outcomes.*

Pending replication, this finding could mean that *intention to reside* may reflect a psychological investment of sorts, perhaps an underlying goal-driven, or reward-driven motivation. To test for other possible relationships, a correlation analysis was run. Indeed, *intention to reside* is significantly linked to both motivational intensity ($r = 0.45$; $p < 0.03$) and strategies undertaken to improve pronunciation ($r = 0.51$; $p < 0.02$). It is

Table 4.2 One-way ANOVA: Intention to Mean rating ($n = 25$)

Groups according to 'intention to reside'	M of Mean Rating	SD	SE	Min. Mean Rating	Max. Mean Rating
1: Intention to stay permanently	3.63	1.4	0.53	1.08	5.17
2: Intention to stay for 2–5 years	5.54	0.44	0.20	4.9	6.0
3: Unsure about permanence	4.65	1.12	0.43	3.17	5.75
4: Certain to leave (within 1 year)	5.16	1.0	0.49	4.0	6.0

	SS	df	MS	F	Sig
Between groups	12.36	3	4.12	3.44	0.04
Within groups	22.75	19	1.20		
Total	35.1	22			

Table 4.3 Two-way ANOVA: Intention and LOR to Mean Rating ($n = 25$)

Groups according to 'intention to reside'	M of Mean Rating	M of LOR	SD
1: Intention to stay permanently	3.63	9.8	1.4
2: Intention to stay for 2–5 years	5.54	2.3	0.44
3: Unsure about permanence	4.65	5.7	1.12
4: Certain to leave (within 1 year)	5.16	1.5	1.0

	Type III SS	df	MS	F	Sig
Intention	3.2	3	1.07	0.95	0.45
LOR	6.9	3	2.3	2.05	0.17
Intended LOR	4.08	6	0.68	0.60	0.72
Corrected total	35.1	22			

therefore significantly connected to specific psychological and cognitive influences on attainment.

Given these findings, *intention* should be accounted for in future studies as a possible mechanism for certain actions or strategies that impact attainment. Further statistical testing may reveal essential connections between affect, cognitive approach and psychological orientation hinging on this particular factor.

(E)merging psychological and social perspectives

This chapter significantly expands the methodological breadth of ultimate attainment studies. It asks several questions that a qualitative analysis can uniquely address, laid out at the beginning of the chapter:

(1) Which aspects of L2 experience should be considered fundamental to ultimate attainment?

(2) How do psychological orientations and experiences in the target language country influence behaviors and goals in the process?

(3) How do constructs such as identity and belonging connect to other potential influences, such as intention to reside, or intention to affiliate with the target language culture?

These questions force the discussion of ultimate attainment beyond its reliance on age as the prevailing influence on SLA. According to the supporting analyses, maturation co-occurs with, and potentially influences, linguistic experience as well as multiple non-linguistic factors (cognitive, social, psychological, etc.). Therefore, preliminary answers to the questions above are outlined below:

(1) Ultimate attainment is a function of psychological and social influences, as much as it is a function of maturation. In fact, the power of maturation may depend largely on its connections to these influences. The significance of specific factors necessarily varies across learners and learning experiences, though some influences do appear to predict attainment consistently.

(2) Attitudes, perceptions of self in L2, and sense of belonging appear closely tied to motivation, which may be the primary operative influence behind both social and cognitive strategies to enhance L2 input and, by extension, fluency. It is highly likely, according to these data (and some existing evidence), that developing experience also influences attitudes. In other words, the relationship is not one-directional. This is what makes a study of individual experience and perceptions so critical to understanding ultimate attainment.

(3) Identity appears to be a complex, often contradictory, construct, not necessarily tied to attainment itself, nor to intention to reside. It should also be understood as separate from motivation. Because of identity's fluid and dynamic nature, formal statistical analyses are not likely to adequately capture its essence. Discrete measures may therefore lead to false interpretations. As for its influence on ultimate attainment, identity, like belonging and perceptions of acceptance, may exercise a primarily indirect influence.

From the analysis offered here, it is apparent that social and psychological considerations are of primary concern to the learner. Language contact opportunities, perceptions of confidence and satisfaction, and attitudes are all closely connected to one another, as well as to actual fluency. In short, each learner appears to *construct* his or her own experience in the target language as a response to both external and internal factors. Perhaps most interesting of all is the conscious effort, and the amount of self-evaluation and reflection, involved in the process.

This issue of consciousness is particularly relevant to current debates in SLA. Up to now, discussions of *conscious* versus *unconscious* control over language acquisition processes overwhelmingly refer to cognitive mechanisms. The patterns of social and psychological adjustments illustrated in this chapter demonstrate that conscious control transcends the cognitive realm; *it is also essentially socio-psychological when language acquisition takes place in the target language community.* These learners consciously seek language input and feedback; they consciously seek greater personal contact with native speakers; they consciously attend to improving their language through social as well as cognitive strategies. These learners consciously attend to their own language acquisition in the interest of attaining certain goals. Their intentions to increase access and improve their fluency are central to their developing experience, and surely to their attainment as well. It therefore makes sense to examine adult SLA considering social and psychological factors *in tandem,* as they operate together, *strategically.*

The emphasis here on socio-psychological adaptation underscores one fundamental difference between classroom and immersion-style acquisition: while some similarities exist between these situations, assimilation concerns are relevant only to the learner residing in-country. There, the implications of language ability for social contact and integration are undeniable. For this group of immigrants, connections to the target language and culture are sometimes conceived of as largely separate. A strong emotional connection to the language itself may carry the individual through difficult social and psychological transitions. Throughout these transitions, native-like attainment is understood to be key to future integration. Each story reveals a tangible self-awareness of the connections between language ability and opportunities for language contact in the surrounding community. For some, these opportunities are seized enthusiastically, for others, especially those who describe their language as less native, that enthusiasm is highly variable. This is the essence of *intention* to embrace one's milieu. Each person pursues opportunities based on perceptions of ability and accomplishment, taking into account attitudes toward the outside community.

The process of acculturation has long been characterized as psychologically and socially difficult, especially where a new language must be acquired (Schumann, 1978). This is understandable, given that language is the vehicle for the expression of traditions, beliefs, and values, even as it marks social, cultural, and ethnic identity (Hamers & Blanc, 2000).[3] Simply put, language connects us to the community. As the means to eventual integration, its significance is deeply personal. Ehlich writes:

> Language contributes to our world orientation in a fundamental way ...
> [it] is the basis for shaping life, for planning and realizing one's own

biography ... it endows common ground, the basis of human existence. (Ehlich, 1994: 113)

The immigrants in this study have, by and large, embraced German as the means by which to secure their belonging in a new culture. The German language has become for them, as Edwards (1985: 17) puts it, 'an emblem of group-ness.'

There is little doubt that in the early phases of acculturation, challenges to group cohesion and individual security are very real, as immigrants face the potential loss of connections to family and heritage community (see Kallmeyer *et al.*, 2000). Furthermore, the acquisition of a new language and the potential loss of a mother tongue force new conceptions of identity and belonging. Overcoming the inherent risks involved in such transformations is worth the struggle, according to Ehlich, if seen in light of new opportunities (Ehlich, 1994: 118; cf. Götze, 1983). Without exception, each participant in this study describes these struggles against a strong framework of appreciation for the opportunities this experience provides. In spite of some personal sense of loss from being far from home, the great majority of these learners feel quite positive about their experiences in Germany and the extent to which they have been able to adapt. Language fluency has played an undeniable role in that adaptation.

Notes

1. Interviews were recorded on audiotape on a Marantz PMD 221; excerpts provided in the following sections have been translated into English.
2. *'Echte Spießer'* is the actual term used, which is slightly derogatory.
3. A final note should be made regarding learner perceptions of cultural difference as reflected in language. Several participants noted that communication style differences are a reflection of cultural difference. For example, humor is not easily translated from one language to the next, and cursing may also be viewed as less serious in Germany than in other cultures (though much of the cursing takes place in English!). One participant noted that his personal communicative style is more direct and emphatic in German, probably because of the 'character' of the German language: ' ... when I speak German I emphasize certain things, things seem more important. I think it has to do with the language itself, but it could also be because I'm more intent on making my point [in German] ...'

Chapter 5
Conclusions and Proposals for Future Research

Throughout this work, I have argued that multiple factors, in combination with one another, may account for age effects to a statistically significant degree. Age of exposure, like length of residence, may give us little indication of the underlying mechanisms responsible for attainment; instead, depending on the individual case, it may be more of an indication of cumulative experience, including constraints on the language learning process from several fronts. Those initiating language acquisition after puberty may be subject to an especially complex combination of influences from social, psychological and cognitive realms.

Putting Age Effects in Context

Clearly, age of exposure is but one factor in ultimate attainment, and not an especially informative one if we consider the results gleaned from Chapters 3 and 4. To isolate the significance of age from its socio-cultural and psychological context is to misconstrue its impact. Critical-period studies have typically done just this, with too little attempt to clarify the nature of its influence. In effect, the absence of focus on individual factors has done little to advance a real understanding of the process. Furthermore, while quantitative analysis has been a valuable tool for verifying factor relationships, it has brought us only so far. How do various aspects of experience operate in practice? How do shifts in their balance over time affect long-term outcomes? These questions cannot be answered through discrete measures alone, much less with an exclusive emphasis on group performance. The individual's perspective must be explored if we are to understand the roles played by these critical factors.

Through an integrated methodology, appropriately measuring the impact of age relative to its concomitant influences is possible. We must discover how the late learner builds L2 experience that reflects his or her personal needs, desires, and styles – cognitively, socially and psychologically speaking. By merging psycholinguistic and sociolinguistic approaches, we may understand how some learners continue on, past predicted stages of non-native-ness. In so doing, the balance of relevant universal and individual influences also becomes clearer.

The combined quantitative and qualitative analyses in this study reveal that critical-period effects may be predicted by a number of experiential and socio-psychological influences, that co-occur with age of onset. The collective evidence leads to several important conclusions.

First, the question of the *strength* of the age factor is a central focus of this study. The tests applied reveal two important pieces of evidence in this regard:

(1) Age exerts some independent influence when tested against other significant factors, such as: length of residence, duration of instruction, intention to reside, personal motivation, satisfaction, etc.
(2) Other variables (specifically, psychological ones) account for a greater percentage of the variance than age of onset. This holds even when AO is combined with length of residence.

In keeping with the theoretical stance outlined above, these findings lead to two important conclusions regarding the impact of AO:

(1) *The nature of maturation's influence is not one of mere conflation; independent effects are found, possibly due to a qualitative shift in neuro-cognitive flexibility. This assertion may be true for the phonological realm, more so than for other levels of language (syntax, morphology, and especially semantics).*
(2) *Given the relative statistical strength of the other variables, maturation's influence is not necessarily primary, at least not to the extent presumed up to now.*

Second, age of onset correlates to multiple factors across a spectrum of learner orientations to the task:

(1) In *the psychological* realm, age of onset correlates to intensity of motivation, sense of fluency, satisfaction with attainment, perceived importance of sounding native, and professional motivational orientation.
(2) In the *social* realm, age of onset correlates to frequency of contact with native speaker interlocutors as well as contexts for primary exposure or experience while in-country.
(3) In the *cognitive* realm, age of onset correlates to duration of instruction, exposure to indirect instruction in the language, and consistency of feedback encountered from native speakers.

These important findings underscore the need to study age effects in tandem with co-occurring socio-cultural and psychological considerations. According to this evidence, and supported by numerous studies from various theoretical approaches, socio-cultural context inherently brings to bear multiple influences on the learning process that coincide with age. Thus, the following generalizations may be drawn regarding *early* SLA:

- *Early exposure predisposes the learner to a greater variety of contact sources, ranging from formal to informal and from personal to professional domains.*
- *Early exposure indicates greater consistency and frequency of personal contact, leading to greater confidence and sense of self in the language – also affecting practice opportunities and fluency itself.*

These generalizations should be verified by future studies set up to investigate maturational effects as a combination of age of onset and specific experiential variables.

Finally, age of onset apparently holds the greatest predictive strength before age 12, and the slope of its linear relationship to outcome decreases appreciably between the ages of 12 and 15, becoming quite weak, even flat, after 15 (see Chapter 3). This finding supports the following arguments:

- *A general learning decline, i.e. exerting effects over time in a steady slope relationship, is not likely the operative mechanism in so-called 'fundamental differences' between late and early learning. Instead, the process of matura- tion, with its concomitant influences, may best predict qualitative changes in language learning.*
- *Because there is still some linearity evident from age 12 to approximately age 15, it is likely that certain factors become increasingly important through adolescence and up to early adulthood. The nature of these factors is social and psychological, as well as neuro-cognitive. For this reason, and because exceptional learning is so frequently noted across studies, a ' sensitive period' is a more apt description of language-learning declines. Clearly, some learners surpass expectations owing to various combinations of optimal experience and/or optimal orientation to the task.*

Based on all of the evidence presented, the idea that ultimate attainment is *primarily* a function of age must be reconsidered. Instead, the impact of age should be understood as *indirect* as well as possibly direct. This requires that we somehow account for other significant factors in the learner's cumulative L2 experience.

Individual and Universal Predictions for Phonological Attainment in SLA

Immigrant language acquisition is arguably the most relevant setting for ultimate attainment studies. In Chapter 2, I noted that ultimate attainment studies have overwhelmingly emphasized universal phenomena in SLA, offering valuable insights on the learning process as well as the nature of potential constraints. Yet these notions can be understood best by appreciating the individual's learning situation. Clearly, such an appreciation is long overdue, since claims of universality do not account for the variation noted in several decades of research. While universal patterns have been substantiated (particularly for morphosyntactic development in uninstructed environments), there are too many exceptions to the rules, and there is too little replication across languages to take these patterns completely for granted. Why do so many exceptions exist? What is the nature of the variation seen? Is cognitive style truly the most powerful influence (as claimed by, for example, Clahsen, 1980, 1984; Felix, 1985; Pienemann, 1987), or are psychological and social factors more critical? How much control does the individual have over the outcome, considering the prevalence of cognitive and social (as well as psychological) style and strategy variation throughout the developmental stages? These are a few of the questions that occupy, and vex, SLA researchers. We may be closest to answering them when we appreciate possible neuro-cognitive constraints *on balance* with operative social-psychological and cultural concerns.

As argued previously, investigating accent is a most promising area for understanding this balance of influences, in part because it is essentially connected to socio-psychological notions of belonging, native-ness, and cultural and linguistic identity. Those participants with the strongest accents according to their own assessments report that more attention is given to their 'foreignness' than for the those with less obvious accents. A few have entrenched accents, and in some cases this has even interfered with their ability to form personal friendships. It is also clear that the phonological realm may be uniquely subject to neurological constraints because of plasticity, or flexibility, which causes changes of both a motor *and* a cognitive nature. This is clear from the extensive research on asymmetrical abilities to accurately perceive and produce new phonetic and phonemic targets.

Acknowledging the salience of accent, raters in this study overwhelmingly cite phonological criteria as the basis for their assessments of native-ness. Their actual ratings verify their reported priority: 79% of written comments on specific task items have to do with pronunciation, on both segmental and suprasegmental levels. (Not surprisingly, the noted features are those targeted by the instruments for their difficulty: vowel length and quality, /R/, /x/, onset /h/, and final voiceless stops /b, d, g/.

The difficulty that some participants experience with these features may be considered a function either of markedness effects, or of possible transfer from L1. I do not believe that they are developmental in nature, as they do not involve simplification, metathesis, substitution, etc., and these learners are likely past such developmental stages. Rather, the non-target production revolves around vowel and consonant qualities such as voicing (for consonants), and laxness and height (for vowels), in addition to slight inconsistencies in intonation and stress. These kinds of inaccuracies are probably due to transfer (Hecht & Mulford, 1987) or to errors in approximation (Beebe, 1984).

The difficulty in pinpointing the source of non-native production is illustrated by a pair of study participants. Toward the end of Chapter 4, I discuss the stories of two 'ethnic' (i.e. identifiably 'non-German')[1] immigrants, Korech and Ahmet. I note that their unique approaches to finding a cultural and linguistic identity diverge according to their attitudes, more so than their actual circumstance. Both participants are firmly rooted in Germany; for all intents and purposes they are members of the middle class given their university student status. However, there is something most interesting about the phonological attainment of these two. They both score within the native speaker range, though not nearly as solidly (with comparable confidence) as some of the other early immigrants. For example, the two French immigrants with early AO score in the 'definitely native' range. Even some of the late learners score closer to native than Korech and Ahmet, including native speakers of Russian, English, and Slovak. If learners with L1s of different language families are able to acquire to native levels, why are these Turkish learners any different? There are no real clues from the interviews, although some particulars of their exposure (and instruction) are certainly different. Still, they end up with very similar ratings. The raters provide some indication of what influenced their assessments: The existing comments stress *phonology,* especially *suprasegmental features.*[2] Syllable stress and intonation are mentioned for both Korech and Ahmet across several tasks, and Ahmet's pronunciation of the isolated word task was deemed 'too perfect' by one rater. What this means exactly is unclear, though Ahmet may have sounded as if he was trying too hard to be accurate.

Consistent with the idea that phonological acquisition may have its own critical period (see Long, 1990), there are no lexical or grammatical errors noted for these two speakers; presumably nothing stood out as identifiably non-native in these realms. Without a closer comparison to the native speaker controls (e.g. through spectrographic analysis), it is not possible to confidently detail the features that led to these assessments. In order to draw stronger conclusions about possible cross-linguistic differences, greater numbers of native Turkish speakers would be needed. Nevertheless, this finding is an intriguing reminder of the possible effects of transfer and fossilization (discussed at length in Chapter 2). Whether such transfer may be attributed to physiological habit, faulty inferences, or even L1–L2 'merger' patterns, as Beebe (1984) puts it, its source is unclear without further analytical instruments.

Here I have shown that the persistence of accent is predicted by a number of factors, spanning cognitive, psychological and social realms, and certainly dependent also upon 'raw' measures of exposure, e.g. age of onset and length of residence. Not enough of these participants have experience with formal phonological training for me to make any solid claims about the efficacy of such training, as in previous studies (Moyer, 1995, 1999). At the same time, these learners clearly spend conscious effort reflecting on the authenticity of their accents; they undertake specific measures to approximate a more native sound even at these very advanced levels, and many desire to sound native. Indeed, this goal is attainable, at least for a few.

Re-thinking the Ultimate Attainment Construct for Future Research

The evidence presented here underscores the fact that *experience*, colored by social and psychological considerations, is uniquely constructed for every learner. Furthermore, *experience,* as relevant to ultimate attainment, can be understood in many ways. The fallacy of viewing experience in simple, discrete terms becomes clear when we consider *length of residence,* often used as a measure of experience. This variable is shown here to correlate significantly to psychological, social and cognitive aspects of experience, as follows:

(1) *psychological*: LOR correlates to satisfaction with attainment, personal sense of motivation toward L2 and sense of native-ness;

(2) *social*: LOR correlates to frequency of spoken contact and intention to reside permanently;

(3) *cognitive*: LOR correlates to duration of instruction and indirect instructional exposure, formal feedback received in the classroom, approach to target language instruction, types of phonological training and feedback in the classroom.

Along similar lines, how does age, per se, affect experience? It holds similar relationships to those outlined for LOR. In addition, the qualitative analysis demonstrates that the impact of age reaches into realms hardly investigated until now. For example, many participants say that as they get older, they are less likely to initiate social contacts, and they are less likely to seek feedback on their L2 fluency. We can comfortably attribute these changes to the socio-pscyhological realm, which holds great significance for attainment. Even more interesting, perhaps, is the confirmation through these data that initiating such strategies not only influences language abilities in unique ways, it is more likely as fluency reaches more native levels. Thus, confidence in ability, real ability, and actions undertaken to improve ability are all related in circular fashion. Furthermore, those with more contacts and greater confidence tend to express a stronger sense of self in the language, i.e. affiliation affects language identity, and vice versa – another circularity that is surely powerful among immigrant learners (even those with early exposure).

For these reasons, general constructs such as AO and LOR provide little explanation for outcomes *on their own* in the sense that they provide indirect measures of L2 experience. What can we glean from them other than *duration of exposure* in isolation from contextual realities? Their impact can be understood only in the context of specific information on *quality of access to L2.* Through investigations of how they impact the development of experience over time, we may understand their unique contributions to attainment.

That said, the 'experience' construct is a conundrum, to be sure. Which aspects of it are most important? How can these be measured effectively and accurately? Clearly, some things are easily measured: instruction, length of residence, etc. Beyond that, I have argued here that a thorough investigation must also ask the essential question: How does the learner *engage* in the process over the long-term? This question presents the researcher with obvious difficulties. Here, I have investigated specific aspects of experience, operationalized according to certain qualities, including:

(1) *duration* of experience, e.g. length of residence, duration of instruction, and years of indirect, formal contact;
(2) *quality* or nature of experience, e.g. contexts for language use (both initially and currently), balance of formal and informal contexts, types of feedback and instruction encountered (including phonological training), passive versus active contexts for language exposure (writing, speaking, listening, etc.), motivational type and types of strategies undertaken;
(3) *consistency* over time, e.g. in terms of frequency of opportunities for personal contact and feedback; motivation to improve language fluency; access to certain contact domains, etc.;
(4) *intensity* or *extent* of certain orientations, e.g. motivation, intention to reside, identity, sense of belonging in TL community and sense of self in TL.

These aspects of experience are all shown to be highly significant according to the quantitative analysis, and are substantiated by the qualitative analysis. The essence of engagement, so critical to attainment, is therefore constructed internally as well as externally. *I would therefore define engagement as a conscious and unconscious structuring of opportunities, as well as attitudes and perceptions, toward a set of goals – the underlying mechanisms for engagement being cognitive, social, and psychological in nature.* In addition, engagement involves changes in orientation, approach, and behavior, and therefore demands a certain amount of effort and risk. For this reason, late learners may be differentially inclined toward it. (This truism may account for a great deal of the variation evident in SLA.) The fact is, adult learners may be well-disposed to certain strategies to adjust to cultural gaps, linguistic gaps, and social gaps, attending consciously to their own weaknesses or discomforts in their own ways. As is clear, engaging optimally in this process can lead to exceptional outcomes.

This empirical study has attempted to take the long view, so to speak, of the acquisitional process, not by testing specific techniques or treatments, but by gathering comprehensive data on the language learning experience of some very advanced learners, whose perspectives on the process are just as important as the raw, quantifiable aspects of it. Through this integrated analysis, I have tried to emphasize individual approach, socio-cultural context, and engagement as key to ultimate attainment. Figure 5.1 represents those emphases, supported by the data analyses.

Figure 5.1 is intended to reflect, as simply as possible, the nature of multi-directional relationships between the primary realms of influence. I term these realms 'processing clusters' here to indicate that they all contribute to the processing of L2 input and feedback, and that they are inherently complex – they involve a number of subordinate factors, for example:

(1)   the 'cognitive processing cluster' includes conscious attention to target forms, learning strategies, feedback uptake, universal and developmental influences;
(2)   the 'psychological processing cluster' includes motivation, attitudes, (flexibility of) identity, risk-taking, confidence and sense of self in L2;
(3)   the social processing cluster includes contact domains, community context for language acquisition, function of L2 in that context, availability of personal/peer relationships with native speakers.

There are two further ways to understand these clusters as I have schematized them. First, they are *all* characterized by such features as *duration, quality, consistency,* and *intensity,* as they all reflect cumulative L2 experience. Second, they are bound together through certain mechanisms, such as flexibility/plasticity, style/preference, intention/behavior, and access/ opportunity, as noted in Figure 5.1. These labels indicate the nature of their interconnections according to the collective findings in this study, and considering the previous evidence for phonological attainment.

Such a schematization is not meant to over-simplify attainment. Rather, it implies that, by examining just one factor (or even several within the same cluster), we are likely to misinterpret critical factors; we are bound to miss important pieces of the puzzle. I maintain that these clusters are *universally significant*, but that the actual significance of each, or the *balance* of their influence, in reality is a question of *individual* orientation.

As a final note on future research directions, the notions of language identity and language function deserve special mention. If issues of community and belonging are central to late language development, we

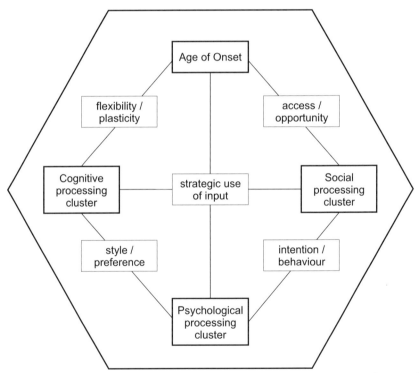

Figure 5.1 Schema of learner experience: An integrated view of critical influences in L2 phonological attainment

must appreciate what it means to learn another language at a point in life when linguistic and cultural identities are already well developed. This has profound implications for the extent to which immigrant language acquirers may desire native-level status in L2. If so, ultimate attainment research should explore individual adaptations to the new language and culture from the viewpoint of social, economic, political and educational realities. Appreciating these realities is critical to understanding potential constraints on attainment. Fishman offers an apt description of the extant gap in the research:

> ... As with most social phenomena ... a purely structuralist or 'outsider' view of language ... is grossly insufficient for capturing the 'insider' experience of that phenomenon. The fortunes and misfortunes of daily life, the camaraderie of shared challenges, the peak experiences of meaningfulness and the depths of despondency ... these all need to be accessible via a socially and emotionally realistic definition of language ... [which] makes us more aware of the intellectual, affective, moral and affiliative aspects of language per se, over and above what any formal linguistic analysis can discern. (Fishman, 1999: 445)

In sum, late SLA is essentially a personal process, one that we hardly glimpse or appreciate in the confines of a structuralist, product-oriented methodology. If we seek a comprehensive model, then methodological approaches must integrate sociolinguistic and psycholinguistic perspectives more effectively. As stated at the conclusion of Chapter 3, a model of SLA must reference multiple sources of influence that operate both independently and interdependently in the process. Experience represents the convergence of these influences in context. *If an essentially interactionist position, combining innate abilities and context, or experience, is widely accepted for first language acquisition, why is it lacking in ultimate attainment research in SLA?*

It should be noted that most of the participants for this study are highly educated immigrants whose programs of study rely on stipends and outside employment. To be sure, their situation is less charged than that of many immigrants to Germany. Yet such differences point to a central problem in the critical-period debate: that of vastly different opportunities afforded to individual learners. For late learners who immigrate to the target language country, cognitive and social barriers to integration must be broken down, often without the advantage of formal instruction in L2. Within their new communities, they must seek out new social networks, learn new ways of self-expression, and develop new senses of belonging. Given these complexities, SLA research must try harder to account for these issues. The situation of most late language learning today begs for closer examination of the learning environment, the learner's cumulative experience, and the learner's developing sense of self as a speaker of the target language.

Approaching these goals requires an integration of methodological inquiry. To that end, this study has explored the significance of cognitive, social, and psychological issues, thereby attempting to bridge existing gaps in prevailing maturational perspectives.

Notes

1. According to their own descriptions, as well as the public discourse in Germany, this is the accepted term to indicate 'not *ethnically* German.'
2. See Moyer, 1999, for findings on the specific importance of suprasegmental training for native-level attainment among classroom learners of German.

Appendix 1
Umfrage/Survey*

Bitte lassen Sie sich genügend Zeit, um die Fragen vorsichtig und vollständig zu beantworten. Das dauert ungefähr 15 Minuten.

Name :_____

A.   Allgemeines/Hintergrund:

(1) Muttersprache(n): (Sprachen, die Sie ständig von Kindheit an gesprochen haben);
(2) Andere Sprachen, von denen Sie 'Passivkenntnisse' haben: (vielleicht Sprachen, die Sie oft zu Hause gehört haben);
(3) Geschlecht: männlich/weiblich;
(4) Alter beim ersten Kontakt mit der deutschen Sprache (d.h. beim ersten Unterricht, Wohnen in einem deutschsprachigen Land, usw ...);
(5) Kontext für ersten Kontakt mit der deutschen Sprache (zu Hause/bei einer Familie, Schule/Uni, Arbeit, usw ...);
(6) bisherige Ausbildung

B.   Deutsch Unterricht:

(1) Deutsch Unterricht über die deutsche Sprache selbst (Monate/Jahre) :
(2) Indirekter Unterricht (über andere Themen, aber auf Deutsch) (Monate/ Jahre):
(3) Gesamter Aufenthaltsdauer in einem deutschsprachigen Land:
(4) Lernmethode(n) für die deutsche Sprache in: (bitte beschreiben)
  • grammatischer Fokus
  • phonologischer Fokus
  • kommunikativer Fokus
  • Fokus auf Uebersetzen
  • anderer Fokus
(5) Wie konsequent waren diese Methoden in Ihrer Erfahrung? Beschreiben Sie Ihre Erfahrung mit diesen Lernmethoden.

C.   Feedback zu Ihrem Deutsch:

(1) Worauf haben sich Ihre DeutschlehrerInnen konzentriert?:
  • Aussprache (Phonologie)
  • Wortschatz und Bedeutung (Lexikon)
  • Wortstellung (Syntax)
  • Pragmatische Kenntnisse oder Interaktionsverhalten
(2) Haben Sie auch Feedback von 'Muttersprachlern' bekommen? Oder haben Sie sich auf andere Bereiche konzentriert? (z. B.: Klarheit der Kommunikation, usw ...)

D.   Kontakt zu Einheimischen/Deutschen:

(1) Bitte beschreiben Sie Ihren Kontakt zu Einheimischen/ Mutterprachlern in Deutschland, z.B: Haben Sie gute Freunde oder wichtige Bekanntschaften mit vielen Deutschen ... usw..?

(2) Würden Sie diesen Kontakt als konstant beschreiben, oder hat er sich mit der Zeit verändert?

(3) Beschreiben Sie bitte Ihren professionellen (beruflichen, akademischen) Kontakt zu Einheimischen/Muttersprachlern. Müssen Sie sich oft in diesem Kontext auf Deutsch ausdrücken?

(4) Hat diese Art von Kontakt mit der Zeit verändert?

E.   Zusammenhänge fürs Deutschsprechen:

(1) Wie oft verwenden Sie Deutsch in Gesprächen mit Muttersprachlern/ Einheimischen (Stunden pro Woche)?

(2) Wieviel Zeit verbringen Sie bei sogenannten 'passiven' Aktivitäten auf Deutsch, z. B. Filme sehen, Fernsehen, Briefe schreiben, usw ... (Stunden pro Woche)?

(3) Wieviel Zeit verbringen Sie beim Schreiben, E-mailen, Lesen auf Deutsch (Stunden pro Woche)?

(4) Gibt es Zusammenhänge, in denen Sie Deutsch exklusiv verwenden?

F.   Motivation und langfristige Ziele:

(1) Bitte schätzen Sie Ihr eigenes Motivationsniveau bezüglich des Erwerbs von der deutschen Sprache:

   -1   2   3 (neutral)   4   5 +

(2) Brauchen Sie fortgeschrittene Deutschkenntnisse für Ihren Beruf oder für weitere Ausbildung?

(3) Wollen Sie Ihre Deutschkenntnisse aus persönlichen Gründen weiter entwickeln?

(4) Haben sich Ihre Gründe fürs Deutschlernen verändert, besonders seitdem Sie hier in Deutschland sind?

(5) Wenn Ihre Motivation mit der Zeit entweder intensiver oder schwächer geworden ist, mit welchem spezifischen Verhalten haben Sie darauf reagiert? z.B.: verbringen Sie mehr/weniger Zeit mit dem Deutschstudium, versuchen Sie mehr Bekanntschaften zu erschließen, suchen Sie Arbeit bei einer deutschem Firma oder einem Geschäft?

Bitte kreuzen Sie die passende Nummer an:

(1) Es ist mir persönlich wichtig, wie ein Muttersprachler/Einheimischer zu klingen:

   starkes Ja 1   2   neutral 3   4   5 starkes Nein

(2) Es gefällt mir, wenn ich als Muttersprachler angenommen bin:

   starkes Ja 1   2   neutral 3   4   5 starkes Nein

(3) Ich bin mit meiner deutschen Aussprache zufrieden:

   starkes Ja 1   2   neutral 3   4   5 starkes Nein

(4) Schätzen Sie Ihre Aussprache ein:
  (1) Ich bin sicher, dass ich wie ein/e MuttersprachlerIn klinge.
  (2) Ich bin ziemlich sicher, dass ich wie ein/e MuttersprachlerIn klinge.
  (3) Manchmal klinge ich schon wie ein/e MuttersprachlerIn, aber nicht konsequent.
  (4) Ich habe einen Akzent in der deutschen Sprache

G. Phonologisches Profil:
Bitte beschreiben Sie Unterricht oder 'Feedback' in Ihrer Lernerfahrung:

(1) Gesteuertes Lernen von der deutschen Phonologie: Beschreiben Sie bitte
  (i)   Methoden, Materialien, technologische Geräte usw., sowie Unterrichtsumfang oder Niveau
  (ii) Phonologiekurs oder extensiver Fokus auf Aussprache
  (iii) gelegentliche Korrektur
  (iv) 'drills' (gezieltes Üben spezifischer Laute)
  (v)   Korrektur des Akzents, bzw. spezifische Silben
  (vi) Korrektur der Satzintonation
(2) Indirektes Feedback oder Korrektur, z. B. im Kontext von Interaktion/ Gespräch mit Muttersprachlern
(3) Häufigkeit
(4) Gezielt auf: Ton, Silbe, Satzintonation, oder vielleicht mehr auf Verständnis/ Kommunikation, usw.
(5) Spezifische phonologische Schwierigkeiten in Ihrer Erfahrung: Laut, Silbenstress, Satzintonation, usw.

H. Lernstrategien:

(1) Haben Sie je auf Ihre eigene Aussprache mit Absicht gearbeitet? Wenn ja, welche Strategien haben Sie verwendet? Zum Beispiel, lesen Sie vor, um Ihren Akzent zu hören oder üben? Haben Sie schwierige Wörter oder Intonationsmuster geübt?
(2) Haben Sie Muttersprachlern genau und bewusst zugehört oder nachgeahmt, um Ihre Aussprache zu verbessern?
(3) andere Möglichkeiten:

* Space for writing was eliminated in this Appendix version of the survey

Appendix 2

Linguistic Tasks*

- *Bitte schreiben Sie Ihren Vornamen auf die Kassette, bevor Sie anfangen.*
- *Es folgen hier 4 Aufgaben, die Sie mit dem Kassettenrecorder aufnehmen sollten. Bitte drücken Sie "Pause/Halt" zwischen jeder Aufgabe (4mal insgesamt).*
- *Innerhalb jeder Aufgabe sollen Sie nicht zu schnell und nicht zu langsam vorgehen. Gehen Sie bitte der Reihenfolge der Aufgaben nach, d.h., wie sie hier gelistet sind. Bitte keinesfalls nochmal aufnehmen oder verbessern! Sie sollen die individuellen Worte, Sätze, usw. auf keinen Fall üben!*

Aufgabe 1:
Bitte lesen Sie die folgenden Wörter in einem für Sie natürlichen Tempo (Pause zwischen jedem Wort):

1. Mühe	9. mürrisch	17. völlig	25. Bücher	33. aufgehen
2. Biene	10. Schublade	18. Ablaut	26. beruhigt	32. durch
3. Schramme	11. Baumwolleindustrie	19. gierig	27. nervlich	33. Röte
4. Nahrung	12. Krankenhausaufenthalt	20. nördlich	28. Wiese	34. jeglich
5. Veränderung	13. März	21. beerdigen	29. bitter	35. lächeln
6. unverzüglich	14. Träume	22. Abschied	30. läuten	36. Zug
7. Psychologie	15. vorenthalten	23. Söhne	31. gehorchen	37. Berg
8. verzweifeln	16. Strom	24. zuallererst	32. Tier	38. Bahn

** PAUSE **

Aufgabe 2:
Bitte lesen Sie die folgenden Texte in einem für Sie natürlichen Tempo:

Text 1: (Über Arten von Verkehrsmittel)

Verkehrsmittel sind alle Fahrzeuge, mit denen Menschen sich fortbewegen oder mit denen Güter befördert werden. Es gibt Verkehrsmittel zu Lande, zu Wasser und in der Luft. Verkehrsmittel müssen nicht unbedingt motorisiert sein. Zu den Verkehrsteilnehmern gehören also auch Fußgänger und Radfahrer.

Als öffentliche Verkehrsmittel bezeichnet man solche Fahrzeuge, die Jeder gegen Bezahlung benutzen darf. Zu den öffentlichen Verkehrsmitteln zählen: die Straßenbahn, U- und S-Bahn, Eisenbahnen und dergleichen mehr. Eine U-Bahn ist ein Zug, der größtenteils unter der Erde fährt. Der Name bedeutet: Untergrundbahn. Auch gibt es U-Bahnen nur in Großstädten. Man wird in den nächsten Jahren viele neue U-Bahnen bauen müssen, weil auf den Straßen der Städte nicht mehr genügend Platz für neue Verkehrsmittel vorhanden ist.

** PAUSE **

Text 2: (Über den Einfluss von Fremdwörtern in der deutschen Sprache)

Hier geht es selbstverständlich nicht gegen Fremdwörter oder um die Säuberung des Deutschen von ausländischen Begriffen. Fremdwörter sind in vielen Kontexten notwendig, in anderen erweitern sie die Möglichkeiten des Ausdrucks.

Das Ausländische bereichert in jeder Sprache das Einheimische eher als es zu bedrohen, obwohl es manchmal Grenzen gibt. Oft ist es eine Frage des Sprachgefühls, wie man mit bestehenden Optionen umgeht, zum Beispiel ob man 'Service' oder 'Dienst' sagt. Das kommt auf Kontext und Sprecher an.

** PAUSE **

Aufgabe 3:

Bitte schauen Sie sich diese Themenliste durch, und wählen Sie eins davon, das Sie kurz besprechen wollen. (Natürlich dürfen Sie auch über Ihr eigenes Thema sprechen.) Sie brauchen nicht mehr als 2 Minuten zu sprechen!

A. Beschreiben Sie eine bedeutsame Erfahrung in Ihrem Leben. Was ist passiert, wie alt waren Sie, *wer* war wichtig in dieser Erfahrung, wie hat Sie diese Erfahrung beeinflusst, usw..?

B. Beschreiben Sie eine sehr wichtige Person in Ihrem Leben. Wie haben Sie ihn/sie kennengelernt? Wie hat diese Person Ihr Leben verändert oder Ihre Meinungen beeinflusst? (das darf auch ein beliebtes Haustier sein)

C. Beschreiben Sie ein Problem oder eine schwierige Situation, mit der Sie kürzlich konfrontiert wurden. Wie haben Sie eine Lösung gefunden? Haben Sie etwas Wichtiges davon gelernt? Wie würden Sie solche Probleme in der Zukunft vermeiden? usw…

D. Besprechen Sie ein Thema, das Ihnen sehr nahe steht. Warum ist dieses Thema/dieses Prinzip so wichtig für Sie (oder überhaupt)? Wie haben Sie sich dafür erstmals interessiert?

** PAUSE **

Aufgabe 4:

Bitte lesen Sie die folgenden Redewendungen und Sprichwörter in einem normalen Tempo:

(1) Reichtum und Pracht verfällt über Nacht.
(2) Lange Qual ist bitterer Tod.
(3) Ein braver Reiter und ein rechter Regen kommen überall durch.
(4) In der Kürze liegt die Würze.
(5) Je länger man lebt, je mehr Art Leben erfährt man.
(6) An Gottes Tafel essen alle aus einer Schüssel.
(7) Hitzige Tränen trocknen bald.
(8) Wer gern gibt, fragt nicht lange.
(9) Das Leben erzieht die großen Menschen und lässt die kleinen laufen.
(10) Was man nicht im Kopf hat, muss man in den Füßen haben.

**PAUSE **

** STOP** Vielen Dank!

* Page breaks between tasks were eliminated in this Appendix version.

Appendix 3
Rater Survey*

Name: _____

The table below outlines several areas that may be most essential to your evaluation of someone's speech in German. Please consider the items below, then rank your top 5 most important if possible (1 = most important, etc.). Feel free to add or define any factors according to your own judgment:

Pragmatics:	Grammar:	Pronunciation:	Other:	Vocabulary:
Style	Word order	Degree of accent	Hesitation	Gender and plural accuracy
Coherence/ organization	Morphology (case, tense, etc)	Stress or rhythm on syllable or across phrase	Speed/Tempo	Idiomatic language
Fluency		Vowel or consonant quality/ precision	Intelligibility/ comprehensibility	
Appropriateness		Intonation or pitch/melody	Regional characteristics	

Top 5 (ranked):

_____

(1) Do your considerations vary according to whether the context is formal or instructional as opposed to natural conversation?
(2) How do you usually respond to speakers with strong foreign accents? (accommodating speech behaviors such as slowing down, listening more intently; forming judgments about the speaker's language ability or other qualities...)
(3) Do you teach German or have you ever? If so, for how many years and at what level (high school, college, beginners, intermediate, etc):
  (i) Do you favor a particular teaching approach?
  (ii) As a teacher, what kinds of error are you most likely to correct ?
(4) Have you yourself ever received explicit instruction on pronunciation in either your native language or in foreign languages, for example, phonetics drills, stress and intonation practice, a course on phonology, etc?

* Space for writing was eliminated in this Appendix version.

Appendix 4

Rating Feedback Sheet*

Please note how long you have been in the USA: _____
Name: _____

You will hear a series of recordings of different speakers reading and speaking German words, phrases and texts. Some excerpts are very brief, others last up to 1 minute. For each different speaker/item, please judge whether you think the speaker is a native German speaker (i.e. German is his/her mother tongue). Also, please assess how confident you are in each item judgment. You may note a particular feature of that speaker's speech that influenced your judgment (e.g. a certain sound, word, stress or into-nation pattern, or any aspect of his/her language).

You may pause between each task to record your response. If absolutely necessary, you may rewind to listen a second time. Thank you very much for your time.

*Aabbreviated list shown below

Speaker/Item	Is this a native speaker?		How confident are you?			Remarks
			Very	Fairly	Not very	
1	Yes	No	1	2	3	
2	Yes	No	1	2	3	
3	Yes	No	1	2	3	
4	Yes	No	1	2	3	

Appendix 5

*Semi-Structured Participant Interview**

A. Experiences coming to Germany; living in Germany; education in Germany

[prompt: general background; need for German fluency; education/instruction in German]

What do you study here? (and where)
How did you get interested in that (subject)?

What would you like to do with that (degree)?
What kind of professional training or degree do you need to pursue those goals?

Do you need to be fluent in German for your career?
Is it important for you to be proficient in German?

How long have you been in Germany?
Do you plan on staying in Germany?
Can you imagine staying permanently?

Did you attend primary or secondary school here in Germany?
What kind of classes were you in? (Sonderklassen, internationale Klassen, Regelklassen)
If so, did you get formal instruction in the German language as well?

B. Personal impressions of Germany; access to heritage culture

[prompt: attitudes; affiliations with language and culture]

Do you feel at home here?
Are there any situations you can think of where you haven't felt "at home"?
Has this changed over time for you?

What kinds of connections do you have to your home country or family?
Do you belong to any formal cultural institutions here?
Are there any support networks you would like to learn about (or belong to)?

Would you say you socialize primarily with Germans or with non-Germans?
How would you describe your own personal contact with Germans?

What are some advantages (or what is the greatest benefit to you) of living/studying here in Germany?

C. Identity/ Belonging

[prompt: sense of well-being, acceptance; linguistic/cultural identities]

Are there specific contexts where you tend to identify yourself only as XX?(explain)
Are there specific contexts where you tend to identify yourself as German? Or can you imagine doing so? In what kinds of situations?

In general, do you see yourself as XX-ish, as German, or as both XX-ish and German?
Can you imagine feeling equally part of German and XX culture?
Has this changed over time?

The interviewer posed all the questions in German; the English is provided here only as an indication of the interview outline.

156

References

Abali, U. (2000) Kulturelle Identität und Sprache: Türkische Schülerinnen und Schüler in Deutschland. *Deutsch lernen* 4, 310–331.

Abuhamdia, Z. (1987) Neurobiological foundations for foreign language. *International Review of Applied Linguistics* 25, 203–11.

Altenberg, E. and Vago, R. (1987) Theoretical implications of an error analysis of second language phonology production. In G. Ioup and S. Weinberger (eds) *Interlanguage Phonology* (pp. 148–164). Cambridge, MA: Newbury House.

Anderson-Hsieh, J. (1989) Approaches toward teaching pronunciation: A brief history. *Cross-currents* 16, 73–78.

Archibald, J. (1993) *Language Learnability and L2 Phonology.* Dordrecht: Kluwer.

Archibald, J. (1997) The acquisition of second language phrasal stress. In S. Hannahs and M. Young-Scholten (eds) *Focus on Phonological Acquisition* (pp. 263–281). Amsterdam: John Benjamins.

Archibald, J. (1998) *Second Language Phonology.* Amsterdam: John Benjamins.

Baker, C. (1992) *Attitudes and Language.* Clevedon: Multilingual Matters.

Barkowski, H., Harnisch, U. and Krumm, S. (1976) Linguistic theory and 'German for foreign workers.' *Linguistische Berichte* 45, 42–54.

Barsalou, L. (1992) *Cognitive Psychology: An Overview for Cognitive Scientists.* Hillsdale, NJ: Lawrence Erlbaum.

Beck, M. (1998) L2 acquisition and obligatory head movement: English speaking learners of German and the local impairment hypothesis. *Studies in Second Language Acquisition* 20, 311–348.

Beebe, L. (1984) Myths about interlanguage phonology. In S. Eliasson (ed.) *Theoretical Issues in Contrastive Phonology* (pp. 51–61). Heidelberg: Julius Groos.

Beebe, L. (1985) Input: Choosing the right stuff. In S. Gass and C. Madden (eds) *Input in Second Language Acquisition* (pp. 404–414). Cambridge, MA: Newbury House.

Berkowitz, D. (1989) The effect of cultural empathy on second-language phonological production. In M. Eisenstein (ed.) *The Dynamic Interlanguage* (pp. 101–114). New York: Plenum Press.

Berry, D. (1994) Implicit and explicit learning of complex tasks. In N. Ellis (ed.) *Implicit and Explicit Learning of Languages* (pp. 147–164). London: Academic Press.

Bialystok, E. (1994) Analysis and control in the development of second language proficiency. *Studies in Second Language Acquisition* 16, 157–168.

Bialystok, E. (1997) The structure of age: In search of barriers to second language acquisition. *Studies in Second Language Acquisition* 13, 116–137.

Bialystok, E. and Hakuta, K. (1999) Confounded age: Linguistic and cognitive factors in age differences for second language acquisition. In D. Birdsong (ed.) *Second Language Acquisition and the Critical Period Hypothesis* (pp. 161–181). Mahwah, NJ: Lawrence Erlbaum.

Bichsel, P. (1995) Es gibt nur eine Sprache. Rede zur Gründung der Arbeits-gemeinschaft zur Förderung des mehrsprachigen Unterrichts in der Schweiz. *Deutsch lernen* 3, 199–209.

Bickerton, D. (1984) The language bioprogram hypothesis and commentaries. *Behavioral and Brain Sciences* 7, 173–221.

Birdsong, D. (1992) Ultimate attainment in second language acquisition. *Language* 68, 706–755.

Birdsong, D. (1999) Introduction: Whys and why nots of the critical period hypothesis for second language acquisition. In D. Birdsong (ed.) *Second Language Acquisition and the Critical Period Hypothesis* (pp.1–22). Mahwah, NJ: Lawrence Erlbaum.

Birdsong, D. (2002) Age and the end state of second language acquisition. Presentation to Applied Linguistics Distinguished Speaker Series, University of Maryland, College Park, February 25.

Birdsong, D. (in press) Second language acquisition and ultimate attainment. In A. Davies and C. Elder (eds) *Handbook of Applied Linguistics*. London: Blackwell.

Birdsong, D. and Molis, M. (2001) On the evidence for maturational constraints in second language acquisition. *Journal of Memory and Language* 44, 235–249.

Bley-Vroman, R. (1989) What is the logical problem of foreign language learning? In S. Gass and J. Schachter (eds) *Linguistic Perspectives on Second Language Acquisition* (pp. 41–68). New York: Cambridge University Press.

Bohn, O. and Flege, J. (1992) The production of new and similar vowels by adult German learners of English. *Studies in Second Language Acquisition* 14, 131–158.

Bohn, R. (1989) Adäquat-folgericht-korrekt-angemessen. Anmerkungen zur Ermittlung und Bewertung sprachlicher Leistungen. *Deutsch als Fremdsprache* 26, 273–278.

Bongaerts, T. Planken, B. and Schils, E. (1995) Can late starters attain a native accent in a foreign language? A test of the critical period hypothesis. In D. Singleton and Z.Lengyel (eds) *The Age Factor in Second Language Acquisition* (pp. 30–50). Clevedon: Multilingual Matters.

Bongaerts, T., Summeren, C., Planken, B. and Schils, E. (1997) Age and ultimate attainment in the production of foreign language. *Studies in Second Language Acquisition* 19, 447–465.

Bongaerts, T., Mennen, S. and Van der Slik, F. (2000) Authenticity of pronunciation in naturalistic second language acquisition: The case of very advanced late learners of Dutch as a second language. *Studia Linguistica* 54, 298–308.

Boyle, J. (1987) Perspectives on stress and intonation in language learning. *System* 15, 189–95.

Brière, E. (1966) An investigation of phonological interference. *Language* 42, 768–96.

Broeder, P. (1991) Talking about people: A multiple case study on adult language acquisition. *European Studies on Multilingualism* 1, 1–198.

Brown, H. (2000) *Principles of Language Learning and Teaching* (4th edn). White Plains: Longman.

Brown, C. (1993) The role of the L1 grammar in the L2 acquisition of segmental structure. *McGill Working Papers in Linguistics* 9, 180–210.

Burgess, J. and Spencer, S. (2000) Phonology and pronunciation in integrated language teaching and teacher education. *System* 28, 191–215.

Buss, S. (1995) Zweitspracherwerb und soziale Integration als biographische Erfahrung: Eine Analyse narrativer Interviews mit türkischen Arbeitsmigranten. *Deutsch lernen* 20, 248–275.

Cargile, A. and Giles, H. (1997) Understanding language attitudes: Exploring listener affect and identity. *Language and Communication* 17, 195–217.

Carroll, J. and Sapon. S. (1959) *Modern Language Aptitude Test*. New York: The Psychological Corporation.

Cessarius, A. and Bolinger, D. (1991) The teaching of intonation: Classroom experiences to theoretical models. In T. Huebner and C. Ferguson (eds) *Crosscurrents in SLA and Linguistic Theories* (pp. 291–303). Amsterdam: John Benjamins.

Chela-Flores, B. (2001) Pronunciation and language learning: An integrative approach. *IRAL* 39, 85–101.

Chun, D. (1988) The neglected role of intonation in communicative competence and proficiency. *Modern Language Journal* 72, 295–303.

Chun, D. (1991) The state of the art in teaching pronunciation. In J. Alatis (ed.) *Linguistics and Language Pedagogy: The State of the Art* (pp. 179–193). Georgetown University Roundtable on Languages and Linguistics. Washington, DC: Georgetown University Press.

Clahsen, H. (1980) Psycholinguistic aspects of L2 acquisition. In S. Felix (ed.) *Second Language Development* (pp. 57–79). Tübingen: Gunter Narr Verlag.

Clahsen, H. (1984) The acquisition of German word order: A test case for cognitive approaches to L2 development. In R. Andersen (ed.) *Second Languages: A Cross–linguistic Perspective* (pp. 219–242). Rowley, MA: Newbury House.

Clahsen, H. (1997) German plurals in adult second language development: Evidence for a dual-mechanism model of inflection. In L. Eubank, L. Selinker and M. Sharwood Smith (eds) *The Current State of Interlanguage* (pp. 123–139). Amsterdam: John Benjamins.

Clahsen, H. and Muysken P. (1986) The availability of universal grammar to adult and child learners: A study of the acquisition of German word order. *Second Language Research* 2, 93–119.

Clément, R., Dörnyei, Z. and Noels, K. (1994) Motivation, self-confidence, and group cohesion in the foreign language classroom. *Language learning* 44, 417–448.

Clément, R., Gauthier, R. and Noels, K. (1993) Language choices in a minority setting: Concomitant attitudes and identity. *Canadian Journal of Behavioural Science* 25, 149–164.

Clément, R. and Kruidenier, B. (1983) Orientations in second language acquisition: The effects of ethnicity, milieu, and target language on their emergence. *Language Learning* 33, 273–291.

Clément, R. and Noels, K. (1992) Towards a situated approach to ethnolinguistic identity: The effects of status on individuals and groups. *Journal of Language and Social Psychology* 11, 203–232.

Clyne, M. (1968) Zum Pidgin-Deutsch der Gastarbeiter. *Zeitschrift für Mundartforschung* 35, 130–139.

Coates, J. (1986) *Pronunciation and Personality*. Bochum: AKS-Verlag.

Cook, V. (1991) *Second Language Learning and Language Teaching*. London: Edward Arnold.

Corder, P. (1983) A role for the mother tongue. In S. Gass and L. Selinker (eds) *Language Transfer in Language Learning* (pp. 85–97). Rowley, MA: Newbury House.

Coupland, N. (1984) Accommodation at work: Some phonological data and their implications. *International Journal of the Sociology of Language* 46, 49–70.

Crookes, G. and Schmidt, R. (1991) Motivation: Reopening the research agenda. *Language Learning* 41, 469–512.

Davies, A. (2003) *The Native Speaker: Myth and Reality.* Clevedon: Multilingual Matters.
DeBot, K. (1980) The role of feedback and feedforward in the teaching of pronunciation: An overview. *System* 8, 35–45.
DeBot, K. (1983) Visual feedback of intonation: Effectiveness and induced practice behavior. *Language and Speech* 26, 331–351.
DeBot, K. and. Mailfert, K. (1982) The teaching of intonation: Fundamental research and classroom applications. *TESOL Quarterly* 16, 71–77.
Derwing, T., Munro, M. and Wiebe, G. (1997) Pronunciation instruction for 'fossilized' learners: Can it help? *Applied Language Learning* 8, 217–235.
DeWaele, J. (2002) Individual differences in L2 fluency: The effect of neurobiological correlates. In V. Cook (ed.) *Portraits of the L2 User* (pp. 221–249). Clevedon: Multilingual Matters.
Dickerson, L. (1975) The learner's interlanguage as a system of variable rules. *TESOL Quarterly 9*, 401–407.
Dickerson, W. (1987) Explicit rules and the developing interlanguage. In A. James and J. Leather (eds) *Sound Patterns in Second Language Acquisition* (pp. 121–140). Dordrecht: Foris.
Dieling, H. (1989) Neue Akzente im Phonetikunterricht: Überlegungen zur Arbeit an der Intonation. *Deutsch als Fremdsprache* 28, 50–54.
Dietrich, R. (1995) The acquisition of German. In R. Dietrich, W. Klein and C. Noyau (eds) *The Acquisition of Temporality in a Second Language* (pp. 71–115). Amsterdam: John Benjamins.
Dittmar, N. (1992) Grammaticalization in second language acquisition. *Studies in Second Language Acquisition* 14, 249–257.
Dittmar, N. and Klein, W. (1975) Untersuchungen zum Pidgin-Deutsch spanischer und italienischer Arbeiter in der Bundesrepublik. Jahrbuch. *Deutsch als Fremdsprache*, 1, 170–194.
Dittmar, N. and Rieck, B-O. (1977) Datenerhebung und Datenauswertung im Heidelberger Forschungsprojekt Pidgin-Deutsch spanischer und italienischer Arbeiter. In H. Bielefeld, E. Hess-Lüttich and A. Lundt (eds) *Soziolinguistik und Empirie. Beiträge zur Problemen der Corpus-gewinnung und -auswertung* (pp. 59–88). Wiesbaden: Athenäum.
Dörnyei, Z. (1990) Conceptualizing motivation in foreign language learning. *Language Learning* 40, 45–78.
Dörnyei, Z (1994a) Understanding L2 motivation: On with the challenge! *Modern Language Journal* 78, 515–23.
Dörnyei, Z. (1994b) Motivation and motivating in the foreign language classroom. *Modern Language Journal* 78, 273–84.
Dörnyei, Z. (2003) Attitudes, orientations and motivations in language learning: Advances in theory, research and applications. In Z. Dörnyei (ed.) *Attitudes, Orientations and Motivations in Language Learning: Advances in Theory, Research and Applications* (pp. 3–32). Best of *Language Learning* Series. Malden, MA: Blackwell.
Dupoux, E. (2003) Plasticity and non-plasticity in speech processing: Late learners and early forgetting. Paper presented to Linguistics Department, University of Maryland, 27 October.
Eckman, F. (1977) Markedness and the contrastive analysis hypothesis. *Language Learning* 27, 315–30.

Eckman, F. (1987a) On the naturalness of interlanguage phonological rules. In G. Ioup and S. Weinberger (eds) *Interlanguage Phonology* (pp. 125–147). Cambridge, MA: Newbury House.

Eckman, F. (1987b) The reduction of word-final consonant clusters in interlanguage. In A. James and J. Leather (eds) *Sound Patterns in Second Language Acquisition* (pp. 143–161). Dordrecht: Foris.

Eckman, F. (1991) The structural conformity hypothesis and the acquisition of consonant clusters in the interlanguage of ESL learners. *Studies in Second Language Acquisition* 13, 23–41.

Edwards. J. (1985) *Language, Society and Identity.* Oxford: Basil Blackwell.

Ehlich, K. (1994) Communication disruptions: On benefits and disadvantages of language contact. In M. Pütz (ed.) *Language Contact and Language Conflict* (pp. 103–122). Amsterdam: John Benjamins.

Ekstrand, L. (1976) Age and length of residence as variables related to the adjustment of migrant children with special reference to second language learning. In G. Nickel (ed.) *Proceedings of the 4th International Congress of Applied Linguistics 3* (pp.179–197). Stuttgart: Hochschulverlag.

Eliasson, S. and Mattsson, D. (1993) Cognitive processing of phonological ambiguity in second language learning. *International Journal of Psycholinguistics* 9, 159–175.

Elliott, A. (1995a) Field independence/dependence, hemispheric specialization, and attitude in relation to pronunciation accuracy in Spanish as a foreign language. *Modern Language Journal* 79, 356–371.

Elliott, A. (1995b) Foreign language phonology: Field independence, attitude, and the success of formal instruction in Spanish pronunciation. *Modern Language Journal* 79, 530–542.

Elliott, A. (1997) On the teaching and acquisition of pronunciation within a communicative approach. *Hispania* 80, 95–108.

Ellis, N. (1994) Implicit and explicit language learning: An overview. In N. Ellis (ed.) *Implicit and Explicit Learning of Languages* (pp. 1–31). London: Academic Press.

Ellis, N. and Sinclair, S. (1996) Working memory in the acquisition of vocabulary and syntax: Putting language in good order. *Quarterly Journal of Experimental Psychology* 49A, 234–250.

Ellis, R. (1985) *Understanding Second Language Acquisition.* Oxford: Oxford University Press.

Elsen, H. (1997) Acquiring verb morphology: German past participles. *Proceedings of the Annual Boston University Conference on Language Development* 21, 160–169.

Esser, H. (1982) Sozialraumliche Bedingungen der sprachlichen Assimilation von Arbeitsmigranten. *Zeitschrift fur Soziologie* 11, 279–306.

Eubank, L. (1992) Verb movement, agreement, and tense in L2 acquisition. In J. Meisel (ed.) *The Acquisition of Verb Placement: Functional Categories and V2 Phenomena in Language Acquisition* (pp. 225–244). Dordrecht: Kluwer.

Faerch, C. and Kasper, G. (1987) Perspectives on language transfer. *Applied Linguistics* 8, 111–36.

Fathman, A. (1975) The relationship between age and second language productive ability. *Language Learning* 25, 245–253.

Felix, S. (1980) Interference, interlanguage and related issues. In S. Felix (ed.) *Second Language Development* (pp. 93–107). Tübingen: Gunter Narr Verlag.

Felix, S. (1981) On the (in)applicability of Piagetian thought to language learning. *Studies in Second Language Acquisition* 3, 179–92.

Felix, S. (1985) More evidence on competing cognitive systems. *Second Language Research* 1, 47–72.

Felix, S. (1991) The accessibility of universal grammar in second language acquisition. In L. Eubank (ed.) *Point Counterpoint. Universal Grammar in the Second Language* (pp. 89–103). Amsterdam: John Benjamins.

Fennell, B. (1997) *Language, Literature, and the Negotiation of Identity.* Chapel Hill: University of North Carolina Press.

Fishman, J. (1999) Concluding comments. In J. Fishman (ed.) *Handbook of Language and Ethnic Identity* (pp. 444–454). Oxford: Oxford University Press.

Flege, J. (1987a) A critical period for learning to pronounce foreign languages? *Applied Linguistics* 8, 162–77.

Flege, J. (1987b) Effects of equivalence classification on the production of foreign language speech sounds. In A. James and J. Leather (eds) *Sound Patterns in Second Language Acquisition* (pp. 9–39). Dordrecht: Foris.

Flege, J. (1991) Perception and production: The relevance of phonetic input to L2 phonological learning. In T. Huebner and C. Ferguson (eds) *Crosscurrents In Second Language Acquisition and Linguistic Theory* (pp. 249–289). Amsterdam: John Benjamins.

Flege, J. (1992) Speech learning in a second language. In C. Ferguson, L. Menn and C. Stoel-Gammon (eds) *Phonological Development: Models, Research, Implications* (pp. 565–604). Timonium, MD: York Press.

Flege, J., Bohn, O. and Jang, S. (1997) Effects of experience on non-native speakers' production and perception of English vowels. *Journal of Phonetics* 25, 437–470.

Flege, J., Frieda, E. and Nozawa, T. (1997) Amount of native language (L1) use affects the pronunciation of an L2. *Journal of Phonetics* 25, 169–186.

Flege, J. and Hillenbrand, J. (1987) Limits on phonetic accuracy in foreign language speech production. In G. Ioup and S. Weinberger (eds) *Interlanguage Phonology* (pp. 176–203). Cambridge, MA: Newbury House.

√ Flege, J. and Liu, S. (2001) The effect of experience on adults' acquisition of a second language. *Studies in Second Language Acquisition* 23, 527–552.

√ Flege, J., Munro, M. and MacKay, I. (1995) Factors affecting strength of perceived foreign accent in a second language. *Journal of the Acoustical Society of America* 97, 3125–3134.

√ Flege, J., Yeni-Komshian, G. and Liu, S. (1999) Age constraints on second-language acquisition. *Journal of Memory and Language* 41, 78–104.

Flynn, S. and Manuel, S. (1991) Age-dependent effects in language acquisition: An evaluation of 'critical period' hypotheses. In L. Eubank (ed.) *Point Counterpoint: Universal Grammar in the Second Language* (pp.117–145). Amsterdam: John Benjamins.

Flynn, S. and O'Neil, W. (1988) *Linguistic Theory in Second Language Acquisition.* Dordrecht: Kluwer.

Fodor, J., Bever, T. and. Garrett, M. (1974) *The Psychology of Language.* New York: McGraw-Hill.

Frischherz, B. (1997) Zweitspracherwerb durch Kommunikation. Eine diskursanalytische Untersuchung zum Zweitspracherwerb türkischer und kurdischer Asylbewerber in der Deutschschweiz. *Bulletin Suisse de linguistique appliquee* 67, 47–65.

Gardner, R. (1979) Social psychological aspects of second language acquisition. In H. Giles and R. St. Clair (eds) *Language and Social Psychology* (pp. 193–200). Oxford: Blackwell.

Gardner, R. (1983) Learning another language: A true social psychological experiment. *Journal of Language and Social Psychology* 2, 219–239.

Gardner, R. (1985a) *The Attitude/Motivation Test Battery: Technical Report.* London, ON: University of Western Ontario.

Gardner, R. (1985b) *Social Psychology and Second Language Learning: The Role of Attitudes and Motivation.* London: Edward Arnold.

Gardner, R. (1988) The socio-educational model of second language learning: Assumptions, findings, issues. *Language Learning* 38, 101–126.

Gardner, R., Lalande, R. and Moorcroft, R. (1985) The role of attitudes and motivation in second language learning: Correlation and experimental considerations. *Language Learning* 35, 207–227.

Gardner, R. and Lambert, W. (1959) Motivational variables in second language acquisition. *Canadian Journal of Psychology* 13, 266–272.

Gardner, R. and Lambert, W. (1972) *Attitudes and Motivation in Second-Language Learning.* Rowley, MA: Newbury House.

Gardner, R., Masgoret, A. and Tremblay, P. (1999) Home background characteristics and second language learning. *Journal of Language and Social Psychology* 18, 419–437.

Gardner, R. and Tremblay, P. (1994) On motivation, research agendas and theoretical frameworks. *Modern Language Journal* 78, 359–68.

Gardner, R. Tremblay, P. and Masgoret, A. (1997) Towards a full model of second language learning: An empirical investigation. *Modern Language Journal* 81, 344–362.

Gass, S. and Selinker, L. (2001) *Second Language Acquisition. An Introductory Course.* Mahwah, NJ: Lawrence Erlbaum.

Genesee, F. (1976) The role of intelligence in second language learning. *Language Learning* 26, 267–280.

Genesee, F., Rogers, P. and Holobow, N. (1983) The social psychology of second language learning: Another point of view. *Language Learning* 33, 209–224.

Gierut, J. (1996) Categorization and feature specification in phonological acquisition. *Journal of Child Language* 23, 397–415.

Giles, H. and Johnson, P. (1981) The role of language in ethnic group relations. In J. Turner and H. Giles (eds) *Intergroup Behaviour* (pp. 199–243). Oxford: Basil Blackwell.

Gonzalez, V. and Schallert, D. (1999) An integrative analysis of the cognitive development of bilingual and bicultural children and adults. In V. Gonzalez (ed.) *Language and Cognitive Development in Second Language Learning* (pp. 19–55). Boston: Allyn and Bacon.

Götze, L. (1983) Deutsch als Fremdsprache in Deutschland: Barriere oder Brücke? *Zielsprache Deutsch* 3, 2–9.

Götze, L. and Pommerin, G. (1988) Bilinguale und interkulturelle Konzepte vor dem Hintergrund der Zweitspracherwerbsforschung. *Zielsprache Deutsch* 19, 31–40.

Graddol, D. (1999) The decline of the native speaker: English as a changing world. *AILA Review* 13, 57–68.

Grosskopf, B., Barden, B. and Auer, P. (1996) Sprachliche Anpassung und soziale Haltung: Zur verstehenden Soziolinguistik der innerdeutschen Migration. *Folia Linguistica* 30, 359–384.

Guiora, A., Beit-Hallami, B., Brannon, R., Dull, C. and Scovel, T. (1972) The effects of experimentally-induced changes in ego states on pronunciation ability in second language: An exploratory study. *Comprehensive Psychiatry* 13, 421–28.

Guiora, A. (1992) The two faces of language ego. A psycholinguistic perspective. *Interface* 7, 19–29.

Hamers, J. (1994) The role of social networks in maintaining the native tongue, in the development of bilingualism, and in the development of literacy. *Bulletin suisse de linguistique appliquée* 59, 85–102.

Hamers, J. and Blanc, M. (2000) *Bilinguality and Bilingualism* (2nd edn). Cambridge: Cambridge University Press.

Hammarberg, B. (1993) The course of development in second language phonology acquisition: A natural path or strategic choice? In K. Hyltenstam and A. Viberg (eds) *Progression and Regression in Language: Sociocultural, Neuropsychological and Linguistic Perspectives* (pp. 439–462). Cambridge: Cambridge University Press.

Harnisch, A., Stokes, A. and Weidauer, F. (1998) *Fringe Voices. An Anthology of Minority Writing in the Federal Republic of Germany.* New York: Berg Publishing.

Harré, R., Clarke, D. and DeCarlo, N. (1985) *Motives and Mechanisms. An Introduction to the Psychology of Action.* New York: Methuen.

Hatch, E. (1983) *Psycholinguistics: A Second Language Perspective.* Rowley, MA: Newbury House.

Hecht, B. and Mulford, R. (1987) The acquisition of a second language phonology: interaction of transfer and developmental factors. In G. Ioup and S. Weinberger (eds) *Interlanguage Phonology* (pp. 213–228). Cambridge, MA: Newbury House.

Hinnenkamp, V. (1990) 'Gastarbeiterlinguistik' und die Ethnisierung der Gastarbeiter. In E. Dittrich and F. Radke (eds) *Ethnizität* (pp. 277–298). Opladen: Westdeutscher Verlag.

Horn, D. (1996) Second language acquisition in the judgment of adult German learners: A report on an empirical investigation. *Lernen in Deutschland* 16, 35–48.

Horrocks, D. and Kolinsky, E. (1996) *Turkish Culture in German Society Today.* Providence: Berghahn Books.

Hudson, T. (1993) Nothing does not equal zero. Problems with applying developmental sequence findings to assessment and pedagogy. *Studies in Second Language Acquisition* 15, 461–493.

Hulstijn, J. (1987) A cognitive view on interlanguage variability. In M. Eisenstein (ed.) *The Dynamic Interlanguage* (pp. 17–31). New York: Plenum Press.

Hulstijn, J. and Bossers, B. (1992) Individual differences in L2 proficiency as a function of L1 proficiency. *The European Journal of Cognitive Psychology* 4, 341–353.

Iandoli, L. (1990) How can the language teacher help students to approximate native pronunciation, intonation, and body language? *Language Quarterly* 28, 22–31.

Ioup, G. (1989) Immigrant children who have failed to acquire native English. In S. Gass, C. Madden, D. Preston and L. Selinker (eds) *Variation in Second Language Acquisition* (Vol. II): *Psycholinguistic Issues* (pp. 160–175). Clevedon: Multilingual Matters.

Ioup, G., Boustagi, E., El Tigi, M. and Moselle, M. (1994) Re-examining the critical period hypothesis: A case study of successful adult SLA in a naturalistic environment. *Studies in Second Language Acquisition* 16, 73–98.

James, A. (1987) The acquisition of phonological representation: A modular approach. In A. James and J. Leather (eds) *Sound Patterns in Second Language Acquisition* (pp. 225–249). Dordrecht: Foris.

James, A. (1989) Linguistic theory and second language phonological learning: A perspective and some proposals. *Applied Linguistics* 10, 367–81.

Jansen, L. (2000) Second language acquisition: From theory to data. *Second Language Research* 16, 27–43.

Johnson, J. and Newport, E. (1989) Critical period effects in second language learning: The influence of maturational state on the acquisition of English as a second language. *Cognitive Psychology* 39, 215–258.

Johnson, J. and Newport, E. (1991) Critical period effects on universal properties of language: The status of subjacency in the acquisition of a second language. *Cognition* 39, 215–58.

Jordens, P. (1996) Input and instruction in second language acquisition. In P. Jordens and J. Lalleman (eds) *Investigating Second Language Acquisition* (pp. 407–449). New York: Mouton de Gruyter.

Jordens, P., DeBot, K. and Trapman, H. (1989) Linguistic aspects of regression in German case marking. *Studies in Second Language Acquisition* 11, 179–204.

Juffs, A. and Harrington, M. (1995) Parsing effects in L2 sentence processing: Subject and object asymmetries and Wh-extraction. *Studies in Second Language Acquisition* 17, 483–516.

Kallmeyer, W., Keim, I. and Tandogan-Weidenhamer, D. (2000) Deutsch-Türkisches: Sprache und kommunikativer Stil von Migranten. *Sprachreport* 16, 2–8.

Kaltenbacher, E. (1994) German word accent in second language acquisition: On the roles of source language target language and markedness. *Linguistische Berichte* 150, 91–117.

Kaye, J. (1989) *Phonology. A Cognitive View.* Hillsdale, NJ: Lawrence Erlbaum.

Kellerman, E. (1983) Now you see it, now you don't. In S. Gass and L. Selinker (eds) *Language Transfer in Language Learning* (pp. 112–129). Rowley, MA: Newbury House.

Klein, W. (1986) *Second Language Acquisition.* Cambridge: Cambridge University Press.

Klein, W. (1996) Language acquisition at different ages. In D. Magnusson (ed.) *The Lifespan Development of Individuals: Behavioral, Neurobiological, and Psychosocial Perspectives. A Synthesis* (pp. 244–264). Cambridge: Cambridge University Press.

Kløve, M. and Young-Scholten, M. (2001) Repair of L2 syllables through metathesis. *IRAL* 39, 103–133.

Kniffka, H. (1992) Cultural identity, life cycles and intercultural communication: Teaching German to adults in Saudi Arabia. *Language Learning Journal* 5, 75–80.

Kolinksy, E. (1996) Non-German minorities in contemporary German society. In D. Horrocks and E. Kolinsky (eds) *Turkish Culture in German Society Today* (pp. 71–111). Oxford: Berghahn Books.

Konig, W. (1991) Welche Aussprache soll im Unterricht 'Deutsch als Fremdsprache' gelehrt werden? Ein Pladoyer für ausgangssprachenorientierte Lehrnormen. *Deutsche Sprache* 19, 16–32.

Krashen, S. (1978) The monitor model for second language acquisition. In R. Gingras (ed.) *Second Language Acquisition and Foreign Language Teaching* (pp. 1–26). Washington, DC: Center for Applied Linguistics.

Krashen, S. (1981) *Second Language Acquisition and Second Language Learning*. New York: Pergamon Press.

Krashen, S., Long, M. and Scarcella, R. (1982) Age, rate and eventual attainment in second language acquisition. In S. Krashen, R. Scarcella and M. Long (eds) *Child–adult Differences in Second Language Acquisition* (pp. 161–172). Rowley, MA: Newbury House.

Kuhl, P. (1986) Theoretical contributions of tests on animals to the special mechanisms debate in speech. *Experimental Biology* 45, 233–65.

Kuhl, P. (1991) Perception, cognition, and the ontogenetic and phylogenetic emergence of human speech. In S. Brauth, W. Hall and R. Dooling (eds) *Plasticity of Development* (pp. 73–106). Cambridge, MA: MIT Press.

Kuhl, P. and Iverson, P. (1995) Linguistic experience and the 'perceptual magnet effect.' In W. Strange (ed.) *Speech Perception and Linguistic Experience* (pp. 121–154). Baltimore: York Press.

Labrie, N. and Clément, R. (1986) Ethnolinguistic vitality, self-confidence and second language proficiency: An investigation. *Journal of Multilingual and Multicultural Development* 7, 269–282.

Lado, R. (1957) *Linguistics Across Cultures*. Ann Arbor: University of Michigan Press.

Lalleman, J. (1987) A relation between acculturation and second-language acquisition in the classroom: A study of Turkish immigrant children born in the Netherlands. *Journal of Multilingual and Multicultural Development* 8, 409–431.

Lambert, W. (1977) The effects of bilingualism on the individual: Cognitive and sociocultural consequences. In P. Hornby (ed.) *Bilingualism: Psychological, Social and Educational Implications* (pp. 15–27). New York: Academic Press.

Lantolf, J. (2000) *Sociocultural Theory and Second Language Learning*. Oxford: Oxford University Press.

Lantolf, J. and Pavlenko, A. (1995) Sociocultural theory and second language acquisition. *Annual Review of Applied Linguistics* 15, 108–124.

Larsen-Freeman, D. and Long, M. (1991) *An Introduction to Second Language Acquisition Research*. New York: Longman.

Leather, J. (1983) Second-language pronunciation learning and teaching. *Language Teaching Abstracts* 16, 198–219.

Leather, J. (1999) Second-language speech research: An introduction. *Language Learning* 49, 1–56.

Lehtonen, J. and Sajavaara, K. (1984) Phonology and speech processing in cross-language communication. In S. Eliasson (ed.) *Theoretical Issues in Contrastive Phonology* (pp. 85–99). Heidelberg: Julius Groos.

Lenneberg, E. (1967) *Biological Foundations of Language*. New York: Wiley & Sons.

Leventhal, H. and Scherer, K. (1987) The relationship of emotion to cognition: A functional approach to a semantic controversy. *Cognition & Emotion* 1, 3–28.

Liebkind, K. (1999) Social psychology. In J. Fishman (ed.) *Handbook of Language & Ethnic Identity* (pp. 140–151). Oxford: Oxford University Press.

Lightbown, P. and Spada, N. (1993) *How Languages are Learned*. Oxford: Oxford University Press.

Lindner, G. (1988) Anwendung der Computergrafik im fremdsprachlichen Phonetikunterricht. *Deutsch als Fremdsprache* 25, 208–213.

List, G. (1989) Zweitsprachenlernen und Probleme der Identität. *Manuskripte zur Sprachlehrforschung* 29, 35–48.

Loeffler, H. (1985) *Germanistische Soziolinguistik*. Berlin: Erich Schmidt Verlag, GmbH.
Long, M. (1990) Maturational constraints on language development. *Studies in Second Language Acquisition* 12, 251–285.
Macdonald, D., Yule, G. and Powers, M. (1994) Attempts to improve English L2 pronunciation: The variable effects of different types of instruction. *Language Learning* 44, 75–100.
MacIntyre, P. (1995) How does anxiety affect second language learning? A reply to Sparks and Ganschow. *Modern Language Journal* 79, 90–99.
MacIntyre, P. and Charos, C. (1996) Personality, attitudes and affect as predictors of second language communication. *Journal of Language and Social Psychology* 15, 3–26.
MacIntyre, P., Dörnyei, Z., Clément, R. and Noels, K. (1998) Conceptualizing willingness to communicate in a L2: A situational model of L2 confidence and affiliation. *Modern Language Journal* 82, 545–562.
Major, R. (1987a) A model for interlanguage phonology. In G. Ioup and S. Weinberger (eds) *Interlanguage Phonology* (pp. 101–124). Cambridge, MA: Newbury House.
Major, R. (1987b) Phonological similarity, markedness, and rate of L2 acquisition. *Studies in Second Language Acquisition* 9, 63–82.
Major, R. (1987c) Foreign accent: Recent research and theory. *International Review of Applied Linguistics* 25, 185–202.
Major, R. (1993) Sociolinguistic factors in loss and acquisition of phonology. In K. Hyltenstam and A. Viberg (eds) *Progression and Regression in Language: Sociocultural, Neuropsychological and Linguistic Perspectives* (pp. 463–478). Cambridge: Cambridge University Press.
Major, R. (2001) *Foreign Accent: The Ontogeny and Phylogeny of Second Language Phonology*. Mahwah, NJ: Lawrence Erlbaum.
Major, R. and Kim, E. (1999) The similarity differential rate hypothesis. In J. Leather (ed.) *Phonological Issues in Language Learning* (pp. 151–183). Malden, MA: Blackwell.
Marinova-Todd, S., Marshall, D. and Snow, C. (2000) Three misconceptions about age and L2 learning. *TESOL Quarterly* 34, 9–34.
Markham, D. (1997) Phonetic imitation, accent, and the learner. *Travaux de l'Institut de Linguistique de Lund* 33, 3–269.
McLaughlin, B. (1987) *Theories of Second Language Learning*. Baltimore: Edward Arnold.
McLaughlin, B. (1990) The relationship between first and second languages: Language proficiency and language aptitude. In B. Harley *et al.* (eds) *The - Development of Second Language Proficiency* (pp. 158–174). Cambridge: Cambridge University Press.
McLaughlin, B. and Heredia, R. (1996) Information-processing approaches to research on second language acquisition and use. In W. Ritchie and T. Bhatia (eds) *Handbook of Second Language Acquisition* (pp. 213–228). New York: Academic Press.
Meisel, J. (1983) Transfer as a second-language strategy. *Language and Communication* 3, 11–46.

Meisel, J. and Clahsen, H. (1985) Principles and strategies of language acquisition: A short description of the ZISA research study. *Scandinavian Working Papers in Bilingualism* 4, 45–56.

Meisel, J., Clahsen, H. and Pienemann, M. (1981) On determining developmental stages in natural second language acquisition. *Studies in Second Language Acquisition* 3, 109–135.

Mellow, D. (1996) On the primacy of theory in applied studies: A critique of Pienemann and Johnston (1987). *Second Language Research* 12, 304–318.

Meng, K. (1995a) Sprachbiographien in einer rußlanddeutschen Aussiedlerfamilie. *Deutsch lernen* 1, 30–51.

Meng, K. (1995b) Sprachfähigkeiten, Sprachentwicklung und sprachliches Handeln bei Aussiedlern in Deutschland – empirische Zugänge. *Deutsch lernen* 1, 68–81.

Michas, I. and Berry, D. (1994) Implicit and explicit processes in a second-language learning task. *European Journal of Cognitive Psychology* 6, 357–381.

Moyer, A. (1995) Ultimate attainment in second language phonological acquisition: Evidence from adult learners of German. Unpublished doctoral dissertation, University of Texas at Austin.

Moyer, A. (1999) Ultimate attainment in L2 phonology: The critical factors of age, motivation, and instruction. *Studies in Second Language Acquisition* 21, 81–108.

Moyer, A. (in press) Accounting for context and experience in German (L2) language acquisition. A critical review of the research. *Journal of Multilingual and Multicultural Development.*

Müller, R. (1996) Innateness, autonomy, universality? Neurobiological approaches to language. *Behavioral and Brain Sciences* 19, 611–675.

Munro, M. and Derwing, T. (1999) Foreign accent, comprehensibility, and intelligibility in the speech of second language learners. In J. Leather (ed.) *Phonological Issues in Language Learning* (pp. 285–310). Malden, MA: Blackwell.

Munsell, P., Rauen, M. and Kinjo, M. (1988) Language learning and the brain: A comprehensive survey of recent conclusions. *Language Learning* 38, 261–78.

Naiman, N., Fröhlich, M., Stern, H. and Todesco, A. (1978) The good language learner. *Research in Education Series* 7. Toronto: Ontario Institute for Studies in Education.

Nation, R. and McLaughlin. B. (1986) Experts and novices: An information-processing approach to the 'good language learner' problem. *Applied Psycholinguistics* 7, 41–56.

Neufeld, G. (1987) On the acquisition of prosodic and articulatory features in adult language learning. In G. Ioup and S. Weinberger (eds) *Interlanguage Phonology* (pp. 321–332). Cambridge, MA: Newbury House.

Neufeld, G. (1988) Phonological asymmetry in second-language learning and performance. *Language Learning* 38, 531–59.

Newport, E. (1991) Contrasting conceptions of the critical period for language. In S. Carey and R. Gelman (eds) *The Epigenesis of Mind* (pp. 111–130). Hillsdale, NJ: Lawrence Erlbaum.

Nihalani, P. (1993) Pragmatics of co-articulation: Towards achieving social acceptability. *IRAL* 31, 39–45.

Noels, K., Pon, G. and Clément, R. (1996) Language, identity and adjustment: The role of linguistic self-confidence in the acculturation process. *Journal of Language and Social Psychology* 15, 246–264.

Norton Pierce, B. (1995) Social identity, investment, and language learning. *TESOL Quarterly* 29, 9–31.

Norton Pierce, B. (1998) Rethinking acculturation in second language acquisition. *Prospect* 13, 4–19.

Norton Pierce, B. (2000) *Identity and Language Learning: Gender, Ethnicity and Educational Change.* London: Longman.

Norton Pierce, B. (2002) Identity and imagined communities in language learning: A research trajectory. Seminar presentation to School of Languages, Literatures and Cultures, University of Maryland, College Park, October 16.

Norton Pierce, B. and Toohey, K. (2001) Changing perspectives on good language learners. *TESOL Quarterly* 35, 307–322.

Nunan, D. (1991) Methods in second-language classroom-oriented research. *Studies in Second Language Acquisition* 13, 249–74.

Nystrom, N. (1983) Teacher–student interaction in bilingual classrooms: Four approaches to error feedback. In H. Seliger and M. Long (eds) *Classroom-oriented Research in Second Language Acquisition* (pp. 169–189). Cambridge, MA: Newbury House.

Obler, L. (1989) Exceptional second language learners. In S. Gass, C. Madden, D. Preston and L. Selinker (eds) *Variation in Second Language Acquisition* (Vol. II): *Psycholinguistic Issues* (pp. 141–159). Clevedon: Multilingual Matters.

Obler, L. (1993) Neurolinguistic aspects of second language development and attrition. In K. Hyltenstam and A. Viberg (eds) *Progression and Regression in Language: Sociocultural, Neuropsychological and Linguistic Perspectives* (pp. 178–195). Cambridge: Cambridge University Press.

Obler, L. and Hannigan, S. (1996) Neurolinguistics of second language acquisition and use. In W. Ritchie and T. Bhatia (eds) *Handbook of Second Language Acquisition* (pp. 509–523). New York: Academic Press.

Obler, L. and Gjerlow, K. (1999) *Language and the Brain.* Cambridge: Cambridge University Press.

Odlin, T. (1989) *Language Transfer: Crosslinguistic Influence in Language Learning.* Cambridge: Cambridge University Press.

Olson, L. and Samuels, S. (1982) The relationship between age and accuracy of foreign language pronunciation. In S. Krashen, R. Scarcella and M. Long (eds) *Child–adult Differences in Second Language Acquisition* (pp. 67–75). Rowley, MA: Newbury House.

O'Maggio, A. (1986) *Teaching Language in Context.* Boston: Heinle & Heinle.

O'Malley, J. and Chamot, A. (1990) *Learning Strategies in Second Language Acquisition.* Cambridge: Cambridge University Press.

Oxford, R. (1990) *Language Learning Strategies.* Boston: Heinle & Heinle.

Oyama, S. (1976) A sensitive period for the acquisition of a non-native phonological system. *Journal of Psycholinguistic Research* 5, 261–283.

Pallier, C., Bosch, L. and Sebastian-Galles, N. (1997) A limit on behavioral plasticity in speech perception. *Cognition* 64, 9–17.

Paradis, M. (1994) Neurolinguistic aspects of implicit and explicit memory: Implications for bilingualism and SLA. In N. Ellis (ed.) *Implicit and Explicit Learning of Languages* (pp. 393–420). London: Academic Press.

Parrino, A. (1998) The politics of pronunciation and the adult learner. In T. Smoke (ed.) *Adult ESL: Politics, Pedagogy and Participation in Classroom and Community Programs* (pp. 171–184). Mahwah, NJ: Lawrence Erlbaum.

Pater, J. (1997) Metrical parameter mis-setting in second language acquisition. In S. Hannahs and M. Young-Scholten (eds) *Focus on Phonological Acquisition* (pp. 235–261). Amsterdam: John Benjamins.

Patkowski, M. (1980) The sensitive period for the acquisition of syntax in a second language. *Language Learning* 30, 449–472.

Pavlenko, A. (2002) Poststructuralist approaches to the study of social factors in second language learning and use. In V. Cook (ed.) *Portrait of the L2 User* (pp. 275–302). Clevedon: Multilingual Matters.

Pavlenko, A. and Lantolf, J. (2000) Second language learning as participation and the (re)construction of selves. In J. Lantolf (ed.) *Sociocultural Theory and Second Language Learning* (pp. 155–177). Oxford: Oxford University Press.

Pennington, M. (1989) Teaching pronunciation from the top down. *RELC Journal* 20, 20–38.

Pennington, M. and Richards, J. (1986) Pronunciation revisited. *TESOL Quarterly* 20, 207–25.

Perdue, C. (1990) Complexification of the simple clause in the narrative discourse of adult language learners. *Linguistics* 28, 983–1009.

Petrenko, A. (1989) Stilistische Varianten der Aussprache im Fremdsprachen-unterricht. *Deutsch als Fremdsprache* 26, 267–272.

Pfaff, C. (1981) Sociolinguistic problems of immigrants: Foreign workers and their children in Germany. *Language in Society* 10, 155–188.

Pfaff, C. (1984) On input and residual L1 transfer effects in Turkish and Greek children's German. In R. Andersen (ed.) *Second Languages: A Cross-linguistic Perspective* (pp. 271–298) Cambridge: Newbury House.

Pfaff, C. (1985) The problem of plurifunctionality in bilingual language acquisition. *Papers and Reports on Child Language Development* 24, 95–103.

Pfaff, C. (1987) Functional approaches to interlanguage. In C. Pfaff (ed.) *First and Second Language Acquisition Processes* (pp. 81–102). Cambridge: Newbury House.

Pfaff, C. (1992) The issue of grammaticalization in early German second language. *Studies in Second Language Acquisition* 14, 273–296.

Pica, T. (1994a) Questions from the language classroom: Research perspectives. *TESOL Quarterly* 28, 49–79.

Pienemann, M. (1987) Psychological constraints on the teachability of languages. In C. Pfaff (ed.) *First and Second Language Acquisition Processes* (pp. 143–168). Cambridge: Newbury House.

Piller, I. (2002) Passing for a native speaker: Identity and success in second language learning. *Journal of Sociolinguistics* 6, 179–206.

Piper, T. (1987) On the difference between L1 and L2 acquisition of phonology. *Canadian Journal of Linguistics* 32, 245–259.

Piske, T., MacKay, I. and Flege, J. (2001) Factors affecting degree of foreign accent in an L2: A review. *Journal of Phonetics* 29, 191–215.

Polka, L and Werker, J. (1994) Developmental changes in perception of nonnative vowel contrasts. *Journal of Experimental Psychology: Human Perception and Performance* 20, 421–435.

Preston, D. (1989) *Sociolinguistics and Second Language Acquisition*. Oxford: Basil Blackwell.

Purcell, E. and Suter, R. (1980) Predictors of pronunciation accuracy: A re-examination. *Language Learning* 30, 271–87.

Ramage, K. (1990) Motivational factors and persistence in FL study. *Language Learning* 40, 189–219.

Rieck, B. (1989) *Natürlicher Zweitspracherwerb bei Arbeitsimmigranten. Eine Langzeituntersuchung.* Frankfurt am Main: Peter Lang.

Rogers, M. (1995) Interpreting interlanguage data: The example of German word order. *Linguistische Berichte* 157, 186–215.

Röhr-Sendlmeier, U. (1990) Social context and the acquisition of German by Turkish migrant children. *Journal of Multilingual and Multicultural Development* 11, 377–391.

Rosenberg, P. (2000) Sprachliche Integration von Rußlanddeutschen. *Deutsch lernen* 4, 355–370.

Rubin, J. (1975) What the 'good language learner' can teach us. *TESOL Quarterly* 9, 41–51.

Rutherford, W. (1995) SLA: Universal grammar and language learnability. In N. Ellis (ed.) *Implicit and Explicit Learning of Languages* (pp. 503–522). London: Academic Press.

Sato, C. (1985.) Task variation in interlanguage phonology. In S. Gass and C. Madden (eds) *Input in Second Language Acquisition* (pp. 181–196). Cambridge, MA: Newbury House.

Sato, C. (1987) Phonological processes in second language acquisition: Another look at interlanguage syllable structure. In G. Ioup and S. Weinberger (eds) *Interlanguage Phonology* (pp. 248–260). Cambridge, MA: Newbury House.

Sayler, W. (1986) Integration in einem fremden Land. Migrationspsychologische Sondierungen. In E. Hess-Lüttich (ed.) *Integration und Identität. Soziokulturelle und psychopädagogische Probleme im Sprachunterricht mit Ausländern* (pp.13–30). Tübingen: Gunter Narr.

Schachter, J. (1996) Maturation and the issue of Universal Grammar in second language acquisition. In W. Ritchie and T. Bhatia (eds) *Handbook of Second Language Acquisition* (pp. 159–193). New York: Academic Press.

Schiffler, L. (2001) Recent neurophysiological studies of the brain and their relation to foreign language learning. *IRAL* 39, 327–332.

Schmidt, R. (1992) Psychological mechanisms underlying second language fluency. *Studies in Second Language Acquisition* 14, 357–385.

Schneidermann, E. (1991) Some neuropsychological characteristics of talented adult language learners. Paper presented to the Second Language Research Forum (SLRF).

Schneiderman, E. and Desmarais, C. (1988a) A neuropsychological substrate for talent in second-language acquisition. In L. Obler and D. Fein (ed.) *The Exceptional Brain: The Neuropsychology of Talent and Special Abilities* (pp. 103–126). New York: Guilford Press.

Schneiderman, E. and Desmarais, C. (1988b) The talented learner: Some preliminary findings. *Second Language Research* 4, 91–109.

Schumann, J. (1978) *The Pidginization Process. A Model for Second Language Acquisition.* Rowley, MA: Newbury House.

Schumann, J. (1994) Where is cognition? Emotion and cognition in second language acquisition. *Studies in Second Language Acquisition* 16, 231–242.

Schumann, J. (1997) The neurobiology of affect in language. Supplement to *Language Learning.* Malden, MA: Blackwell.

Scovel, T. (1981) The effects of neurological age on nonprimary language acquisition. In R. Andersen (ed.) *New Dimensions in Second Language Acquisition Research* (pp. 33–42). Rowley, MA: Newbury House.

Scovel, T. (2000) A critical review of the critical period research. *Annual Review of Applied Linguistics* 20, 213–223.

Searle, J. (2002) End of the revolution (review of Chomsky's *New Horizons in the Study of Language and Mind*). *New York Review of Books* 49, 33–36.

Seidlhofer, B. and Dalton-Puffer, C. (1995) Appropriate units in pronunciation teaching: Some pragmatic pointers. *International Journal of Applied Linguistics* 5, 135–146.

Seliger, H. (1978) Implications of a multiple critical periods hypothesis for second language learning. In W. Ritchie (ed.) *Second Language Acquisition Research* (pp. 11–19). New York: Academic Press.

Seliger, H. (1983) Learner interaction in the classroom and its effect on language acquisition. In H. Seliger and M. Long (eds) *Classroom-oriented Research in Second Language Acquisition* (p. 246–267). Cambridge, MA: Newbury House.

Seliger, H. (1984) Processing universals in second language acquisition. In F. Eckman, L. Bell and D. Nelson (eds) *Universals of Second Language Acquisition* (pp. 36–47). Rowley, MA: Newbury House.

Seliger, H., Krashen, S. and Ladefoged, P. (1982) Maturational constraints in the acquisition of second languages. In S. Krashen, R. Scarcella and M. Long (eds) *Child–Adult Differences in Second Language Acquisition* (pp. 13–19). Rowley, MA: Newbury House.

Selinker, L. (1972) Interlanguage. *IRAL* 10, 209–231.

Selinker, L. (1992) *Rediscovering Interlanguage*. New York: Longman.

Selinker, L. and Lamendella, J. (1981) Updating the interlanguage hypothesis. *Studies in Second Language Acquisition* 3, 201–20.

Skehan, P. (1989) *Individual Differences in Second-Language Learning*. London: Edward Arnold.

Skutnabb-Kangas, T. (1999) Education of minorities. In J. Fishman (ed.) *Handbook of Language and Ethnic Identity* (pp. 42–59). Oxford: Oxford University Press.

Snow, C. and Hoefnagel-Hoehle, M. (1982) The critical period for language acquisition: Evidence from second language learning. In S. Krashen, R. Scarcella and M. Long (eds) *Child–adult Differences in Second Language Acquisition* (pp. 84–92). Rowley, MA: Newbury House.

Sorace, A. (1996) The use of acceptability judgments in second language acquisition research. In W. Ritchie and T. Bhatia (eds) *Handbook of Second Language Acquisition* (pp. 375–409). New York: Academic Press.

Sparks, R. and Ganschow, L. (1993) Searching for the cognitive locus of foreign language learning. *Modern Language Journal* 77, 289–302.

Spolsky, B. (1989) *Conditions for Second Language Learning*. Oxford: Oxford University Press.

Spolsky, B. (2000) Anniversary article: Language motivation revisited. *Applied Linguistics* 21, 157–169.

Stokes, J. (2001) Factors in the acquisition of Spanish pronunciation. *ITL Review of Applied Linguistics* 131–132, 63–84.

Stotzer, U. (1989) Aussprachenvarianten im Kontext, dargestellt an festen Wortverbindungen mit -en Suffixen. *Deutsch als Fremdsprache* 26, 39–44.

Strong, M. (1984) Integrative motivation: Cause or result of successful second language acquisition? *Language Learning* 34, 1–14.
Tan, D. and Waldhoff, H. (1996) Turkish everyday culture in Germany and its prospects. In D. Horrocks and E. Kolinsky (eds) *Turkish Culture in German Society Today* (pp. 138–156). Providence: Berghahn Books.
Tarone, E. (1982.) Systematicity and attention in interlanguage. *Language Learning* 32, 69–82.
Tarone, E. (1987) The phonology of interlanguage. In G. Ioup and S. Weinberger (eds) *Interlanguage Phonology* (pp. 70–85). Cambridge, MA: Newbury House.
Tarone, E. (1988) *Variation in Interlanguage*. Baltimore: Edward Arnold.
Taylor, D. (1977) Bilingualism and intergroup relations. In P. Hornby (ed.) *Bilingualism: Psychological, Social and Educational Implications* (pp. 67–75). New York: Academic Press.
Thornbury, S. (1993) Having a good jaw: Voice-setting phonology. *English Language Teaching Journal* 47, 126–131.
Tomlin, R. and Villa, V. (1994) Attention in cognitive science and second language acquisition. *Studies in Second Language Acquisition* 16, 183–203.
Vainikka, A. and Young-Scholten, M. (1996) Gradual development of L2 phrase structure. *Second Language Research* 12, 7–39.
Van der Linden, E. (1995) Fossilization versus monitor use: A case study. *ITL, Review of Applied Linguistics* 107, 1–16.
Van Lier, L. (1998) The relationship between consciousness, interaction and language learning. *Language Awareness* 7, 128–145.
Van Lier, L. (2000) From input to affordance: Social-interactive learning from an ecological perspective. In J. Lantolf (ed.) *Sociocultural Theory and Second Language Learning* (pp. 245–259). Oxford: Oxford University Press.
Walsh, T. and Diller, K. (1981) Neurolinguistic considerations on the optimum age for second language learning. In K. Diller (ed.) *Individual Differences and Universals in Language Learning Aptitude* (pp. 3–21). Rowley, MA: Newbury House.
Weber-Fox, C. and Neville, H. (1999) Functional neural subsystems are differentially affected by delays in second language immersion: ERP and behavioral evidence in bilinguals. In D. Birdsong (ed.) *Second Language Acquisition and the Critical Period Hypothesis* (pp. 23–38). Mahwah, NJ: Lawrence Erlbaum.
Weinberger, S. (1987) The influence of linguistic context on syllable simplification. In G. Ioup and S. Weinberger (eds) *Interlanguage Phonology* (pp. 401–417). Cambridge, MA: Newbury House.
Werker, J. (1995) Age-related changes in cross-language speech perception: Standing at the crossroads. In W. Strange (ed.) *Speech Perception and Linguistic Experience* (pp. 155–170). Baltimore: York Press.
Werker, J. and Pegg, J. (1992) Infant speech perception and phonological acquisition. In C. Ferguson, L. Menn and C. Stoel-Gammon (eds) *Phonological Development: Models, Research, Implications* (pp. 285–311). Timonium, MD: York Press.
White, L. and Genesee, F. (1996) How native is near-native? The issue of ultimate attainment in adult second language acquisition. *Second Language Research* 12, 233–265.
Witelson, S. (1987) Neurobiological aspects of language in children. *Child Development* 58, 653–88.

Wode, H. (1983) Phonology in L2 acquisition. In H. Wode (ed.) *Papers on Language Acquisition, Language Learning and Language Teaching* (pp. 175–187). Heidelberg: Julius Gross.

Wode, H. (1992) Categorical perception and segmental coding in the ontogeny of sound systems. In C. Ferguson, L. Menn and C. Stoehl-Gammon (eds) *Phonological Development: Models, Research, Implications* (pp. 605–631). Timonium, MD: York Press.

Wode, H. (1994) Nature, nurture and age in language acquisition. *Studies in Second Language Acquisition* 16, 325–45.

Wolff, A. (1991) Phonetik, Ausspracheschulung und Sprecherziehung im Bereich Deutsch als Fremdsprache. *Zielsprache Deutsch* 22, 50–51.

Worbs, M. (1995) Zum Zweitspracherwerb bei jungeren Aussiedlerinnen und Aussiedlern. *Muttersprache* 105, 55–65.

Young, M. and Gardner, R. (1990) Modes of acculturation and second language proficiency. *Canadian Journal of Behavioral Science* 22, 59–71.

Young-Scholten, M. (1994) On positive evidence and ultimate attainment in L2 phonology. *Second Language Research* 10, 193–214.

Young-Scholten, M. (1995) The negative effects of 'positive' evidence on L2 phonology. In L. Eubank, L. Selinker, M. Sharwood-Smith (eds) *The Current State of Interlanguage: Studies in Honor of William E. Rutherford* (pp. 107–121). Amsterdam: John Benjamins.

Young-Scholten, M. (1996) A new research programme for the L2 acquisition of phonology. In P. Jordens and J. Lalleman (eds) *Investigating Second Language Acquisition* (pp. 263–292). Berlin: Mouton de Gruyter.

Yule, G. (1989) The spoken language. *Annual Review of Applied Linguistics* 10, 163–172.

Zuengler, J. (1985) Phonological aspects of input in NS–NNS interactions. In S. Gass and C. Madden (eds) *Input in Second Language Acquisition* (pp. 197–213). Cambridge, MA: Newbury House.

Zuengler, J. (1988) Identity markers and L2 pronunciation. *Studies in Second Language Acquisition* 10, 33–49.

Index

Authors

Abali 131
Abuhamdia 18
Altenberg & Vago 30
Anderson-Hsieh 36, 37
Archibald 28

Baker 41, 104, 127-128
Barkowski *et al.* 6, 125
Barsalou 24
Beck 6
Beebe 31, 38, 142, 143
Berkowitz 41
Berry 33
Bialystok 16, 17, 29, 43
Bialystok & Hakuta 7, 19, 20, 21
Bichsel 1
Bickerton 24
Birdsong 1, 2, 7, 17, 20, 21, 94, 96
Birdsong & Molis 1
Bley-Vroman 9, 44
Bohn & Flege 26, 48
Bohn 37
Bongaerts *et al.*, 1995 23
Bongaerts *et al.*, 1997 2, 12, 23, 39, 40
Bongaerts *et al.*, 2000 23
Boyle 48
Brière 27
Broeder 3, 6
Brown, H. 12, 33, 41
Brown, C. 28
Burgess & Spencer 37
Buss 6, 125, 130, 131

Cargile & Giles 127
Carroll & Sapon 48
Cessarius & Bolinger 48
Chela-Flores 35
Chun 37, 38
Clahsen 6, 141
Clahsen & Muysken 6
Clément 111
Clément & Kruidenier 2, 130

Clément & Noels 2
Clément *et al.*, 1993 2
Clément *et al.*, 1994 2, 40
Clyne 125
Coates 40
Cook 33, 35
Corder 31
Coupland 42
Crookes & Schmidt 39, 40

Davies 12, 46, 113
DeBot 36, 37
DeBot & Mailfert 36
Derwing *et al.* 32
Dewaele 34
Dickerson 26, 32, 33
Dieling 36
Dietrich 3
Dittmar & Klein 125
Dittmar & Rieck 2
Dittmar 3, 125
Dörnyei 39, 40, 49, 130
Dupoux 25

Eckman 27, 28
Edwards 137
Ehlich 1, 137
Ekstrand 16
Eliasson & Mattsson 28
Elliott 34, 35, 39
Ellis, N. & Sinclair 29
Ellis, N. 29, 33
Ellis, R. 3, 31
Elsen 6
Esser 6
Eubank 6

Faerch & Kasper 29
Fathman 16
Felix 6, 29, 33, 141
Fennell 3, 5
Fishman 147

175

Subjects